Mysteries of English G

Despite a history of hundreds of years of research analysing aspects of English grammar, there are still open problems which continue to baffle language researchers today. Such 'grammar mysteries' arise for a number of reasons: because the language is changing; because different speakers of the language adhere to distinct norms and thus introduce and maintain variation in the system; because there are differences between the grammar of spoken and written English. This book illuminates some of the complexities of the subject, the areas where new discoveries await and why it matters.

Through a series of accessible and engaging case studies on various aspects of grammar, from multiple negation to possession, the authors present grammar as an intellectual challenge. This book brings out into the open questions about language usage to which we still do not have good answers in a bid to make variation overt and to revel in the mystery of the English language.

Aimed at both the interested general reader and the beginning student of English language and linguistics, this is a fresh take on grammar.

Andreea S. Calude is a Senior Lecturer in Linguistics at the University of Waikato, New Zealand. She has a background in mathematics and linguistics and researches (spoken) grammar, language evolution, loanwords and just about any quantitative language-related question she can get data on. She is the Editor-in-Chief of *Te Reo* – the Journal of the Linguistic Society of New Zealand and the co-editor of *Questions About Language,* with Laurie Bauer (2020).

Laurie Bauer FRSNZ is Emeritus Professor of Linguistics at Victoria University of Wellington, New Zealand. He is the author of over twenty books including *The Oxford Reference Guide to English Morphology* (2013), which won the LSA's Leonard Bloomfield Prize. In 2017 he was awarded the Royal Society of New Zealand's Humanities Medal.

Mysteries of English Grammar

A Guide to Complexities of the English Language

Andreea S. Calude and Laurie Bauer

LONDON AND NEW YORK

First published 2022
by Routledge
2 Park Square, Milton Park, Abingdon, Oxon OX14 4RN

and by Routledge
605 Third Avenue, New York, NY 10158

Routledge is an imprint of the Taylor & Francis Group, an informa business

British Library Cataloguing-in-Publication Data
A catalogue record for this book is available from the British Library

Library of Congress Cataloging-in-Publication Data
Names: Calude, Andreea S., author. | Bauer, Laurie, 1949- author.
Title: Mysteries of English grammar: a guide to complexities of the English language / Andreea S. Calude and Laurie Bauer.
Description: Abingdon, Oxon; New York, NY: Taylor and Francis, 2022. | Includes bibliographical references and index.
Identifiers: LCCN 2021016733 | ISBN 9780367710248 (hardback) | ISBN 9780367710279 (paperback) | ISBN 9781003148999 (ebook)
Subjects: LCSH: English language–Grammar.
Classification: LCC PE1112 .C256 2022 | DDC 425–dc23
LC record available at https://lccn.loc.gov/2021016733

ISBN: 978-0-367-71024-8 (hbk)
ISBN: 978-0-367-71027-9 (pbk)
ISBN: 978-1-003-14899-9 (ebk)

DOI: 10.4324/9781003148999

Typeset in Times New Roman
by Deanta Global Publishing Services, Chennai, India

To Paul and Winifred for their constant support

Contents

Tables

Preface

Andreea and Laurie

This book is not an English grammar: it makes no attempt to cover everything you might want to know about the way English works as a language. Rather it is a book about aspects of the grammar of English: it picks out some of the interesting parts and stirs up the mud at the bottom of the linguistic pond in its search for gems. It tries to explain why people might not know what is the right thing to say or to write (beyond mere ignorance), and what keeps different versions of a particular grammatical pattern in use. It also tries to point out some of the complexities of grammar that we all deal with on a daily basis. Unlike other books of grammar (though not all!), our book provides details of the language and the patterns observed but also about the people who search for these patterns (linguists). In some chapters, we illustrate problems and issues which researchers are struggling to solve as well as the methods they use to do so, unveiling the process by which we study language and difficulties which our methods present us with. Knowledge about grammar is an emerging and ongoing field of inquiry, and by no means a completed task.

In order to do this, we have to look at the way people really use language – what they actually say and write as opposed to what they might think they say or write (which is different again from what somebody else might think they ought to say and write). Because we both live in New Zealand, we have often used brief excerpts from New Zealand media for illustrative purposes. We cite quality New Zealand newspapers like the *Dominion Post* and the *New Zealand Herald*, we cite the prestigious RNZ National (Radio New Zealand), especially in news and current affairs programmes. This is simply because the material is readily available to us. We do not believe that the language of the New Zealand media is any different in relevant ways from the language of the media in Australia or the United Kingdom (and although there are sometimes marked differences from the language of North America, we point out where this may be relevant to our discussion).

We would like to thank Winifred Bauer, Jessie Burnette, Paul James and David Trye for their readings of drafts, enthusiastic support and general help. We are also greatly indebted to Routledge editors, especially Louisa Semlyen and Eleni Steck for their belief in our ideas, and the referees for their thoughtful comments and suggestions.

1 Introduction

Laurie and Andreea

Setting the scene

English is currently the most described language in the world. We say this not only because of the number of very detailed grammars of English such as Jespersen (1909–1949), Quirk et al. (1985) or Huddleston & Pullum (2002), and not only because we have been writing grammars of English for a very long time, one of the earliest works being Bullokar's *Pamphlet for Grammar* in 1586 (Linn 2006, p. 74). While both these factors are clearly important, it is the range of constructions which are part of English that have been subject to detailed consideration by generations of grammarians and linguists, either trying to provide a better description of English, or trying to prove some theoretical point about the way grammar works. The descriptions do not always agree (for various reasons, some of which we will consider here), but they are available for consultation, and they provide a very detailed description of more of the grammar of English than has been attempted for any other language. It might thus seem that yet another book about English grammar would be a waste of time. Surely, it has all been done, and the job of English grammarians has now been rendered redundant.

In this book, we argue that this is far from being the case. Researchers who work in the field of English grammar are still making new discoveries, finding new regularities and providing new insights. There are many reasons why we might not know precisely what is going on in grammar, not only in English, but in other languages, too.

Variation in language

First, we should note that English is not a homogeneous language. There are many varieties of English, where 'variety' is a technical term that encompasses dialects, styles, genres, even patterns which may be indicative of the individual speaker or writer. The examples given in (1)–(3) are ways of saying the same thing in different varieties.

(1) a. I've not finished it.
    b. I haven't finished it.

DOI: 10.4324/9781003148999-1

(2) a. I don't know whom to trust.
b. I don't know who to trust.

(3) a. I have a friend lives in Auckland.
b. I have a friend who lives in Auckland.

In the United Kingdom, (1a) is more likely to be heard in the north (Scotland and northern England), (1b) in the south; (2a) is much more formal than (2b), with the result that (2b) is more likely to occur in spoken language and (2a) is often confined to some kinds of written language (Microsoft Word suggests changing (2b)). The sentence in (3a) illustrates a structure which can be heard, but is not generally accepted, and which is found more often in informal styles and in some dialect areas, while (3b) is the standard form (the form of the language which is deemed most prestigious and used in formal contexts). Different varieties may use different grammatical patterns (they may also be different varieties because they sound different – in Lancashire, England, *wood* may rhyme with *cud* – or use different words altogether – *slater* and *woodlouse* are both words to denote the same creature), so that a person from Perth, Australia, may use different grammatical patterns from a person from Perth, Scotland, a lawyer may use different grammatical patterns (speak a different variety) from a carpenter, a man may use different grammatical patterns from a woman, a woman may use different grammatical patterns in addressing her daughter and in addressing her grandmother, and so on.

One particular kind of variety is brought about by language change: things which used to be normal in English are now no longer normal. In the late 1800s, (4a) was the ordinary way of expressing the meaning, and (4b) did not exist, though today speakers would probably find (4a) very odd (see Strang 1970, pp. 98–9).

(4) a. The house is building.
b. The house is being built.

Language changes all the time, and once the time-depth is great enough, the old seems odd and the new seems normal. But while the change is actually occurring and both forms can be found, change can cause some confusion. Such periods of confusion can sometimes be very long, and then we often find that the speech of younger speakers is systematically different from that of older speakers. This confusion sometimes gives rise to statements of what 'should' be done, which can have the effect of prolonging the life of a moribund construction.

Descriptive and prescriptive grammar

Notions of what should be done in grammar are called 'prescriptive' or 'normative' statements. Prescriptive ideas, ideas about the way language ought to be, have several origins. In some cases, a grammarian will describe what he or she believes is the case in the language of people who are thought to use the 'best' English – often literary writers, biographers and historians – and this gets interpreted as meaning that everyone should copy this usage.

In some instances, the copied usage is a minority one. For example, it is probably the case that for the majority of English speakers around the world (though more often in some areas than in others), *I never did it last week* is a perfectly normal statement, even though, in standard English, *never* is incompatible with *last week*, and *I didn't do it last week* would be the expected form.

In other cases, it may be suggested that English grammar should follow a pattern that is found in some other language (a language with high cultural prestige, often Greek or Latin). For example, the class of prepositions is so-called because in Latin, the corresponding set of words occurred before (pre-) noun phrases. In English, they are also found in that position, but the same forms also have another use in expressions like *come out, drop in, put up,* and in other places where they do not always occur before a noun phrase. Lowth (1762) knew that what we now call 'preposition stranding' was 'an Idiom which our language is strongly inclined to' [sic] (quoted in Huddleston & Pullum 2020, p. 202), and it was later authors who tried to impose what they perceived as a Latin pattern on English and left us with awkward normative statements such as 'Never end a sentence with a preposition' (to which, of course, the response may be 'What would I want to end a sentence with a preposition for?' or 'What would I want to use a preposition to end a sentence up with for?').

In a third set of cases, grammarians may describe an older pattern and readers may take it as implying (whether that is the author's intention or not) that the newer pattern replacing it should not be used (as is illustrated with *whom* in (2a)).

By contrast, so-called 'descriptive' statements about language claim to do no more that state what grammatical patterns can be observed in usage. They may also try to provide explanations of the observed patterns, and the more modern grammars may indicate where there are differences of opinions on such matters. The three major grammars cited above are all descriptive in this sense, but all descriptive works may end up being used normatively, for example in second-language teaching situations.

What becomes of interest then, is how people know what general usage is, and how to identify appropriate data for description. Many writers make up their examples (as we have done to this point), and assume that their readers will agree with them about what is or is not part of English. In fundamental sentences like (5), that may well be true, but there are plenty of instances where we might disagree, and the disagreement may be minor or major.

(5) The cat sat on the mat.

For example, in the third decade of the twenty-first century there is likely to be disagreement about the sets in (6)–(7); even if individual speakers are consistent in their own usage, there may be disagreement between speakers.

(6) a. I'm bored with this game.
 b. I'm bored of this game.

(7) a. Have you any money?
 b. Do you have any money?
 c. Have you got any money?

Sources of evidence

To avoid the bias of citing one's own personal intuition – which, in some cases, may change from day to day – many grammarians prefer to cite examples of usage from users who have, as far as we can tell, not been consciously manipulating their usage when they produced the relevant material (and we do this quite often in this book). It is possible, of course, for people to make mistakes in their usage – or at least, to say things which they would wish to correct if they had more time. Making mistakes is particularly easy to do when speaking as opposed to writing, but it can happen in any language medium. To avoid such errors, we would ideally like to see a particular pattern repeated from several authors, but it is often difficult to find suitable examples. To maximize the chances of getting good data, linguists and grammarians these days frequently use corpora.

A corpus is a large body of data selected in such a way as to provide usage from many people, and entered into a computer database to allow for easy searching. Corpora can be anything from a few thousand words of running text to billions of words of running text, depending on when the texts in the corpus were collected and how they were gathered and treated. Typically, for example, corpora of spoken English are smaller than corpora of written English, because a lot more work is involved in entering and editing data for a corpus of spoken language than for one of written language. Older corpora (from the late twentieth century), which took material from printed media, tend to be smaller than modern corpora which take material from internet sources. We provide examples from a number of corpora in this book, and the corpora used are listed in our set of references, along with the books that we have consulted.

Some corpora are parsed, which means that each word is assigned to a word class, such as noun, verb, adjective and so on. Because most of the parsing is done automatically, using artificial intelligence and statistical techniques, there are to date still problems involved in doing this. Though it is rarely completely accurate, in principle it makes it easy to distinguish between *standard* ('a flag') and *standard* ('normal'), or to see what nouns fit into the noun slot in *a high* [Noun] *for* (for example, we can have *high hopes/regards/praise for*, but not, *high corpus for*). While corpora allow us access to a great deal of good data, the data has been democratized, in the sense that the data in such collections is typically the written usage of everyday writers, with no priority given to writers who are considered models of the best usage, as was typically the case in earlier descriptions, including dictionaries.

What is grammar?

We have not yet considered the meaning of the word *grammar*, a word that has an unfortunately large number of meanings among linguists and grammarians (Crystal 2015, Bauer 2021).

In one usage, grammar is the science of the study of all language phenomena. This might involve phonetics (is the [s] sound in *cuts* in *She cuts the grass every week* systematically different from the [s] sound in *cuts* in *She has several bad cuts on her hand* ?), phonology (are the rules for stressing nouns different from those for stressing verbs in English?) and pragmatics (can you give an order by making a statement?) – incidentally, the answers to all of these questions is 'yes'.

A more restrictive use of grammar omits these factors, and keeps the word 'grammar' for two things: syntax (the way in which words are ordered and how that relates to the meaning of larger units) and morphology (the way in which meaningful elements go together to make up words, so that we can have *wasp-ish-ness* but not **wasp-ish-ity* or **wasp-ity-ish*). (The asterisk is a device conventionally used by linguists to show that what follows is not good English.)

This latter is the main sense in which we will use the word. *A grammar* (not just *grammar* any more) will also be used, as it has already been used in the second example, to denote a description of a language or a part of a language focusing on these questions.

Grammars, in this sense, focused heavily on regularities in the language. Their interest was to uncover and document regular patterns in the language. A typical example of such a regular pattern might be how verbs are adjusted for different persons (first, second, third). The left-hand side in (8) gives the Latin version of the how the verb meaning 'love' is 'conjugated' and the right-hand side gives the English version.

(8)
a. amo 'I love'
b. amas 'you love' (just one person)
c. amat 'he/she/it loves'
d. amāmus 'we love'
e. amātis 'you love' (more than one person)
f. amant 'they love'

You can immediately spot that Latin makes a lot of changes along the way, while English does not. Linguists term these 'paradigms', for instance the above pattern shows the present tense verb paradigm in Latin and English. We can show other paradigms too, such as, different tenses in English, as in (9).

(9)
a. infer (basic form, infinitive)
b. infers (third person singular present tense form)
c. inferred (past tense form, past participle form)
d. inferring (present participle form)

On the basis of this paradigm, we can then predict that the past tense and past participle form corresponding to *travel* will be *travelled* (as long as *travel* belongs to the same paradigm as *infer*; *think* does not).

Paradigms can involve regularities of single words, like (8) or (9), or they can be extended to groups of words (phrases) or larger combinations of words. This kind of approach to grammar is now called a 'constructional' approach.

Constructions are patterns of words which recur with a fixed meaning. Sometimes constructions are very specific (as with the examples in (10)), and sometimes they are very general (as with the examples in (11)). In either case, a certain amount of substitution is permitted within the general meaning assigned to the construction.

(10) a. [T]hat girl is one twist short of a slinky. (Kleypas, Lisa 2015. *Brown-eyed girl*. New York: St Martin's, p. 89)
b. They are both [...] two paving stones short of a patio. (Cole, Martine 2016. *Betrayal*. London: Headline, p. 262)

(11)					
	a.	My uncle	gave	my sister	a doll.
	b.	Father Christmas	gave	me	a jigsaw puzzle.
	c.	The cat in the hat	gave	us all	a big shock.
	d.	I	showed	my wife	the report.

In (10) we have a construction which, whatever words are used, means 'not very clever'; in (11) we have what is sometimes called 'the double object construction', where certain verbs can take two objects (direct and indirect, the thing given and the person it is given to).

A very different metaphor is the notion of a descriptive rule. A descriptive rule is a rule which tells you what is happening. Depending on the work you happen to be reading, it may be formulated in anything from ordinary prose (e.g. 'The indirect object precedes the direct object' in (11)) to a formula whose elements are theoretically determined (e.g. 'V NP NP', where 'V' is short for 'verb' and 'NP' is short for 'noun phrase', for the same sentences in (11)). More modern formal grammars tend to take the latter approach.

How many answers are there to a question?

A question such as *Which side of the road do they drive on in Japan?* has a single and verifiable answer. People drive on the left in Japan, and you can go to Japan and see for yourself that this is the case. A question like *Why did people vote for Brexit in the referendum?*, on the other hand, has multiple answers. We can easily list a few: they were misled by propaganda; they were not deflected from important issues by the arguments presented in the anti-Brexit propaganda; they wanted to control immigration; they wanted Britain to be great again; they could not imagine ever trying to get a job in Europe; they did not think that it was important that a country should keep its word on alliances; they did not understand the economic advantages of the EU; they thought the EU was overriding their own democracy. You can probably add to this list. The thing about a question of this type is that there is not just one right answer, and that more than one answer can be true at the same time. Also, the answer may be different for different subgroups of people.

Questions about language are more often like the Brexit question than like the side-of-the-road question. There may be multiple answers, people may disagree about which of them are important, different people may behave as they do due to different sets of answers. If you ask a question such as:

(12) Is it *She went to lay on the bed* or *She went to lie on the bed*?

there is not necessarily a single right answer. Who you are and who you are speaking to, what message you want to convey, where you come from and whether or not you are attempting to speak standard English may all be relevant factors in an answer. On the other hand, a question such as

(13) Is it *a stationery car* or *a stationary car*?

may have a single answer, provided that you make assumptions about expecting standard spellings and standard situations.

Multiple answers, or the inability to give a single, simple answer, should not be a sign that the question is silly or that the person expected to answer does not know what they are talking about. The lack of a unique answer is implicit in some questions, and where the answer depends on identity, personality or a myriad of social factors, the lack of a single answer is not a cop-out. The chapters in this book are not intended to provide definitive answers to the questions they raise. Nor are they intended to provide an exhaustive list of every question raised in connection to the topic of the chapter at hand. Our goal is to take readers on a grammatical journey into the kinds of problems that those who study grammar (and particularly for us, English grammar) ask. We would like to provide readers with a chance to think about language – and possibly to think about language in a new way.

Why are there grammar mysteries?

Finally, we come to the notion of a mystery. There are several reasons why a particular piece of usage might be considered a mystery:

- We don't know what is going on; perhaps we are unable to determine any regular pattern – things are messy; perhaps we can see some regularities, but do not understand what drives the patterns we find; perhaps we just do not yet know what the relevant patterns are. If there are genuinely no patterns, the system is presumably unknowable, so this is a situation we do not expect to find, and do not want to find. In such cases, we must try to find something that makes it in principle possible to learn the grammar. There is a big difference between the unknown and the unknowable.
- We know what is going on, but it does not seem to be predictable. This might be because speakers can manipulate the patterns in subtle ways that we cannot fully discern.
- We know what is going on, but we do not know how the mind determines what will actually be said.

- We know more or less what is going on, but we do not know how to successfully capture the patterns we see within a neat theoretical framework (a grammatical model).

The last of these questions has exercised the minds of a lot of linguists over the last half-century, and although the discussions are frequently fascinating, they tend to be rather technical. Accordingly, we shall not deal in detail with the last point here, and to the extent that we do, it will just be in general terms. This should not be taken to mean that we do not care about these models. If we are really going to teach computers to use human language, it will involve creating such models that can be interpreted by artificial intelligence. It is just that, for our purposes, choosing a particular model and introducing the technicalities it involves would interfere with our purpose of drawing attention to the puzzles which are at the core of what we are interested in.

Put simply, this book is about some of the bits of English grammar that we do not understand properly. This is odd. At one level, we must surely understand the grammar well enough to use it on a daily basis: we find it easy to say what we want to say, but very difficult to introspect about how we go about putting these utterances together. And there must be regularities ('rules' if you wish) involved. If there were not, we could never make any mistakes (because a mistake implies that we have done something wrong, and if there are no rules or regularities, there is no right or wrong). Yet we all know that we are perfectly capable of making mistakes when we talk and write, and text, even in our native language. If there were no rules, moreover, foreigners would not be able to get things wrong when they talk in our language, but we do recognize typical 'foreigner' errors (*I knowed the answer, He go home early*). We also know that poets and advertising people are capable of extending our language and saying things in ways that have never been said before (*Eat Fresh, Because you're worth it*). What is the difference between extending our usage and making a mistake? Is it a matter of degree, or is there a difference of type?

Who is this book for and how should it be read?

We wrote this book because we find English grammar fascinating and because we are convinced that much of what people like us find interesting will be equally interesting for those who are not familiar with the field of linguistics. Much of language study is hidden behind fancy terms and paywall academic journals but we feel that at least some of this content should be made accessible for a wide audience.

Hence our book is intended for a non-specialist public, for English users and speakers, for advanced learners of English as a second or foreign language, for language enthusiasts and grammar fanatics – for anyone with an interest in and curiosity about language.

The chapters are not connected to each other, although their arrangement was decided upon on the basis of complexity to some extent. Regardless, readers can pick and choose the order in which they read each chapter. The list of chapters is not exhaustive – there are many more English grammatical bits that we could have discussed, but we chose a list of those constructions that we, as grammarians, find interesting and perhaps straightforward to write about for a non-specialist audience. We have deliberately tried to make the language jargon-free wherever possible, and only introduced terms if we deemed it absolutely necessary. Each term is explained in the relevant chapter, but for convenience, we also include a chapter at the end of the book with some short definitions and examples for easy reference (see Glossary).

Wrapping up

The questions and mysteries we raise in the chapters of the book are in many ways neither completely new (some have been the focus of many research articles), nor entirely problematic (despite the gaps in current understanding of English grammar, we can still all get by using the language to communicate with one another). As language researchers, we find these questions not just captivating but also of practical importance. In the end, if we do not know how English grammar works in detail, how are we supposed to teach foreigners our language, and how can we edit texts so that they use a standard form of the language? Some people may not care: as long as we can understand one another, all is well. Others care very deeply. But whether you care or not, there is a fascinating intellectual puzzle here: what is going on, and how must the mind work to deal with the complexities of our language? If, as some have argued (Simpson 1994, p. 1894; Chomsky 1972, p. 100; Fry 2019), language makes us human, trying to see how language works is probing the very essence of our humanity.

References

Bauer, Laurie 2021. *The linguistics student's handbook.* 2nd edition. Edinburgh: Edinburgh University Press.

Bullokar, William 1586. *Pamphlet for grammar*. London: Denham.

Chomsky, Noam 1972. *Language and mind.* Enlarged edition. New York: Harcourt Brace Jovanovich. (For the 3rd edition: DOI:10.1017/CBO9780511791222)

Crystal, David 2015. *A dictionary of linguistics and phonetics*. 6th edition. Malden, MA: Blackwell. doi:10.1002/9781444302776

Fry, Stephen 2019. Interview on the BBC, 3 July.

Huddleston, Rodney & Geoffrey K. Pullum (eds) 2002. *The Cambridge grammar of the English language*. Cambridge: Cambridge University Press. doi:10.1017/9781316423530

Huddleston, Rodney & Geoffrey K. Pullum 2020. Modern and traditional descriptive approaches. In Bas Aarts, Jill Bowie & Gergana Popova (eds), *The Oxford handbook of English grammar*, 201–221. Oxford: Oxford University Press. doi:10.1093/oxfordhb/9780198755104.013.15

Jespersen, Otto 1909–1949. *A modern English grammar on historical principles*. Seven vols. London: Allen and Unwin. doi:10.4324/9780203715987

Linn, Andrew 2006. English grammar writing. In Bas Aarts & April McMahon (eds), *The handbook of English linguistics*, 72–92. Malden, MA: Blackwell.

Quirk, Randolph, Sidney Greenbaum, Geoffrey Leech & Jan Svartvik 1985. *A comprehensive grammar of the English language*. London: Longman.

Simpson, J.M.Y. 1994. Language. In R.E. Asher (ed.), *The encyclopedia of language and linguistics*. Vol 4. Oxford: Pergamon.

Strang, Barbara M.H. 1970. *A history of English*. London: Methuen.

2 What you must say, what you can say and what you do not say

Grammar and norm

Laurie

Setting the scene

This chapter is unlike the others in this book, in that it is not focused on a particular grammatical point, but rather on how we are supposed to interpret grammatical statements. There is a general feeling – among linguists as well as among non-linguists – that if something is allowed by the grammar, then it is a piece of good English (in our case). We will see that this is far from being the case, and that grammatical adequacy is only part of what you need to know to speak natural-sounding English. This has huge implications for language teaching. If it is not enough to know the grammar of the language in order to be able to speak it appropriately, then how can we formulate the extra information, and are teachers aware of how to teach the extra layers of complexity?

What you must say and what we want to say

Roman Jakobson is credited with the insight that languages differ not in what you can say, but in what you must say (Jakobson 1959). Before we look at this in more detail, let's consider a couple of simple examples to illustrate the point.

In Tariana, an Arawakan language of South America, you would have great difficulty in translating a basic English sentence such as *The dog bit him*. Not because dogs don't bite people occasionally, but because in Tariana you have to specify whether you know this because you yourself saw it happen, whether you know this because you heard it happen, but did not see it, whether you know it because you deduce it from the fact that, for example, he has a scar that looks like a dog bite, or whether you know it because somebody else told you about it (Aikenvald 2003, p. 287). You cannot remain neutral, you have to specify. A marker for evidentiality is present on the verb, and verbs must carry such marking. To our ears this seems unnecessarily specific. But consider another example. If you report that you met a friend in the street, and that friend told you something, you are obliged in English to refer to that friend as either *he* or *she* (possibly *they*, but otherwise avoiding this would be very long-winded and would sound odd). That is, you have to tell your interlocutor the sex of the person involved. In many languages of the world, including Finnish,

DOI: 10.4324/9781003148999-2

Mandarin and Māori, you would not have to be so specific. You could remain noncommittal about the sex of the friend. So is it too specific to give information about the sex of one's friend in English? In French or German, you would have to specify the sex as soon as you mentioned the friend: you would have to distinguish between *un ami* ('male friend') and *une amie* ('female friend') in French, for example. This is as specific as English, but the distinction hits even earlier. Is this too much information? Of course, specificity or amount of information is not really the point at all. It's just that information of different kinds is built into the systems of different languages, and so cannot be avoided. Some of the things we have to mention in English are discussed elsewhere in this book: countability, present relevance and so on. Speakers of languages that do not have definite articles (e.g. Finnish, Russian, Urdu) have great difficulty in deciding when to use the word *the* in English; speakers of languages that do not automatically mark past tense on every relevant verb (e.g. Chinese, Thai) have great difficulty in remembering to make every past verb overtly past. And we have great difficulty if faced with a language like Tariana that requires information on evidentiality, or languages which demand that we specify whether something we have is owned alienably (someone could take it away from you) or inalienably (it is part of you), because we are not used to working with such categories. It's not so much that languages force you to say too much or too little; rather it's a matter that languages choose where to be more specific and where to be less specific, and all languages provide a large amount of redundant information – information that you could deduce from what you can see or what you already know.

Perhaps the more extraordinary part of Jakobson's statement is that languages do not differ in what they can say. This is extraordinary because we all know that there are words in other languages for which we have no counterpart in our own. English has borrowed *kudos* from Greek, *prestige* from French and *mana* from Polynesian because it apparently has no suitable word of its own for the concept. We use the German term *Schadenfreude* because we do not have an English counterpart. And in some cases, we are told about words from other languages which we have not borrowed and yet cannot easily translate.

A relatively recent example to come to widespread attention is the Danish word *hygge* (which the Danes seem to have borrowed from Norwegian). *Hygge* can be both a noun and a verb. As a noun it implies relaxation, comfort and warm feelings; as a verb it implies having a good time and feeling safe and at ease. English does not have a single word that encapsulates all of that, but we can highlight different parts of it, and we can explain it all with paraphrases, as I have just done. In the same way, even if we do not have an ending on a verb to say that 'I know this because I saw it myself', we can say that in several different ways (one being the very way I have just explained it).

The general principle seems to be that even if we cannot say everything with the same degree of precision and economy in all languages, what we can say in one language we can say in any language. This is an astounding fact that we take for granted: for example, we assume that a good translator can translate any text into any other language without losing anything of value (although it may not be possible to conjure up the same associations and emotional background).

What are the limits of grammar?

Everyone agrees that while (1a) is a sentence of English, (1b) is not.

(1) a. I hope to finish this before teatime.
    b. Syntax my working not is.

What is more, we would expect our grammar to tell us this, somehow: perhaps by assigning a structure to (1a) and failing to assign one to (1b), perhaps by having rules which allow for (1a) but not for (1b), perhaps in some more overt way. In other words, by some method or another, a grammar provides a distinction between what is possible in terms of that grammar and what is not. This allows us to distinguish between grammatical structures like (1a) and ungrammatical ones like (1b).

Note that the word *grammar* is being used in a quite specific way in the last paragraph, one which may strike you as odd, though it is one which is widely current within the linguistic community. Here *grammar* means something like 'a set of statements (rules, constraints, constructions, etc.) which specifies what is part of the language for which the grammar provides a description'. This is just one of many ways in which the word *grammar* is used by linguists and grammarians (see, for example Crystal 2015, Bauer 2021). Of course, using the word *grammar* in this way involves a figure of speech. Since grammars in this sense are written by humans, the grammar itself is merely a record of their decisions. We could – and some linguists do – take a step even further back and view the grammar in this sense as something in the mind of the speaker of the language, developed over the period of language acquisition, in which case we have another sense of *grammar,* which is the information from that grammar as deduced and extrapolated from observed linguistic behaviour by grammarians and linguists. Whichever of these you choose to adopt, the grammar still provides information about what is part of the language being described (in our case, English) and what is not.

But now we come to the difficult point. How picky is the grammar, and how much does the grammar leave to our general way of thinking about the world? Consider (2).

(2) The cars are speeding down the road and it's likely to crash.

This looks like a mistake: surely either we mean *car is* or we mean *they're*. We expect our grammar to make sure that number is coherent in our sentences. Similarly with, say, countability (see more in Chapter 6). Example (3) should be ruled out by our grammar.

(3) I saw many money lying on the table.

What then about gender? Is (4) equally ungrammatical?

(4) a. My aunt came to visit and he gave me a present.
b. After he gave me a present, my aunt went home.

If we stress *he* in (4a) (so that it no longer refers to the same person as *my aunt*), possibly if we assume that my aunt is transgendered, we may be able to force a reading of it which is possible. But in the normal conditions under which we use English, (4a) is odd and (4b) is even harder to make into a normal sentence of English. Is it ungrammatical? Consider (5).

(5) My toothbrush is pregnant and is trying to kill me.

Under normal circumstances, *pregnant* must be predicated of an adult female mammal (*This mare is pregnant* is fine, *This stallion is pregnant* is not, and neither is *This kitten is pregnant*, nor *This hen is pregnant*). *Pregnant*, a fortiori, cannot be predicated of a toothbrush. Neither do we assume that a toothbrush has the power to plan any events, let alone murder. As McCawley (1971, p. 219) observes, 'A person who utters [(5)] should be referred to a psychiatric clinic, not to a remedial English course'. In other words, there is nothing wrong with the sentence (5), except that the likelihood of its being spoken outside of a linguistics class is so small as to be non-existent. And, as McCawley points out, the grammaticality of (5) is confirmed by the fact that (6) seems perfectly normal.

(6) I dreamt that my toothbrush was pregnant and was trying to kill me.

Another famous example that makes the same point is Chomsky's (1957, p. 15) sentence reproduced in (7).

(7) Colourless green ideas sleep furiously.

To what extent should we expect subjects and verbs to be coherent, and take it that the coherence is determined by the rules of grammar, and to what extent should we leave that to speakers' knowledge of the way the world works? If we try to make it part of the grammar, then we can say that (8) is not a grammatical sentence of English, because bricks are not edible; if we leave it up to our knowledge of how the world works, we can say that eating bricks is odd, but if it happens, we have to be able to talk about it, just as we can describe attested examples of pregnant women eating coal – even though we might think coal is inedible.

(8) I have just eaten a brick.

If (8) is ruled out because bricks are not edible, that implies that our grammar contains a list of edible, potable, throwable, visible (and so on) things, and yet the sentences in (9) might be perfectly acceptable if toys were involved, if cookies were made in artistic shapes, or if there was smoke in the air.

(9) a. He threw a mountain at me.
 b. He threw a house at me.
 c. I ate a castle.
 d. I saw the wind move down the alley.

Overall, then, it seems better to say that such matters are not part of grammar at all, even if this means that (5) and (7) are grammatical sentences of English, and so is (10).

(10) Because the man with the clouds in his potatoes seemed populated, we contradicted seaweed and pursued radiators.

But that brings us back to sentences like (3). Does that mean that (3) is now to be considered a sentence which our grammar should acknowledge as part of English? And if not, why is (3) different from (5)? Furthermore, if (7) or (10) is a perfectly good sentence of English, then what is our grammar telling us, and is it telling us enough to be of any value?

The answer here no doubt depends upon a whole interlocked series of beliefs held by the analyst. The obvious conclusion, though, is that grammar tells us about the major syntactic structures, but leaves out most of the detail to a matter of what we want to say. The sentence in (10) is weird not because it breaks any rules of grammar, but because it does not make sense in our world to put those words where they are in that sentence. If we replace some of the relevant words, we end up with (11).

(11) Because the man with the holes in his shoes seemed violent, we took care and avoided conflict.

At the same time, some of what we might think of as grammar, might be related not to the structures involved, but to the particular words we choose. Just how much of the structure is lexically determined (fixed by the words involved) may be controversial and difficult to determine, but some things seem fairly clear.

Lexically determined structures

The words which are most obviously constrained in the structures with which they occur are verbs. The verb *kiss* demands a kisser and a kissee; the verb *give* demands a giver, a recipient (sometimes in a phrase beginning with *to*) and a gift; even though *donate* might seem as if it means much the same as *give*, *donate* demands a donor and a gift, but the recipient must be in a phrase beginning with *to*. *Snore* requires only a snorer. We are not free to mix and match (see (12)–(15)).

(12) a. He kissed her hand.
b. *He kissed the duchess her hand.
(13) a. He gave his wife a pearl necklace.
b. He gave a pearl necklace to his wife.
c. *He gave to his wife.
(14) a. He donated $1000 to the church roof fund.
b. *He donated the church roof fund $1000.
(15) a. He snored.
b. *He snored his wife.
c. *He snored his wife a restless night.

Sometimes we can break the bounds of these constructions to gain a particular effect, and some constraints are easier to break than others, but they are fairly robust. With a sentence like *He kissed like a man who had never kissed a woman before* we have to reconstruct the kissee to make sense of the sentence. In *I gave at the office* we have to reconstruct the gift (money) to make sense of what is said. If we say of a person that *He drinks heavily*, we not only reconstruct something drinkable (such as tea or cocoa), we specifically reconstruct alcoholic drink. These reconstructions are possible partly because we know what to expect with these verbs.

Some adjectives work in much the same way. We have to know, because of the individual adjective involved, that it is *bad at Latin*, *familiar with the book*, *intent on her work*, *interested in cooking*, *proud of her son* and so on (see Chapter 10, on adjectives).

Because these are lexical, they are often variable or unstable. We can say *She started learning to drive* or *She started to learn to drive*; we can say *She's angry with her sister* or *She's angry about her sister*, or *She's angry at her sister*, possibly with subtle distinctions between them. If they are unstable, they can change easily. While I would say *I will deal with the problem*, many younger people say *I will deal to the problem*. We both find the other's form puzzling (see Chapter 3, on prepositions).

Beyond syntax and lexis: how we really talk

How do you say goodbye to a friend? How do you greet a friend? How do you enquire after another person's health? How do you tell the time? In all of these different examples, you'll probably find that you have a number of alternatives available to you. Consider saying goodbye. At least the phrases in (16) are possible in English.

(16) Goodbye.
See you (later).
Spot you later.
Laters.
Cheerio.

Adieu.
Ciao.
Sayonara.
Good day.
So long.
Take care.

You can probably think of some others, as well. The expressions in (16), though, are not all equally available. *Laters*, in my experience, is used only by children (though my personal experience of it is limited, and I'm sure it's really much wider than that). *Good day* is definitely British and formal. *Ciao* and *Sayonara* are stylistically rather odd: you may have a very fixed idea of the kind of person who would use them. So although you have a number of choices, and you can recognize an even wider range of choices, your possibilities are quite limited. Under normal circumstances, I would not expect you to be able to say any of the expressions in (17).

(17) Fare thee well.
Until we see each other again.
Until we meet again.
Go in peace.
Love.

The point about the expressions in (17), of course, is that they are translations of what you would say in a number of other languages. *Fare thee well* is now old-fashioned in English, *Until we see each other again* is precisely what you say in French (*au revoir*), German (*auf Wiedersehen*), Russian (*do svidania*), Italian (*arrivederci*), Romanian (*la revedere*) and other European languages. The point I want to make here is that there are a large number of potential things you might say, things which would fit the grammatical patterns of English, but you don't say them. The same is true of the other types of expression that were mentioned above. You don't greet someone in English by asking, *How much do you earn*? or *Have you bathed yet?*. You don't tell the time by saying *It's ten minutes after half an hour to two o'clock.* Yet there are languages where such things are perfectly normal.

There are some things we can say, and a host of things that we never say, even though they are perfectly grammatical. This is not a matter of grammar; it is not a matter of choosing the right patterns to go with particular words. It is a matter of culture, which, for present purposes, we might gloss as habits of language use.

Now consider a very different example. There are many words in English which you can use if you want to say that something is of more than normal size. Words like *big* and *large* spring easily to mind, and can be used with a wide range of nouns: you can have *a large appetite* or *a large zebra*. You do have to remember that *a big man* or *a big woman* is large in size, while *a big boy* or *a big girl* is likely to be mature enough to understand the realities of the world, so things are not necessarily always straightforward, but the use of these words is relatively widespread. There are some other terms, though, which are far less easy to use as widely as these two. Consider the expressions *an astronomical figure, a bouncing baby, a bumper crop, a goodly sum, a great rate, a high price, a substantial contribution, a tidy sum* and so on. These adjectives are far more restricted in the nouns they can occur with. That doesn't necessarily mean that they are limited to just one noun (perhaps *bouncing* is limited to *baby* – though it probably means 'healthy and energetic' these days, rather than just 'large' as suggested by *The Oxford English Dictionary*; in *a bouncing bomb* it has a different meaning). Many of these adjectives can occur with a range of nouns, especially nouns related in meaning, sometimes more than you might expect. Some examples are given in (18).

(18) astronomical: figure, costs, number, prices.
bumper: crop, harvest, issue, year.
considerable: amount, degree, interest, number, time.
goodly: amount, number, profit, quantity.
high: degree, proportion, risk, speed, standard.
substantial: amount, contribution, part, proportion, sum.
tidy: amount, sum.

As will be clear from the examples in (18), some nouns can occur with many of these adjectives: *sum* can go with *astronomical, considerable, goodly, substantial, tidy*. Sometimes the adjective is fussier, sometimes the noun. Words with a restricted set of words with which they are typically associated are said to collocate. The tightest collocations are restricted to just one possible word: *kith and* ____; *vim and* ____; *rise and* _____ (as an instruction to wake up). Most are not that particular, but they do restrict the choices of what we might say, even though this has nothing to do with grammar. Grammar can provide the pattern, but it doesn't tell us which synonym to use. Sometimes, though, the collocation can affect the grammar.

This has been discussed in particular detail with respect to idioms. Idioms are expressions which have a syntactic structure, but where the words involved in that structure do not allow us to interpret what the expression means. The words *to buy the farm* seem to mean 'to purchase the agricultural area', but they actually mean 'to die'; the literal meaning of the words does not help you find the actual meaning in real usage. *To buy the farm* is an idiom. With some idioms (though by no means all), the grammar is fixed. We can say *He bought the farm*, but *The farm was bought by the bank* does not mean that the bank died, and *The farm was bought by John* does not mean that John died. *Buy the farm* allows for variation in tense, but does not allow passivization, (**The farm was bought* does not work in the idiomatic sense of the expression) in the way that *buy the cheapest kind of butter* would.

The examples that have been given above illustrate some of the ways in which what we actually say is restricted, not by grammar or the lexical structure of individual words, but by the way language is used. In the 1950s, this was called the norm of language (Coseriu 1952), though the term has rather fallen out of favour in recent years. To show why it is important, let us consider a final example.

There is something called an *atomic bomb*. There is something called an *atom bomb*. They are the same thing: the two expressions are synonymous. In attributive position you can use an adjective, or you can use a noun (see Chapter 10, on adjectives). The grammar allows both structures. As well as *atom bomb* and *atomic bomb*, we have the expression *nuclear bomb*. But we do not have the expression **nucleus bomb*. If the grammar allows both structures, why do we have both in one case, and only one in the other? Similarly, we have *canine tooth* which means the same as *dog tooth*, but we have *dog star* with no corresponding **canine star* (which would mean a dog used to film *Lassie* or *Rin Tin Tin*).

The answer is that some things are part of language usage, part of the norm, while other things are not. Sometimes there can be two synonymous expressions which are both part of the norm. Sometimes different expressions arise specifically to denote different things.

Wrapping up

Overall, then, we first have to acknowledge that the grammars of different languages are not the same: they force us to provide different information. They might not prevent us from saying what we want to say, but they make some things more neatly sayable in some languages than in others. Once we look at the grammar of one language, though, there are things that are permitted by the grammatical rules that we never say. Just occasionally, we find things that are not permitted by the grammar that we do say: *if you please*, *How do you do*? These tend to be left-overs from a time when they were grammatical. If we find something that is grammatical but which we don't say, it might be because there is a lexical constraint, it might be because it is a collocation, it might be because it is an idiom, but overall we can summarize this as saying, it is because it is not part of the norm. We are not only bound by the grammar, we are also bound by the norm. So sometimes the reason that things are not said that way in English is simply that we don't say that.

What should I read?

Unfortunately, our sources do not tell us in what language you can greet someone by asking how much you earn, and so on; we just hope we are not promulgating false information. We do know that some questions are likely to come up earlier in some languages than in others. For some people, it is normal and polite to ask how old an interlocutor is – and in languages where seniority is important for pronominal usage, this may be vital for further communication. In other languages, it is not necessary, but still polite. In English, we have a fixed answer to such a question: 'As old as my tongue and a little older than my teeth'. This response basically says, 'This is none of your business', and is used because English speakers apparently find it odd to reveal their age, and impolite to ask it of people between about 21 and 75. The language that says *ten minutes after half an hour to two o'clock* is Danish. On examples like telling the time and saying goodbye, see Pawley & Syder (1983). On formulaic language in general see Wray (2012).

References

Aikhenvald, Alexandra Y. 2003. *A grammar of Tariana.* Cambridge: Cambridge University Press. doi:10.1017/CBO9781107050952

Bauer, Laurie 2021. *The linguistics student's handbook.* 2nd edition. Edinburgh: Edinburgh University Press.

Chomsky, Noam 1957. *Syntactic structures.* The Hague: Mouton.

Coseriu, Eugenio 1952. *Sistema, Norma y Habla.* Montevideo: Facultad de Humanidades y Ciencias, Instituto de Filología, Departamento de Lingüística.

Crystal, David 2015. *A dictionary of linguistics and phonetics.* 6th edition. Malden, MA: Blackwell. doi:10.1002/9781444302776

Jakobson, Roman 1959. On linguistic aspects of translation. In Reuben A. Brower (ed.), *On translation*, 232–239. Cambridge, MA: Harvard University Press.

McCawley, James D. 1971. Where do noun phrases come from? In Danny D. Steinberg & Leon A. Jacobovits (eds), *Semantics*, 217–231. Cambridge: Cambridge University Press.

Pawley, Andrew & Frances Hodgetts Syder 1983. Two puzzles for linguistic theory: Nativelike selection and nativelike fluency. In Jack C. Richards & Richard W. Schmidt (eds), *Language and communication*, 191–225. London: Routledge.

Wray, Alison 2012. What do we (think we) know about formulaic language? An evaluation of the current state of play. *Annual Review of Applied Linguistics* 32(1): 231–254.

3 *Over and out*

Prepositions

Andreea

Setting the scene

One of the most wonderful sources of joy in my life is watching my kids acquire language. It is also one of the most agonizing processes to witness, which from time to time yields great research questions, but mostly results in misunderstandings, slammed doors and unmade beds. Because my daughter is eighteen months older than my son, she often takes it upon herself to impart her vast additional wisdom to her younger brother. I recently heard her say to him *technically, you are not going on the airplane, Danny, you are going in the airplane*. Of course, she is right (it is preferable to be inside the plane rather than on top of it), but she is also wrong, because conventionally, English speakers use the preposition *on* (or *by*) when talking about flying somewhere. And while we are talking about *on* and *in*, namely prepositions, I myself had some trouble deciding whether *impart* should be followed by *with* or by *to* (does one impart something *with* someone, like *sharing with* or impart something *to* someone, like *reporting to*?).

As noted by Andrew Pawley and Frances Syder in their much-cited 1983 article (see Chapter 2, on norm), a large part of language use is highly conventional. The use of prepositions is especially so. We use certain combinations of words because *that's just the way we say it*. Add to this the fact that prepositions are also notoriously frequent, and it is easy to see why these little, almost unnoticed words make life difficult. Prepositions are troublesome for linguists, in their endeavours to capture and explain language use, and for learners, in their efforts to learn how to use prepositions appropriately. Why do we say *by accident* but not **by purpose*, opting for *on purpose* but not allowing **on accident*? And what on earth can one do with *error*? Sharing the same semantic domain does not seem to guarantee consistency of structure – we use different prepositions with nouns that mean roughly the same thing (*mistake, error, purpose, accident*).

(1)	✔ by mistake	* by error	* by purpose	✔ by accident.
	* on mistake	* on error	✔ on purpose	* on accident.
	* in mistake	✔ in error	* in purpose	* in accident.

DOI: 10.4324/9781003148999-3

Even if much of language is conventional, can it really be the case that so much of what we say is recycled and stored in our mental lexicon? Does this imply that individual prepositions have no fundamental meaning? Let's look at some examples of idiomatic prepositional use more closely.

Riding the preposition train: why it's hard to get anywhere these days

One domain in which prepositions show variation within a language, as well as when translating from one language into another is that of means of transport. If you've learnt English as a second language, you are probably familiar with the can of worms I am about to peer into. I learnt English as a teenager and my native language, Romanian, seemed to handle everything differently from English. Studying linguistics has taught me that variation in this particular lexical domain exists across many languages, and Romanian and English are by no means a unique pair in this respect. Nevertheless, Romanian and English make the point adequately.

In English, we go *on foot* or *by foot* but never **with the foot* as we would in Romanian (*cu piciorul*). Similarly, we travel places *by bus* or *on the bus*, in Romanian we say *cu autobuzul* 'with the bus', but we come *in the car* or *by car* not **on the car* or **with the car* (like we do in Romanian, *cu maşina* 'with the car'). Interestingly, it seems more natural to ride *in a taxi* than to go *by taxi* (though admittedly, the latter is acceptable), despite the fact that a taxi is a type of car, so you would expect the same preposition in both cases. We can only go *by bike* not **with the bike* or **on the bike* (*on your bike* is allowed but it means something else entirely, namely 'go away!', and you can *sit on your bike* or *get on your bike*, you just can't travel *on your bike*, although physically you do); which is precisely what we say in Romanian, *pe bicicletă* 'on the bike'. You can also say *get your skates on,* meaning you better hurry up, which, like the expression *on your bike*, may felicitously be uttered when neither skates no bikes are in sight. We fly *on the plane* and ride *on the train*, or even skip the preposition altogether in American English: *ride the train* (for me, this expression conjures up images of Indiana Jones–type individuals holding on to the side of the train), though *flying the plane* can only be done by pilots never by passengers (all being well). Neither being (physically) *on the train* nor *on the plane* makes good sense of course, though a more sensible option might be to arrive *by train* (in Romanian we fly *cu avionul* 'with the plane' and go *cu trenul* 'with the train').

And while we are on the topic of buses, why are English-speaking children encouraged to sing songs about the *wheels on the bus* (*go*[ing] *round and round*)? What kind of buses are these? (Surely, wheels ought to be located underneath a bus, or on the bottom, but not on top of it?)

These examples show that travelling and means of transport present variation across languages. These topics are not the only problematic grounds for prepositions. As Taylor articulates beautifully in his book on linguistic categories (1995, p. 109), 'In English, you put gloves *on* your hands and a ring *on* your finger; in Italian gloves go *sulle* [on] *mani*, but a ring goes *al* [to] *dito*' and 'In German, you go *auf* [on] *Urlaub*, you live *auf* [on] *dem Lande*, and you meet people *auf* [on] *einer Party*, while in English you go *on* holiday, you live *in* the country, and you meet people *at* a party' (all translations of prepositions are my own).

So how do we aptly navigate prepositional uses across languages? They seem to pose difficulties in translation. But even within one single language, we face certain problems. Once we know how to use a preposition, we might be able to come up with a valid story of how we came to use it that way, but it is not easy to tell *a priori* which preposition will show up in the first place. In some cases, we have to work harder to come up with the story than in others, and some uses remain mysteriously idiomatic.

Slippery meanings

Before we consider the most enigmatic uses of various English prepositions, let's first discuss the nature of meaning. Regardless of theoretical inclination, all linguists think of language as being made up of some kind of analysable building blocks. Words are the most salient type of building block, though it has been convincingly argued that an objective and cross-linguistically implementable definition of what a word is still eludes us (e.g. Bauer 2000, Dixon & Aikhenvald 2003, Haspelmath 2011).

Be that as it may, many sentences can be parsed by splitting them up into words and considering their meaning. Sure, some parts are idiomatic – for instance, *by and large* (see Chapter 11, on double *be*) – but for the most part, the general meaning of a sentence can be deduced from the meaning of its parts, where the parts can be words, phrases or even constructions (larger groupings of words, for example, [what's this X doing in my Y], where X and Y are open slots which can be filled in by various elements, with the condition that X is not usually expected to be found in Y).

Inferring the intended meaning can be problematic when we are dealing with a word (form) which spans multiple meanings. Multiple meanings arise in cases where a given word has multiple but unrelated meanings (homonyms), like the word *bank*, which could mean the bank of a river or the bank where money used to be kept, but more recently, where debt is accrued. Multiple meanings can also arise when a word has multiple, but *related* meanings. We call this 'polysemy'. The utterance *the boy is in the room* implies the boy is physically located inside the room, but *the chapter will be written in the next two weeks* no longer invokes the literal sense of the preposition *in*. Here, we are dealing with a related derived meaning which likens time to a container, within the space of which the writing of the chapter is metaphorically thought to take place.

English prepositions are well-known for their polysemy. Consider the following sentences:

(2) John's cat was on the radio yesterday.
(3) Mary walked under the bridge.
(4) Martin travelled to Spain for work.

In (2), the cat could be sitting physically on top of the radio or it could be that (s)he was recorded on a radio programme (while John was being interviewed or rang one of the radio stations), the walk in (3) could be taking place entirely under the bridge, or the bridge may be just one of the landmarks passed by Mary on her way, and the travel in (4) could be to satisfy current job requirements (he travelled on business) or because Martin wanted to look for a new job altogether (quite the opposite of satisfying his current job requirements). The ambiguity in these sentences rests on the interpretations of *on*, *under* and *for*.

Two puzzles emerge from such semantic ambiguity. First, where does one sense end and another start? In other words, can we set out consistent and objective boundaries between senses, and if so, how? Secondly, how do speakers know which sense is intended? These questions go well beyond the use of prepositions and probe the very heart of the language system itself, which is why prepositions have found themselves at the core of many important theoretical debates and linguistic studies.

Unsurprisingly, linguists disagree with one another in how to answer these questions. For example, structuralist semanticists take on an Aristotelian approach to meaning, in which senses can be reliably disentangled on the basis of componential features and then stored in our brains in a dictionary-like fashion. So *queen* has the features [+ruler] and [+female] and *king* has the features [+ruler] and [–female] (or [+male]).

But is this a realistic view of how words are dealt with by speakers? This approach does not seem to reflect the fact that meaning is organized and hierarchical. For instance, the use of the preposition *around* in *He planted daffodils around the garden* seems closer to the general, more basic meaning of *around* than its use in *He suddenly turned around to face her.* Yet the dictionary entry list of senses for *around* does not capture this organization.

A different approach is put forward by cognitive linguists, who reject the idea of necessary and sufficient features, and view senses as fuzzy, hierarchical and overlapping, with some senses being more central and others more peripheral. For example, both *apple* and *tomato* are types of fruit, but an *apple* is a better example of a fruit (more central member of the class of fruits) than a *tomato*. They also propose that a form may develop additional related senses which typically arise from bodily experience and are thus extensions of the original, physical sense. So even though, languages differ in how they might extend the analogy of the original sense of say, a given preposition, once such an extension takes place, it can be traced back to its primary sense, grounded in its spatial, physical embodiment. A case in point of how this works is the preposition *over*.

Why we will never get over *over*

There can be no doubt that in linguistic circles, *over* is the most famous preposition in the English language. A Google Scholar search suggests more than 100,000 academic publications have been written on this preposition alone, and not just about English *over* but also its equivalents in other languages – though recall that equivalence is not always easy to determine. In many ways, *over* is really quite ordinary and not unlike other English prepositions, it just so happens that the first articles to cause a stir about the slippery meaning of prepositions focused their attention on it.

In one extensive study, Tyler and Evans (2003) identify no less than 15 distinct senses of the preposition. And theirs is a conservative count. It is not only linguists of different theoretical persuasions who disagree with one another about how to conceptualize meaning, cognitive linguists also disagree amongst themselves about where to place the boundary between senses. Here is a pair of sentences to illustrate the nature of the disagreement (discussed in Tyler & Evans 2003, pp. 40–1):

(5) The helicopter hovered over the ocean.
(6) The hummingbird hovered over the flower.

The meaning of *over* in (5) and (6) is essentially identical, it has to do with coverage, but there is one subtle difference: the coverage of the ocean is partial in (5), whereas the coverage of the flower is either absolute or at very least, larger proportionally than the coverage of the area of the ocean in (6). On this basis, one of the grandfathers of cognitive linguistics, George Lakoff, argued in his 1987 book that *over* designates separate senses in the two sentences. But arguing against this conclusion, Tyler and Evans (2003) maintain that the difference in meaning between (5) and (6) can be deduced from the context. In other words, we can grasp the difference in coverage in the two sentences from what we know about oceans and what we know about flowers, and not from the sense of the preposition *over*.

Tyler and Evans propose that, in general, two senses should be analysed as distinct if one sense entails additional information which the other does not, and so long as – crucially – this additional information cannot be deduced from the context. But how much of the extent of coverability is deduced from the context in (5) and (6)? All of it, according to Tyler and Evans, which is why they analyse the two uses of *over* in (5) and (6) as denoting one single sense. Clearly, the matter is still open for discussion.

Of course, the importance of the additional information needs to be taken into account, too. But are there all that many situations in which it really matters whether the cover is full or partial? And if there are such situations, using the word *completely* could solve any ambiguity. So are those examples necessarily instantiating distinct senses or not?

These sentences aside, sifting through further examples of *over* in English, it is pretty clear that regardless of how many senses we posit for *over*, there are certainly at least a few different ones to disentangle. The primary sense has to do with a spatial location locating one entity above another, like in the earlier examples (5) and (6). Here are some other extensions of this primary sense (a short explanation of each sense is given in square brackets). Perhaps the 100,000 articles about *over* is not so unreasonable after all.

(7) My Lego brick tower fell over. [downward movement]
(8) Simba crossed over the Pridelands boundary. [dynamic movement]
(9) Flip the pancake over. [circular motion]
(10) The winter is now truly over. [finished, completed]
(11) Temperatures remain over 25 degrees. [more than]
(12) He put his hand over his mouth as he sneezed. [cover]
(13) Over and Over again (song title by Nathan Skyes). [again, repetition]
(14) It is often dry over February through to March. [temporal, duration]
(15) My husband often chats with our neighbour over the fence. [direction from one side to another]
(16) Covid 19: UK university students fuming over restrictions. (*NZ Herald* headline, 28 September 2020) [about]

Why can you *put on weight* but not *put off weight*?

Prepositions can also pose problems when used with certain verbs, termed 'phrasal verbs'. Like their congeners in other Germanic languages, English phrasal verbs like *get off, get on, get out, come out, go away, put on* are tricky for non-native speakers of English because their meanings are highly idiomatic and not deducible from their parts.

As an example, let's take the verb *put*. You can *put on a show* meaning you perform a show, *put on a shirt* meaning you will wind up wearing a shirt (not performing it) and *put on weight* meaning you are increasing your weight – all of these meanings are conventional. *Putting on makeup* does not mean increasing the makeup you already have (though that will be a consequence), but rather using makeup on one's face. No one *puts on intelligence* despite being able to *put on weight* (but if grammatically allowed, that would most likely be interpreted as faking intelligence, not increasing it). Incidentally, **putting off weight* is not an English expression either and the reasons for this remain unclear. On the other hand, *putting off writing the chapter* is grammatically acceptable but practically not recommended. *Putting off the doctor's appointment* means delaying the appointment, while *putting off my cousin* could mean making a bad impression on the person or delaying his visit (it is ambiguous). These examples show that it is not just the verb – in our case *put* – but also its object (*my cousin, the doctor's appointment, weight, a belt, a show*) that need to be taken into account when deciding whether an expression is grammatical or not, and if so, what its meaning might be.

Phrasal verbs are not just challenging for learners, but also for linguists because they present analysis problems: it is not straightforward to decide whether the preposition forms a structural unit with the preceding verb, or with the following noun phrase. So, in the sentence *Sampras knocked Agassi out, out* relates more closely to the verb *knocked* in order to create the (idiomatic) phrasal verb meaning of *defeated.* And in *Rapunzel looked out her tower window, out* relates more closely to the noun phrase *her tower window* to indicate direction. Word order is sometimes used to differentiate the two situations: if the verb is separated from the preposition, it forms a unit with it, if not the preposition forms a unit with the noun phrase instead. But even that is not always a sufficient rule. The status of *out* in the sentence *He remembered to put out the rubbish* is less clear in this respect: does it relate more closely with *put* or with *the rubbish*? It certainly is not clear that *out* forms a unit with *the rubbish* here.

One solution is to view phrasal verbs as a fuzzy grammatical category, with some clear-cut, prototypical cases of strongly phrasal verbs at one end of the continuum (the *knocked out* type) and with other similarly clear-cut and prototypical cases of strongly non-phrasal verbs at the other end of the continuum (the *looked out of* type) and a number of mildly phrasal cases (the *put out* type) in between these extremes (see criteria proposed by Dixon 1982).

The status of prepositions

Another trouble with prepositions is their lexical status. Linguists classify words into (among others) lexical classes (or parts of speech): nouns, verbs, adjectives, adverbs, conjunctions, pronouns, demonstratives and prepositions, based on properties of the class members. These classes are in turn classified as primarily grammatical (fulfilling structural roles, say the articles *a, the* or conjunctions *and, but*) or primarily referential (words we intuitively think of as having 'meaning', like *house, tree, run, nice, fast*). There is a whole lot to say about lexical classes and problems of classification here which I am putting aside because our main interest lies with classifying prepositions.

Prepositions have their own class because they exhibit various properties unique to them. The trouble is, that there are various exceptions to all these properties, and there is resulting uncertainty as to whether prepositions align with grammatical or referential meaning.

First, prepositions are prototypically said to have the broad function of locating entities in space or time (for example, Matthews 2005, p. 292) – except we have seen this broad definition has plenty of exceptions too, there are idioms and phrasal verbs to deal with. Their function – in as far as that function holds – makes it difficult to decide whether they should be grouped with grammatical words or with referential words. Most linguists place them in the referential group, though in many ways, they can be said to take on a structural role, expressing relationships between words and phrases.

Secondly, English prepositions prototypically occur before a compulsory noun phrase. The sentence **The mug is on* is not acceptable (unless if we are dealing with some futuristic mug that can be turned on and off) because the location of the mug is missing (*on* what?). Except that some prepositions are perfectly grammatical without a following noun phrase: *Just come around* [no noun! You know where] *at nine*, (the South African and American English use of noun-less *with*) *I hear there is a party at Glenn's, do you want to come with* [no noun! Obviously with me/us]?, or the fashion-related sentence: *Black is in again.* And then there are also phrasal verbs which are followed by a prepositional phrase not a noun phrase, like *he jumped out of the window*.

Thirdly, the form of prepositions does not change, we do not add bits of words (morphemes) to create new variants of these, as we do with other referential words. Take the noun *group*, we can have *group*, *groups*, *grouping*, *ungroup*, *regroup*, *regrouping* and so on. But now think about *of*. It's just *of*. This is perhaps the most sturdy property of prepositions. English prepositions don't usually incorporate additional morphemes, but they do sometimes take part in compounds, such as *without*, made of two prepositions stuck together, *with* and *out*. The only real trouble with prepositions like *without* is indeed its prepositional status. *Without* can certainly be used as a preposition: *I left without him*. But there are sentences where it does not function as a preposition: [Mother to toddler asking for TV:] *Maybe you just need to go without today*, unless we want to say that *without* remains a preposition but the accompanying noun phrase, say *TV*, is deleted because it can be understood from context (termed 'ellipsis'). Below is another example of such a complex preposition: *within*.

(17) National Party leader Judith Collins is facing criticism from within over policy decisions that at worst are improvised and at best did not consult the party's own spokesperson. (*New Zealand Herald*, 6 October 2020)

Wrapping up

Although some parts of language may follow predictable patterns, others do not. Prepositions present various idiosyncrasies in meaning and take part in phrasal verbs and other combinations which pose problems of analysis. At their core, they are used to locate various entities in space or time. Yet, prepositions function in similar ways to more traditional grammatical words, linking nouns to each other or a noun phrase to a given verb. These different functions place prepositions at the crossroads between grammatical and referential content, lurking in the no-man's land between semantics and syntax and keeping both learners and linguists on their toes.

What should I read?

Lindstromberg (2010) offers a clear and accessible account of the meanings of over 90 English prepositions. For a practical guide to English phrasal verbs for language teachers or learners see Hart (2017). Lakoff (1987) and Taylor (1995) provide detailed accounts of meaning, categorization, and the organization of senses into central/core versus peripheral meanings. Their books are not jargon-free but are rewarding reads which cover some important tenets of cognitive linguistics and the link between language and culture.

References

Bauer, Laurie 2000. Word. In Geert Booij, Christian Lehmann & Joachim Mugdan (eds), *Morphologie/Morphology: An international handbook on inflection and word-formation* (Volume 1), 247–256. Amsterdam: De Gruyter.

Dixon, Robert 1982. The grammar of English phrasal verbs. *Australian Journal of Linguistics* 2(1): 1–42. doi:10.1080/07268608208599280

Dixon, Robert & Alexandra Aikhenvald 2003. Word: A typological framework. In Robert Dixon & Alexandra Aikhenvald (eds,) *Word: A crosslinguistic typology*, 1–41. Cambridge: Cambridge University Press.

Google Scholar. Available online at https://scholar.google.com/

Hart, Carl 2017. *Ultimate phrasal verb book.* New York: Simon and Schuster.

Haspelmath, Martin 2011. The indeterminacy of word segmentation and the nature of morphology and syntax. *Folia Linguistica* 45(1): 31–80. doi:10.1515/flin.2011.002

Lakoff, George 1987. *Women, fire, and other dangerous things: What categories reveal about the mind.* Chicago: Chicago University Press.

Lindstromberg, Seth 2010. *English prepositions explained.* Amsterdam and Philadelphia: Benjamins.

Matthews, Peter H. 2005. *The concise Oxford dictionary of linguistics*. Oxford: Oxford University Press.

Pawley, Andrew & Frances Hodgetts Syder 1983. Two puzzles for linguistic theory: Nativelike selection and nativelike fluency. In Jack C. Richards & R.W. Schmidt (eds), *Language and communication*, 191–226. London: Routledge. doi:10.4324/9781315836027

Taylor, John 1995. *Linguistic categorization: Prototypes in linguistic theory*. Oxford: Oxford University Press.

Tyler, Andrea & Vyvyan Evans 2003. *The semantics of English prepositions: Spatial scenes, embodied meaning and cognition.* Cambridge: Cambridge University Press.

4 *You'll never get nowhere*

Double negatives

Laurie

Setting the scene

Until the 1960s, adultery was the only reason for which divorce could be granted in the state of New York. And adultery was hard to prove, unless your spouse cooperated and did not object to being found in error. Couples who wanted a divorce had to travel to another state, where divorce on other grounds was legal. If you were rich enough, you went to Nevada where, after being a resident for just six weeks, you could gain a divorce without even notifying your spouse. You did have to swear that you intended to continue to reside in Nevada, however. The point of the story is not to either glorify or denigrate divorce, but to point out that human laws vary from area to area and from period to period (no-fault divorce is now legal in New York State). The same is true of other human constructs – certainly of linguistic ones. The rules that govern language are not the same everywhere, or across time. What seems like a good argument in one place and at one time may not hold at another as the language changes, and we may (in the case of language) find remnants left behind from the rules of an earlier period.

One of the most familiar of all prescriptive rules in English is the rule against the double negative (Crystal 1984). The appeal is to logic. If, in mathematics, $1 - (-1) = 2$, it is clear that two negatives make a positive. By the same logic, (1) must mean that 'he gave me something': the negative in *didn't* must cancel out the negative in *nothing* to make a positive.

(1) He didn't give me nothing.

Not only would the French (and speakers of many other languages, including Italian and Russian) be horrified by this idea, since *Il ne m'a rien donné* 'He not me has nothing given' is the standard way of saying 'He didn't give me anything' in French, but we will see that the logic that applies to sentences like (1) – and there is logic – is not the mathematical logic to which appeal was made just above, but a different linguistic logic.

We will begin the investigation with a double negative to which nobody objects, and then move on to other types.

DOI: 10.4324/9781003148999-4

A standard double negative

There is a double negative where one of the negatives is a prefix on an adjective which is apparently perfectly acceptable. Some examples from the British National Corpus (BNC) (Davies 2004–) are presented in (2).

(2) a. such decisions were not uncommon.
b. Caroline's experience as portrayed in that video is not unusual.
c. could they reasonably have regarded illness in pigs as a not unlikely consequence of that breach?
d. I was not unhappy to be sitting opposite an attractive lady [...]

Most of these could be seen as negating a sentence with a negative adjective in it: *I was not happy, I was not unhappy*. But (2c) seems to imply that *not unlikely* is itself an adjective phrase, and that only the adjective is negated not the whole sentence. The other sentences in (2) can be read the same way. And this is in accordance with the usual reading of such constructions, because *not unlikely* is not a negation of *unlikely*, it is another step on the way from *likely* to *unlikely*. Although you may disagree with the ordering in (3), we seem to have a sequence of degrees of unlikeliness as set out there.

(3) likely   not unlikely   not likely   unlikely

Quirk et al. (1972) call this 'local negation', and compare it with what happens in *Not a word was spoken*, where only the noun phrase is negated and not the whole sentence.

A case where double negatives do cancel out

The argument for two negatives cancelling each other out gains some weight from the fact that there are places where this is precisely what happens. Some examples, again from the BNC, are given in (4).

(4) a. You can not not react to Dorothy [...]
b. God could not not exist.
c. you can not not know that you are involved in an activity of communication [...]

The sentence in (4b), for example, denies that it is possible for God not to exist, and is equivalent to *God must exist*. The negation is complicated because the movement from *cannot* to *must* is not necessarily obvious, but the two *not*s do cancel each other out, just as prescriptivists would have it. The same is true (without the complication of the modal verb) in *Nobody has nothing to offer* (Quirk et al. 1972, p. 379), equivalent to *Everyone has something to offer* in meaning, but the two do not occur in the same positions in discourse, where *Nobody has nothing to offer* is likely to come after a statement to the contrary: *Chris has nothing to offer. That's not true; nobody has nothing to offer.*

The usual double negative

English has a set of words (*any*, *anyone*, *anything*, *anywhere*) which occur in negative environments. Consider the examples in (5).

(5)	He has some money.	*He hasn't some money.	He hasn't any money.
	She saw someone.	?She didn't see someone.	She didn't see anyone.
	They bought something.	?They didn't buy something.	They didn't buy anything.
	We went somewhere.	*We didn't go somewhere.	We didn't go anywhere.

The examples with question marks before them are fine if they are direct denials of a statement to the contrary, but otherwise are odd. There are more of these non-assertive, negative environment words (Quirk et al. 1972, pp. 376–7), but the examples in (5) are sufficient to make the point.

That may be the current standard usage, but it was not always general usage, and, indeed, is not general usage once we move away from the very narrow confines of standard English. There is another version of the sentences in (5), with negative words and no sentence negation: *He has no money*, *She saw no one*, and so on. In related languages, such as Dutch and German, this is the only possibility here, the non-assertive words do not exist. When my children were learning Dutch, they complained that saying (the equivalent of) *I speak no Dutch* was to falsify the situation: they spoke some Dutch, but not enough to converse fluently. This is an Anglophone reaction. Dutch doesn't use the different constructions to make the distinction. This raises the question of whether the extra negative is in the sentence negation (as in *I don't speak Dutch*) or in the nominal negation (as in *I speak no Dutch*). The way to be safe, is to keep both ('on the same principle that we drive in two or three nails instead of one', as Curme 1931, p. 139 puts it): it may be pleonastic, but it makes sure that the negative is conveyed. So we find, as we have found for centuries, *He hasn't got no money*, *She didn't see nobody* and so on.

Mathematical logic and linguistic logic

There is a widespread story about double negatives that has been doing the rounds for years. A school teacher is talking to an English class about double negatives, and making the (mathematical) point that two negative make a positive. 'But', he adds, 'it is never the case that two positives make a negative'. From the back of the class a voice is heard, saying 'Yeah, yeah'. The two-positives-make-a-negative rule is absolutely not mathematical. But it is linguistic, whether you say *yeah yeah* or *yeah right* or something else. And if there is a linguistic rule which allows two positives to make a negative and no corresponding mathematical rule, it follows that linguistic logic is not the same as mathematical logic.

Consider also sentences like those in (6).

(6) a. I didn't give nothing to nobody.
b. She didn't see nobody nowhere.

The examples in (6) have three negatives in them. If we are going to be strictly mathematical, two negatives make a positive, but the third makes things negative again. Of course, the examples in (6) are negative, but the prescription finds them just as objectionable as a double negative. If the argument is purely mathematical, the sentences in (6) ought to be blameless.

Linguistic logic is not mathematical. In linguistic logic, the more you insist on the negative, the more negatives you pile up, the stronger the negation becomes. So if someone asks you. 'Do you think it will rain?' and you answer, 'No, no', you think it will not rain, you are not making a positive: you cannot say, 'No, no, it will rain'.

Some messier bits of negation

We can begin this section with a rather trivial example, which nevertheless makes a point. There is, in British English, an expression *I couldn't care less* meaning, in effect, 'I don't care'. There is nothing particularly noteworthy about this expression, except that its equivalent in American English – a growing use since the 1960s – is *I could care less* (although many Americans are conscious of this being rather odd: see Barber 1998 under *care*, Merriam-Webster n.d., Fogarty 2020). The more general, and more surprising, point is that sometimes speakers do not know whether what they want to express requires a positive or a negative.

Another place where the same thing happens can be seen in (7), where we have examples from the BNC.

(7) a. I wonder whether a new radical approach should be taken [...]
b. And a handful of critics is beginning to wonder whether Ireland has not concentrated a little too hard on attracting inward investors [...]
c. I wonder if one of the clerks could just put it before us [...]
d. And I wonder if we do not need to enquire into the theological basis of both.

In (7) we see expressions with *wonder whether* or *wonder if*, and some are followed by positive expressions, some by negative. The question is, would these examples mean something different if we swapped positive and negative? That is, if we said *I wonder whether a new radical approach shouldn't be taken*, would it mean anything different from (7a)? And if we said *And a handful of critics is beginning to wonder whether Ireland has concentrated a little too hard on attracting inward investors* would it mean anything different from (7b)? We can probably agree that, even if we think there is a difference, it is a very subtle one. And that being the case, it seems that there are places where we cannot really tell the difference between positive and negative. Those places are, of course, not random. We know there is a difference between *Come into the garden, Maud* and *Don't come into the garden, Maud*, but our grammar allows us in some places to say that positive or negative may mean the same.

Interestingly, it seems we may be less likely to tie ourselves in knots this way than our great(-great)-grandparents. Jespersen (1917) cites Darwin as saying (8).

(8) [I]t never occurred to me to doubt that your work...would not advance our common object in the highest degree.

Unless (8) is just an error (which Jespersen doesn't appear to believe, and Fowler 1968 under *not* cites a similar example), it seems to me that it is a form of English which is no longer in current usage. I could be wrong, but perhaps we are collectively sorting out some of these excrescent negatives. If I am wrong, there is another kind of multiple negation here, with *never*, *doubt* and *not* all contributing negative values to the sentence, and yet the overall meaning being positive ('I think your work will advance our project').

Another type which seems to have fallen out of fashion is illustrated by (9) (from Partridge 1963, p. 198).

(9) I know nothing, nor you neither.

This is another double negative, and is more lucidly phrased as *I know nothing; nor do you.* There are more complicated versions of this kind of structure, of the form *Do not X and do not Y neither*, found in the eighteenth and nineteenth centuries, but the *neither* has now yielded to *either*, making the negation clearer.

Yet another kind of negative has the devil as a negative marker. Some more examples form the BNC are in (10).

(10) a. 'Do you hear from her at all?' Her tone was light but tense. 'Devil a word,' replied her mother.

b. 'But we leave tomorrow!' she exclaimed. That took him by surprise. 'The deuce you do! Well I shall see to that.'

Devil a word means 'not a word' and *deuce* is a euphemism for 'devil', and the speaker who produces it seems to be denying that the departure will take place. Just why the devil should be a negating force (even if he is not a force for good) is obscure. I'm sure we could speculate about it.

Wrapping up

Negation feels easy, but obviously is not. Not only are there varieties of English which use different rules for negation, even within standard English there are places where negation becomes puzzling. There is some slight evidence that we may be getting rid of some of the worst excesses, but bureaucratic language can always be relied upon to come up with questionable usages. Certainly the standard variety of English uses fewer markers of negation than was once the case, and examples like (11) from Chaucer and (12) from Shakespeare are rarely found in literary styles today.

(11) He neuere yet no vileynye ne seyde In al his lyf unto no maner wight.
He never yet no evil not said in all his life to no kind of person.
'He never said anything evil to anyone of any rank'.

(12) I haue one heart, one bosome, and one truth, And that no woman has, nor neuer none Shall mistris be of it, saue I alone. (*Twelfth Night* II.i: Viola disguised as a man)
'I have one heart, one bosom, and one truth, and no woman has it and none shall ever be mistress of it except for me'.

What should I read?

For readable introductions to double negatives see Crystal (1984) and Cheshire (1998). For a full discussion of negation in a number of languages see Jespersen (1917).

References

Barber, Katherine (ed.) 1998. *The Canadian Oxford Dictionary*. Toronto: Oxford University Press.

Cheshire, Jenny 1998. Double negatives are illogical. In Laurie Bauer & Peter Trudgill (eds), *Language myths*, 113–122. Harmondsworth: Penguin.

Crystal, David 1984. *Who cares about English usage?* Harmondsworth: Penguin.

Curme, George O. 1931. *A grammar of the English language. Vol III: Syntax*. Boston: Heath.

Davies, Mark 2004. *British National Corpus* (from Oxford University Press). Available online at https://www.english-corpora.org/bnc/.

Fogarty, Mignon 2020. www.quickanddirtytips.com/grammar/could-care-less-versus-couldnt-care-less. Posted 16 Jan, accessed 4 May 2020.

Fowler, H.W. 1968 [1926]. *A dictionary of modern English usage*. 2nd edition revised by Sir Ernest Gowers, corrected. London: Oxford University Press. For a more recent edition: doi:10.1093/acref/9780199661350.001.0001

Jespersen, Otto 1917. *Negation in English and other languages*. Det Kongelige Videnskabernes Selskab. Historisk-filologisk Meddelelser I, 5. Copenhagen: Høst.

Merriam-Webster n.d. Is it 'could' or 'couldn't care less'? www.merriam-webster.com/words-at-play/could-couldnt-care-less, accessed 4 May 2020.

Partridge, Eric 1963 [1947]. *Usage and abusage*. Harmondsworth: Penguin.

Quirk, Randolph, Sidney Greenbaum, Geoffrey Leech & Jan Svartvik 1972. *A grammar of contemporary English*. London: Longman.

5 *All the way from the Ukraine*

The definite article

Andreea

Setting the scene

Learning to drive a car involves choosing between learning to drive an automatic car and learning to drive a manual car. People tend to have a strong preference for one or the other. The two types are very different because in an automatic car, the driver does not need to select gears themselves, the car sorts it all out for them. In contrast, in a manual, the driver is forced to choose gears, and even though this can become automated with practice, the selection still needs to be made every time, regardless of whether the driver is fully aware of it or not. This same distinction applies to languages with regard to the definite article: some languages require speakers to commit to using a definite or indefinite (or sometimes generic) version of a noun (*the car* vs *a car*, or *cars* in general), other languages do not enforce such commitment on their speakers.

English is one of those languages which forces speakers to think about the definite article: the most frequent word in the English language is *the*. We thus think and talk a lot about it. In practice, we don't limit ourselves to using the definite article to point out the definite, familiar or recently mentioned, but we use it for much more. More, in fact, than we can sometimes reasonably explain. And because we use *the* so much, we are often not even aware of the complexities it presents. But before I come to all that, let me first explain how *the* is typically used in English.

English has two main articles: (definite) *the* and (indefinite) *a(n)*. There is also a zero article, and although we don't hear or say it, linguists know it is there, e.g. *Students are people too*. In deciding between *a(n)* X, *the* X and simply X (here's a decision you didn't even know you were making) speakers weigh up two main factors: whether the entity in question (the noun X) is a specific one, and whether the person you are talking to is familiar with it (Bickerton 1981). So *a car* is any generic car, whereas *the car* is a specific one or one that has just been mentioned or is close enough that I can point to it. A bird is any bird your mind conjures up: *a sparrow* for me because I am European, *a tui* or *a kiwi* for my daughter as she is growing up in New Zealand. But, as it happens, *the bird on our fence* is neither of these; that bird is a specific albeit rather nondescript bird whose name is unfamiliar to me. When talking about multiple entities, we can also leave out the

DOI: 10.4324/9781003148999-5

definite article: *other birds are pretty too*, or put it in: *the other birds on our fence are pretty too*, depending on whether we are thinking of generic birds or specific birds, and on how much is said about them. In short, *the* is used when the noun following it has a unique reference or is familiar to the speaker (usually because it is physically present or has just been referred to).

However, over the years, it has become clear that *the* is working overtime, in more functions than previously assumed. In some cases, it appears in places it is not expected to be for no good, explicable reason; for instance, with certain collective nouns (*the government voted on the abortion bill today* vs *government voted on the abortion bill today*; it is unclear what the difference between these two expressions is, if any). In other cases, it turns up in contexts which already express inherently definite meanings (*the Ukraine* – why *the*? as far as I am aware there is only one Ukraine). More than that, in some of these contexts, it seems to have attracted additional meanings (*is that the wife calling?*) and in other contexts it contrasts, not just with the indefinite article *a* but also with *my* and *your* and with some plurals (*Romanians are everywhere nowadays* vs *The Romanians are everywhere nowadays*). So how do we really use *the* in English?

Definite articles and place names: where on earth is *the* Naki?

Given the rule of thumb mentioned above, one might expect the definite article to be redundant with names (i.e. proper nouns), which are inherently definite, specific and ideally uniquely identifiable. Let's start with place names and then consider other proper nouns.

If you have ever visited New Zealand, you may have noticed that for locals, the definite article (*the*) seems to 'come and go' as the speaker pleases in certain place names. So I might accurately say that *My friend is from the Waikato (region)* or simply *He is from Waikato*. Someone can come from *Taranaki* but not from *The Taranaki*; however, they could hail from *the Naki* (this being a common shortening of *Taranaki*).

It is not just names of regions and provinces that can vary with respect to *the*. In New Zealand, we have *The North Island* and *The South Island*, but also *North Island* and *South Island* (though admittedly, the article-less form is not acceptable in all contexts or by all speakers). And then there is *Cook Strait* and *the Cook Strait*: Radio New Zealand discussed an event taking place 'in the Cook Strait' (RNZ Rural News, 12:30, 11 March 2020), and a few months later, the same news site announced that 'Some Interislander ferry services are cancelled from this afternoon with 6m waves forecast in Cook Strait' (RNZ News site, 12:44, 1 July 2020).

When presented with any variation, the linguist's first instinct is to look for a pattern. Like a second Marie Kondo, we want to tidy up the system, to find a neat rule and arrange all examples accordingly, so that there's a place for everything. Bauer (2016) feels that, for some place names used in lists, especially in weather forecasts, inclusion or exclusion of *the* could be a matter of what precedes the place name: when following *and* or a preposition (*in, on*), the article tends to be deleted. Perhaps deleting articles helps keep things short in weather forecasts where space is at a premium. Another explanation might be that we are looking at a change in progress, whereby a fossilized version of [determiner + place name + noun] (*the X Island, the X region*) is losing its head noun (*island, region*) but not the article. Neither of these fully explains the data, and more examples are needed (partly because place names are not frequent to begin with). So, we still have untidy examples and uncategorized cases.

Beyond New Zealand English, there is also variation in certain country names: *(the) Sudan, (the) Ukraine, (the) Yemen, (the) Lebanon.* It has been proposed (Berezowski 1997, Langendonck & Velde 2009) that where there is variation, a general rule might be that when proper nouns are used as names referring to countries understood to be administered and organized by humans, the general article is dropped. However, when used descriptively to refer to regions or geographic areas in which the direct human involvement is backgrounded, the definite article is retained. Their idea is that when we refer to *the Ukraine,* we think of it as humanly governed and organized, and when we drop *the*, we think of Ukraine as a geographical area. Unfortunately, it is not entirely clear why this distinction should apply to Ukraine but not to the Netherlands (we can have *the Netherlands* but not **Netherlands*).

Definite articles and collective nouns: is that *the* Americans?

But wait, there's more. When *the* turns up with certain collective nouns, it suddenly attracts additional meanings and undertones beyond definiteness itself. While it is true that language can be and often is creative and ever-changing, and that we could conjure up new and exciting sentences never heard before, the reality is that in our everyday lives, we tend to recycle phrases which we have said and heard before (see also Chapter 2, on norm). One consequence of this is that in time, over thousands of language exchanges, speakers begin to make associations between different word combinations and certain ideas. For example, while the verb *cause* can mean 'to bring something about', it turns out that in actual use, *cause* is always negative: something can *cause a commotion*, *cause a disaster*, *cause a catastrophe*, but never *cause someone to fall in love*, *cause a success*, *cause a triumph* or *an achievement*. So, to put it more accurately, *cause* really means 'to bring about something undesirable'. There is no lexical reason why *cause* could not be used positively; we just don't use it that way.

So, what associations have speakers been making between *the* and the nouns it precedes? The first is something that might be thought of in terms of distancing. *The* can be used to demarcate the speaker's distance from the noun following it. Here are some sentences to illustrate the point (from Acton 2019, pp. 53–4):

(1) The Americans do love cars!
(2) Americans do love cars!
(3) We Americans do love cars!

In (1) and (2), the speaker is distancing themselves from the group identified by the collective noun *Americans*. In fact, it is very likely that the speaker uttering (1) is not American at all, signalled by *the* (exclusive of speaker), whereas, in (3), they certainly are, signalled by *we* (inclusive of speaker). It seems strange to think of *the* as being in semantic opposition to *we*, but the sentences above show precisely that. It seems stranger still to associate the definite article with distance because its function is precisely the opposite: *the* is typically used to discuss people, events and things which are familiar. It is almost as if *the* points out familiar entities for both speaker and listener, or entities which, while familiar to both speaker and listener, at the same time, distant (in some way) from the speaker. Moreover, the distancing use of the definite article is not available to all nouns, it only seems to apply to nouns that denote nationalities or groups (collective nouns).

Acton (2019) found that in political discourse, American English speakers were much more likely to use [*the* X] (e.g. *the Republicans*) if they were trying to distance themselves from the people referenced by the noun following the article. Here is an example (Acton 2019, p. 60):

(4) Paid for by Bernie 2016 (not the billionaires). (from US Senator Bernie Sander's presidential campaign website)

But here is an example where *the* is used to refer to a particular party as a unified front (also from Acton 2017, p. 60), rather than expressing distance:

(5) The Tea Party Patriots depend on grassroots activism where it counts: near you. Local Groups are the backbone of our activities across the nation. (The website of the 'Tea Party Patriots')

So a good way to sum up what *the* is doing in these examples is to say that it adds emotional colour.

Definite articles and loaded nouns: is that *the* wife?

Matters get yet more complicated, because the use of *the* can trigger more than just mere distancing. It can apparently translate to downright mockery. Consider these next sentences:

(6) Oh who is that calling, is that the wife?
(7) Oh who is that calling, is that your wife?

In (6), according to Acton (2019, p. 61) *the wife* attracts a mocking and derogatory tone, although he does admit that in some circles, it could even be thought to express deference (in other words, the exact opposite). For at least some of us, it can also be playful and affectionate. Whatever the intended connotations, (6) would probably most likely be used in informal, spoken situations. Comparatively, the tone of (7) is (exclusively) neutral. Whatever the precise difference, the point is that there is definitely a difference between (6) and (7), and depending on the speaker and situation, the use of *the* adds emotional colour to what is being said.

Here are some more examples illustrating differences in emotional colour involving *the*. Compare the earlier example of *the wife* in (6) with *the friend* and *the one* below:

(8) Is that *the* [accented] friend or is that just a new friend?
(9) Is she the one?

In these sentences, the definite article signals a special relationship that is probably seen in a positive light, particularly in (9). Finding *the one* is usually considered a good thing, unless it results in the derogatory version of *the wife* in (6). As Biber et al. (1999, p. 264) accurately state, phrases containing the definite article 'require extensive pragmatic inferencing on the part of the addressee'. Just how the addressee is able to unpick this extensive pragmatic inferencing is not entirely clear but the context is also likely to help. We also don't know how much of the heightened emotion comes from the definite article and how much is of it arises from the context alone.

Sentences like *Have you seen the cat?* (something my husband often seems to ask, much to my daughter's annoyance: *He has a name you know!*) or *Have you brought in the washing?* (something I often ask him) are not necessarily trying to imply distance, but they do seem 'emotionally loaded' in other ways (*the cat* could be seen as playful and affectionate, *the washing* could be seen as deliberately foregrounding the joint nature of the problem, *it's not just my washing for that matter*). So why is it OK to use the definite article in these examples, when the nouns in question are neither previously mentioned in the discourse nor uniquely identified in the linguistic context?

Grannis (1972) explains these uses by recourse to what he calls the 'conspiracy of uniqueness' between speaker and hearer. Never mind that everyone knows there to be plenty of cats around and plenty of washing in the world, if the speaker and hearer mutually agree to conspire in pretending that the cat and the washing in question are unique (for the purpose of their interaction), then the definite article is fine in those sentences.

Following on from Grannis (1972), Matt Gardner and Sali Tagliamonte (2020) investigate which types of nouns are more likely to occur with the possessive *my* and which ones would be used with the definite article *the*. They code a large corpus of English and test for a myriad of possible factors, ranging from who the speakers are to the nature of the ownership relationship (whose *wife/car/washing* is it really?) and the formality of the interaction. What they find is that the big factor tipping the scale towards *the* or *my* has to do with the likelihood of the nouns in question being communally owned. Nouns which are considered to be periodically communally owned occur with *the*. Nouns which are individually owned tend to occur with the possessive *my*, *your* and so on. So *car, cat* and *dog* would frequently take *the*: *where is the car/cat/dog?* meaning (more accurately) 'where is our car/cat/dog?'. In contrast, nouns more likely to be uniquely or individually possessed (in Western culture, a prime example would be *wife*), do not so readily occur with *the*. Interestingly, aside from romantic partners and body parts (*my right arm* is hopefully mine and mine alone), there is little else that consistently occurs with the definite article. This trend might also explain why, according to Matt Gardner and Sali Tagliamonte (2020, p. 250), *the wife* is 'most stigmatized culturally'.

Definite articles and generic singular nouns: going to *the* hospital?

Upon learning that British Prime Minister Boris Johnson had been admitted into hospital, following his diagnosis with Covid-19, US President Trump is quoted in *The Guardian* as saying 'Hey, it's a big move going to *the hospital*, he's a great gentleman, I hope he's ok' (*The Guardian*, 6 April 2020). A few weeks later, another article from *The Guardian* reported: 'About 8,000 more people have died in their own homes since the start of the coronavirus pandemic than in normal times, a Guardian analysis has found, as concerns grow over the number avoiding going to *hospital*' (*The Guardian*, 8 May 2020). So which one is correct or better? Actually, they are both correct.

You may have already spotted a difference between English varieties. American English and British English have different preferences: the first example is a quote from the US president; the second is (probably) written by a British English journalist. It has indeed been long noted that the British tend to leave out the article (Quirk et al. 1985, pp. 277–9 and Biber et al. 1999, pp. 261–3). Crucially, variation exists within the English spoken in England itself, not just across English varieties. It seems reasonable to assume that a system which has allowed variation in the use of *the* within it will also ripple out to further variation in new varieties of it.

Finnish linguists Markku Filppula and Juhani Klemola (2017) set out to investigate definite article use across English varieties and looked at no fewer than ten varieties: American English, British English, Canadian English, East African English, Hong Kong English, Indian English, Irish English, Jamaican English, Philippines English and Singaporean English. They carefully analysed examples of real language interactions (corpora) by extracting typical phrases where there is variation in definite article use (according to Quirk et al. 1985, pp. 277–9 and Biber et al. 1999, pp. 261–3).

They found that, as confirmed by others, British English omitted *the* most often, while American English used it more often, though not the most on their scale. Jamaican English and Canadian English were closest to British English in their preference for omitting *the*. At the other end of the continuum, the Asian varieties of English, Hong Kong English and Indian English used the definite article the most, with American English coming in third (2017, pp. 162–3).

But why would this be? We don't know for sure. One possibility is that we are looking at effects arising from postcolonial contact varieties (the term refers to contact between two languages, here a native variety, such as Chinese, and an incoming colonial one, in this case, English – of course, it is contact between speakers of those languages, because languages do not exist in vacuum, in absence of any speakers). While language contact could explain the patterns found in Irish English, many of the Asian languages in contact with English do not have a definite article at all (for instance, Hindi and Chinese) so the native language cannot be the source of the inclination towards high uses of the definite article. Various theories have been put forward (Sand 2003, Siemund 2013), but we still have not arrived at a definitive explanation.

Wrapping up

For something so short and insignificant-looking, the English definite article poses some tough questions. First, there is variation in its use with proper nouns: most do not have it, some country names have it in some sentences but not in others. So what is the exact different between *Ukraine* and *the Ukraine*? Second, when used with certain collective nouns, like *Americans* and *Republicans,* but also with some other nouns, like *wife* or *cat*, it seems to add various shades of emotional colour. But here too, questions remain unanswered. Is the definite article the source carrying these emotional overtones, or is it the surrounding context, or is it a combination of the two? And how do we explain wider differences in patterns across English varieties as a whole?

What should I read?

Bauer (2016) is highly readable and easy to follow, as is Filppula & Klemola (2017). Acton (2019) is a bit more technical but rewarding for those interested in a full treatment of this topic.

References

Acton, Erik K. 2019. Pragmatics and the social life of the English definite article. *Language* 95(1): 37–65. doi:10.1353/lan.2019.0010

Bauer, Laurie 2016. Why is there nothing to do in the Manawatu? *New Zealand English Journal* 29/30: 1–10.

Berezowski, Leszek 1997. Iconic motivation for the definite article in English geographical proper names. *Studia Anglia Posnaniensia* 32: 127–144.

Biber, Douglas, Stig Johansson, Geoffrey Leech, Susan Conrad & Edward Finegan 1999. *Longman grammar of spoken and written English.* Harlow: Longman.

Bickerton, Derek 1981. *Roots of language*. Ann Arbor: Karoma. doi:10.26530/OAPEN_603354

Filppula, Markku & Juhani Klemola 2017. The definite article in World Englishes. In Markku Filppula, Juhani Klemola, Anna Mauranen & Svetlana Vetchinnikova (eds), *Changing English: Global and local perspectives* (Vol. 92), 155–168. Berlin: Walter de Gruyter.

Gardner, Matt & Sali Tagliamonte 2020. The bike, the back, and the boyfriend: Confronting the "definite article conspiracy" in Canadian and British English. *English World-Wide* 41(2): 225–254. doi:10.1075/eww.00047.gar

Grannis, Oliver 1972. The definite article conspiracy in English. *Language Learning* 22: 275–289. doi:10.1111/j.14671770.1972.tb00088.x

Langendonck, Willy van & Mark van de Velde 2009. The function of (in)definiteness markers with proper names. In *Proceedings of the 23rd international congress of onomastic sciences*. Canada: York University.

Quirk, Randolph, Sidney Greenbaum, Geoffrey Leech & Jan Svartvik 1985. *A comprehensive grammar of the English language*. London: Longman.

Sand, Andrea 2003. The definite article in Irish English and other contact varieties of English. In Tristram Hildegard (ed.) *The Celtic Englishes III*, 413–430. Heidelberg: Winter.

Siemund, Peter 2013. *Varieties of English: A typological approach*. Cambridge: Cambridge University Press.

6 *A large amount of exceptions*

Countability

Laurie

Setting the scene

Derwing (1973, p. 124) tells the story of how his daughter, at the age of three, discovered that orange juice came from oranges. She knew the words *orange* and *orange juice*, and could use them perfectly appropriately, but she suddenly had the insight that they were related. The story is a nice one, and tells us something about the way in which language works. Even when the language provides clues (like the form *orange* in both expressions), we do not need to see the link to use the words properly. We can use the words *health* and *filth* even if we do not know that they are related to *heal* and *foul,* respectively. Where grammar is concerned, our overt knowledge is usually even less. And one area where this is noticeably true is in the area of countability. We use the grammatical systems of countability effortlessly, but we have little perception of what it is we are doing, and why even the label may not help us much.

Countability is usually treated as the difference between two classes of noun: 'countable' or 'count' nouns on the one hand, and 'uncountable' or 'mass' nouns on the other. Count nouns can be counted (*one book*, *two books*), mass nouns cannot (**one knowledge*, **two knowledges*). We will see other differences between the two in a moment. Countability is not something that native speakers think about much, but if you look in grammars or dictionaries for foreign language learners, you will find nouns discussed and overtly marked. It is an important category in English, often because of the way certain quantifiers, like *some*, *few* and *much* are used.

But what is the problem? *Books* are countable because you can see them and point to them individually, while *knowledge* is sort of amorphous and cannot be divided into neat little packages, and at first glance, the distinction might seem more to do with the nature of the world than with grammar. Things are not that simple, though.

First of all, what is a countable noun is not simply a matter of the way the world is constructed. It is partly a matter of how we perceive the world, or, the way our language categorizes the world for us (and we can argue about whether this is the same thing or not). In English, *information* is a mass noun (we cannot have **two informations*), but in French *information* (meaning the same thing) is often used

DOI: 10.4324/9781003148999-6

in the plural, so it is countable. *Research* is another mass noun in English, but the German translation *Forschung* is frequently used in the plural. *Spaghetti*, a word which we have borrowed or stolen from Italian, is a mass noun, but in Italian it is a plural noun, and you find things like (1).

(1) Ecco gli spaghetti. Mangiamo gli.
Here is/are the (plural) spaghetti (plural). Let us eat them.

Most surprisingly, except in special legal uses, the word *money* is not countable in English, even though money is one of the most obviously countable things you can think of.

The reason that this is so important for foreign learners of English is that it has implications for a number of ways in which the noun can be used. If we stick with *book* and *knowledge* as our examples of countable and mass nouns respectively, we find the differences in usage illustrated in Table 6.1.

These facts about English are not particularly surprising, and not at all mysterious. There are, though, complications with the system, some of which are fairly trivial, and some of which are rather more telling.

Less and *fewer*

The first is that the system is changing – just a little bit. Before the First World War, we could have added two extra lines to Table 6.1. It would have allowed *fewer books* but not **less books*, and *less knowledge* but not **fewer knowledge*. By the middle of the twentieth century, *fewer* was losing ground (Partridge 1969), and these days *less* is by far the more common form both for count and for mass nouns. With twenty-twenty hindsight, it is perhaps not surprising that this was a weak point in the system. First of all, there were places where a choice between the two was possible: should it be *less than four hours* or *fewer than four hours*? *Hours* is plural, so we might expect *fewer*; on the other hand, *four hours* is a lump of time, not just a tally of hours, and *less* is appropriate under such circumstances. Also, *less than five pounds* might mean £4.10, but *fewer than five pounds* suggests a round number of pounds. Furthermore, if we want to talk about greater numbers

Table 6.1 Contrasting usages with count and mass nouns

a.	*book	knowledge
b.	a book	*a knowledge
c.	five books	*five knowledges
d.	many books	*many knowledges
e.	*much book	much knowledge
f.	*a piece of book	a piece of knowledge
g.	*some[i] book *but* some books	some knowledge

[i] In these examples, *some* is to be pronounced as [sm] with no vowel or a minimal vowel, not as in *Some mothers do have 'em*, where *some* rhymes with *come*.

or amounts, we have to use *more*: *more books*, *more knowledge*. If we need only one word for one extremity, why should we need two for the other? And thirdly, *few* was also proving difficult to use (Fowler 1968), so that *few*, *fewer* and *fewest* were all under threat. Although *less* with countables is now the dominant form, there are still some speakers who use the old system, and that is why we get letters in the press complaining about supermarket signs with messages such as *Less than 10 items*. *Item* is a count noun, *less* in the old system goes with mass nouns.

This change to the system is not, in the wider scale of things, particularly important. *Less* has changed its function and *fewer* has been replaced. This does not change countability, it just changes one of the ways in which countability is indicated grammatically, one of the ways in which it is marked. Because it has been the subject of so much prescriptive comment, it has taken on an importance out of all proportion to its effect on the language system, and made countability seem threatened.

Coffee and *cake*

The second complication is one that has always been here. Some nouns arise in both count and mass constructions. As an example, consider the word *cake*. We can have *a cake*, *five cakes*, *many cakes*, and we can also have *cake* (as in *Cake is good for children*) and also *much cake* (*How much cake have you eaten?*), *a piece of cake*, and, in the old system, *less cake*. You can find the same pattern with many words denoting food and drink: *beer*, *cheese*, *chocolate*, *coffee*, *curry*, *ice-cream*, *pasta*, *tea*, *trifle*, *wine* and so on.

At first, this might seem like a minor consequence of the items in the real world coming in large masses sometimes, and sometimes in portion-sized lumps. But when we look a bit further, this is not really a sufficient explanation. Because when we think of things that are typically mass nouns, we can nearly always use them in count noun patterns as long as we mean 'types of X'. For example, although *butter* is typically a mass noun (*How much butter do we have?* **Can I have a butter, please?*), we can quite easily say *There are dozens of butters on the supermarket shelves these days*. Similarly with *jam*, *honey*, *margarine*, *milk*, *spaghetti*, *yoghurt* and so on. We can push this further. If you imagine a story set in the siege of Paris, when people had to eat rats, then *Would anyone like some ([sm]) rat?* becomes normal (*[sm]* is pronounced as indicated in Table 6.1). And if you imagine a children's story about bookworms, *Would anyone like some index?* becomes possible. While there is no absolute free-for-all (*knowledges* is still very awkward, even if you mean 'types of knowledge', *informations* is still odd, *furnitures* is surely impossible – although we can have *pieces of furniture*), even *bread*, which most of the time is a mass noun with the count counterpart *loaf*, can be countable when it means 'types of X'.

This is interesting. It means that we do not have words listed in our heads as count or mass nouns, it means that somehow we are calculating that we need a count or a mass use of a noun, and then using the relevant patterns to give the meaning we want. It also means that when we come across a new noun, the syntactic pattern it occurs in tells us something about its meaning. For example, if we do not know the modern meaning of *tweet*, the headline (from the *New Zealand Herald* of 29 December 2019) *Tweets that have come back to bite Donald Trump*, tells us that a tweet is something that you can count.

Masses of quantifiers

Now let us turn to another minor mystery. Over the years, English has had a large range of vague quantifiers: things like *a bunch of*, *heaps of*, *loads of*, *masses of*, *stacks of*, *tons of* and others. It may help to think of these things as complex determiners. *A bunch of* implies that the things collected are countable, as does, for example, *a number of*, but most of these expressions can be used indifferently with count or mass nouns. We can have *heaps of books* or *heaps of information* (in the latter case, of course, figurative *heaps*). One such expression, however, seems to require mass nouns, and that is *amount of*. *A large amount of information* is fine, *a large amount of book*s was not at all fine until quite recently. It had to be *a number of books*. Yet for some reason, *amount* has become a quantifier which does not distinguish between count and mass nouns. We find examples like those in (2).

(2) a. There were [...] a certain amount of mothers and prams [...]. (Christie, Agatha 1965. *At Bertram's Hotel*. Leicester: Thorpe (large print) edition, 2010, p. 139)
b. There would be just the right amount of people on the street. (Van Lustbader, Eric 1989. *French Kiss*. London: Grafton, p. 111)
c. They've got a fair amount of members here. (Satterthwait, Walter 1992. *A flower in the desert*. Toronto: Worldwide, p. 119)
d. An even greater amount of members. (RNZ National, Two Cent's Worth, 15 December 2019)

It is not clear to me why this development took place. Maybe, originally, the use of *amount* with, for instance, *people*, was intended to depersonalize them and turn them into a faceless mob; but if that is the case, the distinction was rapidly lost, and *amount* is today just another vague quantifier. More likely, it was just bringing *amount* into line with other words like *heaps* which are not fussy about countability.

Neither of the recent developments (the loss of *fewer* or the emergence of *amount* with count nouns) really attacks the core of the grammar of countability. Instead, it changes the grammar associated with two words. These are relatively minor changes. The next set of potential changes seems more serious.

Much and *little*

One of the uses of *much*, as we have seen, is as determiner with uncountable nouns, as in (3).

(3) How much information do you need?

But *much* has a number of other uses in English, including things like *how much* and *not much.* So when we see something like (4) (from the British National Corpus (BNC), Davies 2004–), we have to very careful in our analysis, and note that this is not the same *much* we found in (3).

(4) [T]eachers use questioning to check up on how much children have taken in.

On the other hand, we find instances where *much* followed by a noun which looks plural is precisely the *much* we found in (3). Examples, again from the BNC, are in (5).

(5) a. a few more won't make much odds.
b. I don't have that much brains, but I'd say I had good common sense.
c. and really very much thanks to Fox.

In the examples in (5), the apparently plural nouns following *much* are really mass nouns, and not the plural of the form with no *-s* (*odd, brain, thank*). So although the examples in (5) look odd, they actually show countability working well. However, there are other instances (and yet again, the examples come from the BNC), where we find *much* followed by a genuinely plural noun, and here the general pattern of countability in English grammar seems to be broken.

(6) a. No, can't, too much children there.
b. Unless you'd er think of America, but they've got so much problems there that they've got to look within themselves now haven't they?
c. Did you notice much differences in the work once you got promoted [...?]
d. But there wasn't much students then, we had about four of five in the beginning.
e. and after much tears and heartache we've come up with the winner.
f. How much copies is that then? In simple terms?
g. it doesn't sound as if people had much inhibitions about coming up to you and asking you.
h. Because he's got so much decorations up.
i. got so much dreams
j. young man paid such interest in the garden and paying so much compliments.

These examples come from spoken English, and we have no information as to whether the speakers involved are speakers of standard English or of some other variety. Nevertheless, there are sufficient such examples for it to become clear that this is not just an error, even if this particular pattern is not very common, and even if *much dreams*, for instance, is really intended to pattern with the examples in (5).

One possibility is that the pattern we see in (6) is a trace of a new pattern and that the language is just beginning to change. One of the findings that historical linguists have reported repeatedly over the last half-century or so is that change often starts in non-standard varieties and then spreads into standard varieties. So we could be seeing the very first traces of a change coming in from some non-standard variety, which one day will become normal in standard English (just like *The house is being built* that was mentioned in Chapter 1, Introduction).

But we do not know. An alternative hypothesis might be that *much* is becoming generalized to new environments, just like *less*, discussed above, because it has so many functions, and because it can easily occur in front of plural nouns (as in (5)). And yet another hypothesis might be that some of these patterns (if not all) are remnants of earlier forms of English. The examples in (7), again from the BNC, look as if they are parallel to the examples with *amount* cited above: *deal* is typically used with mass nouns.

(7) a. I agree that we have a great deal of things to learn from the United States [...]
 b. there are a great deal of economies to be reached [...]

Strang (1970, p. 139) points out that the restriction of *deal* to mass nouns is an eighteenth-century phenomenon, and that before that it could be used with either mass or count nouns.

A rarer pattern is that illustrated in (8).

(8) We're getting very little results from it. (RNZ, National, Morning Report, 16 April 2015)

The sentence in (8) does not mean that the results were small, only that there were few of them. So *little*, in this sense, should also go with mass nouns. The more examples we find of nouns used countably with the grammar of mass nouns or vice versa, the less stable the whole system of countability looks. At the moment, majority usage does not threaten this, but there are sufficient signs of weakness for us to wonder what might happen next.

What would it look like if English did lose countability?

Would it be possible for English to lose countability? Countability is not just the ability to count things, so plurality could still remain in the system without it. The grammatical feature of countability involves the use of determiners as set out in Table 6.1. So instead of having *much* and *many*, we would have to have a single word or expression covering both, like German *viel* 'much, many' or French *beaucoup de* 'much, many'. We already have an expression like that: *a lot of*. *A lot of* can be used with countables (*a lot of books*) and with uncountables (*a lot of knowledge*). We would have to lose the distinction between *less* and *fewer*, but as has already been shown, we are already losing that, and many speakers can already have *less books* and *less knowledge*. Quantifiers would have, in general, to fit with both countable and uncountable uses of nouns, and again this is already happening with things like *stacks of books*, *stacks of knowledge*, *an amount of books*, *an amount of knowledge*. We would have to allow *some* (unstressed) to occur with both singular and plural nouns, including those which are now used countably. Since we can already have *some butter* and *some butters*, we are well on the way here, too.

What is perhaps less clear is whether all nouns would have to be able to occur in both the singular and the plural. We have very few that occur in only one form (*knowledge* and *measles* being examples), so although we have not reached any such goal – if it is even necessary – we are potentially well on the way towards it. This means that we can use English, for the most part, as though it has singular and plural but no countability already. The difference between *sm books* (plural) and *sm knowledge* (singular) must then depend on the perception that there are several books but only one knowledge – which is the perception at the heart of countability – but we can express this solely in terms of number, without making appeal to any other grammatical feature.

What this suggests is that it is not only possible to lose countability as a grammatical feature, but that some varieties of English may already be well on track to doing so. And that would, in turn, explain why *fewer* is being lost and *amount* is being reassigned.

What should I read?

On the notion of countability in general, and how much more complicated it is than I have explained here, see Murphy (2010) and, especially, Wierzbicka (1988). On the whole question of language affecting our perceptions (so-called 'linguistic relativity'), specifically with relation to countability, see Lucy (1992). On the more general topic of language change, a good introductory book is Aitchison (1981).

References

Aitchison, Jean 1981. *Language change: Progress or decay?* London: Fontana. [Later editions are published by Cambridge University Press. doi:10.1017/CBO9780511809866]

Davies, Mark 2004. *British National Corpus* (from Oxford University Press). Available online at https://www.english-corpora.org/bnc/.

Derwing, Bruce 1973. *Transformational grammar as a theory of language acquisition*. Cambridge: Cambridge University Press.

Fowler, H.W. 1968 [1926]. *A dictionary of modern English usage*. 2nd edition, revised by Sir Ernest Gowers. London: Oxford University Press. For a more recent edition: doi:10.1093/acref/9780199661350.001.0001

Lucy, John 1992. *Grammatical categories and cognition*. Cambridge: Cambridge University Press. doi:10.1017/CBO9780511620713

Murphy, M. Lynne 2010. *Lexical meaning*. Cambridge: Cambridge University Press. doi:10.1017/CBO9780511780684

Partridge, Eric 1969 [1947]. *Usage and abusage*. Harmondsworth: Penguin.
Strang, Barbara M.H. 1970. *A history of English*. London: Methuen.
Wierzbicka, Anna 1988. *The semantics of grammar*. Amsterdam and Philadelphia: Benjamins. doi:10.1075/slcs.18

7 *The author has finished this chapter last year*

The present perfect

Andreea

Setting the scene

Outside linguistics circles, English is not widely known for its elaborate and magnificent grammatical artillery; indeed, some people will go as far as claiming that English has no grammar at all. Especially when compared to a language like Latin – famous for its case system, verb conjugations and…for being dead (but I digress). Aside from the disquieting implication that there is nothing to study for those of us whose day job is to research English grammar, there are larger issues at stake in defending the claim that English does indeed have a grammatical system.

Now, if we were to build a defence for the claim, a good place to start looking for traces of grammatical structure is in how the language deals with time. Many of the world's languages employ grammatical means for organizing events in time (what grammarians call 'tense', not because it is stressful – that can be just an unfortunate by-product – but because it comes from the Latin word *tempus* meaning 'a portion of time' via the Old French word *tens*, meaning 'time'). Not every language marks time (for example, most famously, the Amazonian language of Pirahã, Everett 2005), but in a world where (arguably) time is money, languages are pushed to express time in some form or another, and grammar is often enlisted in the task (other means could be adverbs or adverbial phrases, like in Chinese, *zuotian* 'yesterday' or *2020 nian* 'the year of 2020' can be used to specify the timing of a given event).

Right on-(linguistic)-trend, English does have grammatical means for marking time. There is a (simple) present tense, for example, *English has grammar,* albeit a rather unexciting one but nevertheless it plays a part in signalling time. The only form of the present tense verb which changes is for the third person singular, unlike languages like German, Romanian or Russian which change verb forms for many, if not all different persons (see Table 7.1). There is also a (simple) past tense, such as *English had grammar*, typically used in narratives and fiction. And arguably, there is a future one, formed with the verbs *will* or *going to*, as in, *English will have a grammar*. The question of whether English has a structural future tense or not is debatable because some people believe using a helping verb like *will* is cheating (Palmer 2014) and not really grammatical machinery *per se.*

DOI: 10.4324/9781003148999-7

Table 7.1 Present tense verb forms in English, German, Romanian and Russian

English (Germanic)	*German (Germanic)*	*Romanian (Romance)*	*Russian (Slavic)*
I speak	ich spreche	eu vorbesc	govorju
you speak	du sprichst	tu vorbeşti	govorish
he/she speaks	er/sie spricht	el/ea vorbeşte	govorit
we speak	wir sprechen	noi vorbim	govorim
you speak	ihr sprecht	voi vorbiţi	govorite
they speak	sie sprechen	ei/ele vorbeşc	govorjat

Be that as it may, no one would argue against the fact that English does have ways of expressing future events.

Simple tenses aside, English also has a system of tenses for forming what we call the 'perfect' pattern. Far from being perfect ('perfect' has to do with being 'finished' rather than with being 'faultless'), the perfect tenses employ an auxiliary (*have* in English) together with the main verb specifying the action, and come in three flavours: the present perfect (*English has had a grammar*), the past perfect (*English had had a grammar*), and the future perfect (*English will have had a grammar*). Among these, the present perfect raises a whole lot of questions which current theory is still grappling with – a whole lot more grammar than we can currently handle, as it turns out. But before I turn to these questions, let me first attempt to convince you that tenses in (English) grammar are not strongly bound to time in real life. For example, just because a form carries the label 'present' does not mean that English speakers actually use it to refer to events which take place at the time of speaking.

Tense is not (true) time

As many learners of English will have discovered, the labels that we associate with various grammatical patterns in English are nothing more than guidelines for typical uses of those forms, not strict rules for how they are interpreted. Taking the simple present tense as an example and scanning English sentences uttered by native speakers, we can see that this tense is not just used to refer to the 'here and now' (*I am so fed up with this lockdown*, or *Here comes the bride!*). But it is also used to express habitual events (*I get up daily at about 7am*), repetitive or cyclic events which may not even occur at the time of speaking/writing (one could utter in June or any other time of year: *Christmas is always such a merry occasion*), or lasting states that are true at the time of speaking/writing but which go well beyond this time, spilling into both past and future (*The Cookie Monster loves cookies*).

You might be forgiven for thinking this is a mere semantic quibble. After all, these events do surround the present time, even if they are not strictly speaking confined to it, so in many ways, we are still dealing with the present. But what do you make of the passage in (1), from the website www.history.com?

(1) September 1st. Germany invades Poland. On this day in 1939, German forces under the control of Adolf Hitler bombard Poland on land and from the air.

Here, the present tense clearly references events which (mercifully) are slipping further and further into our past. The use of the (grammatical) present tense to refer to past events, labelled the 'historic present' or 'scientific present', is neither an error, nor poor linguistic style. In examples like these, the present form is used to express events in a dynamic and animated manner, allowing the hearer or reader to feel like an active observer of their unfolding over time (in the case of historic present especially) while still maintaining their relevance to the 'here and now' (particularly in the case of the scientific present). The present tense form is nothing but an illusionary trick to direct the attention of the hearer (or reader) to a particular desired state of affairs.

The converse is also possible: the present tense can be used to refer to what is in reality, a future event. Consider for instance: *My train leaves at six pm next Tuesday* or *My son turns seven in November*. The events in these sentences are interpreted as taking place at a time following speaking time; in other words, sometime in the future relative to speaking time. Such 'scheduled/planned present' uses are similarly not grammatical faux pas, but part of the repertoire of native and perfectly capable English speakers.

It might therefore help to think of tense as a grammatical pointer (linguists use the term 'deixis') towards one direction or another, which can flex as needed, according to the speaker's needs.

Unpacking the present perfect tense in English

Having seen the flexibility of tense uses in English, let's now turn our attention to the present perfect. Despite seeming fairly inconspicuous, the present perfect certainly has some surprises in store. Judging by its label, one might guess that the present perfect denotes an action which is happening 'here and now' (the present bit) and which is completed (the perfect part – for a discussion of aspect in English grammar, see Chapter 9, on the progressive). One issue which has been troubling linguists is the question of whether the present perfect is a kind of 'tense', in agreement with, for example, Pullum & Huddleston (2002, p. 116), or a kind of 'aspect', a position held by the older grammar, Quirk et al. (1985, p. 189), but also by the *Longman grammar of spoken and written English* by Biber et al. (1999, p. 460) (see discussions in Ritz 2012 and Werner et al. 2016). While these positions might represent what appear to be purely theoretical disagreements between two possible grammatical roles, more radical proposals have also been put forward.

Hübler (1998) argues that the function of the present perfect is not at all grammatical but solely pragmatic; being a device which signals the speaker's strong emotional attachment to the proposition and thus, not related to timing at all. We will see more about what this means shortly, but for now, it is important to note that the precise interpretation of the present perfect remains a matter for debate, and one which can only be reliably investigated by examining real language data.

More recent analyses have taken to analysing the exact specifics of how speakers actually use the present perfect construction in actual situations. This research has uncovered four main uses of the present perfect in English, each being quite precise in its function, and more troublingly for linguistic theory, not all uses have explicit relevance to the 'here and now' (Ritz 2012, Yao 2016 and just about any article on the present perfect).

First, in sentences like *We've been besties since forever*, the present perfect conveys actions or events which started in the past (sometimes a distant past at that) and continue to the time of speaking (or writing). Despite being a present tense, the focus here is not on the continuation of the event into the 'here and now', though that is also part of the meaning, but rather on the extended duration of the period which the event spans. In other cases, its focus might be the exact time when the event started, as given in the sentence *Mickey Mouse has been around since 1928*. The durative interpretation arises from the use of the present perfect in conjunction with durative adverbials like *since X* or *for X*.

Secondly, there are examples like *I have never drunk rakia in my life*, in which the present perfect expresses an experiential or existential situation and often appears together with a negator like *never* or *not*.

Thirdly, there are sentences like *He cannot come out right now because he has broken his leg*. Here, the present perfect tense stipulates results or consequences, depicting ongoing and almost stative-like events; although the breaking event has happened, its consequences are to be felt for a long time to come – that broken leg will certainly take a while to heal – and it is on these consequences that the focus of the action is directed.

Finally, and now we come to the use of most interest for our purposes here, the present perfect can be employed to express 'hot news'; a vivid and self-explanatory label which linguists have embraced ever since the early 1970s when McCawley (1971) coined it. While the 'hot news' use of the present perfect is itself no longer terribly newsworthy, it is surely its most famous use of all, since much linguistic literature is dedicated to it (McCawley 1971, Klein 1992, Schwenter 1994, Ritz & Engel 2008, Schwenter & Torres Cacoullos 2008, Ritz 2010 and many others). Here is a selection of examples in which the present perfect stipulates 'hot news', taken from English-language newspapers around the world on 9 April 2020:

(2)
a. Freezing, Coatless Woman Has Decided It Is Spring. (*The Onion headline*)
b. To the distress of wordists, a dictionary has confirmed the lexical veracity of 'irregardless'. (*The Guardian*)
c. A transcriber has made an unfortunate blunder during today's Covid-19 update when they miscaptioned Prime Minister Jacinda Ardern's comments on live TV…she urged people to 'enjoy your staycations', [but] the words were captioned on TV to say 'enjoy your Steak Asian'. (*New Zealand Herald*)

In examples (2a-c), the woman's decision that spring had arrived, the dictionary's confirmation and the transcriber's subtitle blunder are all deemed newsworthy and significant for the reader, despite being past events (for all intents and purposes). The significance for the reader stems from the fact that the consequences of these (admittedly past) events have implications for the 'here and now'. In other words, what these examples have in common is their relevance to the present.

While some have argued that the 'hot news' present perfect ought to be grouped together with resultative uses of the present perfect (the broken leg example) or with experiential present perfect cases (the rakia example) (Michaelis 1998, Howe 2013), others strongly believe that the 'hot news' present perfect is a separate category in its own right. The latter position rests on the idea that 'hot news' present perfect uses can introduce new topics in the discourse and highlight their importance (Schwenter 1994). Regardless of what we call it, the fact remains that the 'hot news' present perfect is not actually referencing a present action. So how might one explain the use of a present (tense) form to refer to a past event? And why would it be used to signal 'hot news'?

It has been suggested that by means of its longer and more complex form (involving two separate verbs, the auxiliary *have* and the main verb), the 'hot news' perfect can draw extra attention to the event in question. In line with the iconicity and economy principles described by Haiman (1980), language will afford more complex and longer expressions to more important or more complex information. Pushing this point further, we can see Hübler's position (1998), which does away with the grammatical aspect interpretation altogether, and emphasizes the pragmatic dimension of the present perfect. He argues that the longer form of the present perfect signals a stronger emotional attachment compared to the alternative lighter form of the simple past. Thus, that which is deemed to exert more (cognitive) effort is coded by greater linguistic effort.

The road not taken **– the present perfect is not replacing the simple past in English**

Predicting the linguistic future proves no easier than predicting the stock market. One possible way to attempt predictions of this sort (and most linguists wisely don't!) is by looking at what has been taking place in (genetically) similar languages. So if we want to know how English might evolve in future, we may want to take a look at what other Indo-European languages are doing. As regards the present perfect, Indo-European languages, like French and German, exhibit an increase of the present perfect over time, to the extent that we see it entirely dominating the narrative landscape. In these and other Indo-European languages, the simple past tense has been altogether dethroned by the ever-prevailing present perfect (Bybee et al. 1994). In French, the well-known *passé composé* is taught to many a French learner as the basic narrative tense of choice, perfectly compatible with adverbs of past time, such as (the French for) *yesterday* and *last week*.

It might sound odd that tenses would 'fight it out' like this, but grammatical structure is nothing but recurring habit, as speakers are sensitive to associations and frequencies of use. The historic trajectory of the present perfect in Indo-European languages is elegantly explained by Schwenter (1994, p. 1007), who describes the 'hot news' present perfect as holding 'the most tenuous relation between a past event and the present'. This tenuous relation allows the present perfect form to have its eye on the past, while 'talking' in the present. Over time and with sustained use, the (weak) present link becomes eroded, less important and in the end, altogether lost, and its eye to the past dominates. And so it is that a new narrative tense is born, at the expense of other tenses previously conscripted into the role (usually the simple past, if there is one in the language). It must be noted that, in collaboration with his colleague Torres Cacoullos, Schwenter (2008) went on to revise his original explanation of the connection between 'hot news' and the past as a result of his analysis of Spanish. Regardless of the exact details, proximity of the events described to the present (time) remains a clear relevant factor.

A look at history confirms the trend proposed by Schwenter for French too. Apparently, prescriptive French grammarians from the sixteenth century would frown at the use of the *passé composé* in contexts which referenced events occurring further in the past than the previous 24 hours. By the eighteenth century, however, these norms relaxed considerably and the *passé composé* was allowed to cast its net further into the past than the 24-hour limit (see Yao 2016, p. 131 and Fournier 2004 cited in Ritz 2018, p. 139).

Well, the French grammarians of the sixteenth century might be very pleased with modern English indeed! In contrast to its genetic cousins, the English present perfect appears to resist any such change, according to Yao (2016). The sustained and continued use of the 'hot news' present perfect in narratives depicting newsworthy information endures, but there is no indication that it is about to take over as the tense of choice for narratives more generally. Despite an increase in frequency of use, the English present perfect does not seem to run wild and unconstrained (Elsness 2009, Hundt & Smith 2009, Yao 2016), prompting linguists to wonder why English is doing something different.

Non-standard present perfect uses – surprisingly surprising

Alas, not everyone agrees that English is doing something different! Analyses of Australian English exhibit what Marie-Eve Ritz and others term 'non-standard' uses of the present perfect. Another use, another puzzle to explain in what is already a rather messy picture!

Ritz found present perfect examples whose interpretations remain in keeping with 'hot news' readings, but which do allow past adverbials (contra previous analyses, especially of American English). What is more, these uses take on a vivid mirative function – expressing surprise – and bearing a strong rhetorical function (Ritz 2010, 2018). Non-standard present perfect examples seem to resemble temporal progressions, where a simple past tense verb might have otherwise been found, behaving like the new narrative tense on the block, but with a twist: an accompanying overtone of surprise.

Ritz's data (2010, 2018) is primarily comprised of police media releases. Also investigating the present perfect in police language, Cox (2005) uncovers similar uses of the present perfect in New Zealand English. The non-standard present perfect sentences identified by linguists like Ritz do more than just attention grabbing (a function attributed to the 'hot news' type), and, at the same time, they do more than merely illuminate a narrative sequence: they have the added value of surprise. The speaker is signalling their surprise at the sequence of events described, thereby increasing their emotional involvement with the content of the utterance. So here we have a grammatical device marking tense (and aspect), which is not just used to the anchor events in time, but also to express the speaker's own reaction to these events (in other words, a pragmatic function). Hübler would be pleased with this analysis. Here are two examples illustrating the non-standard present perfect from Ritz (2018):

(3) It will be alleged that on October 20, 2005 the woman has stolen the man's vehicle and has then been involved in a traffic crash in the car park of the Phoenix Shopping Centre in Spearwood. The vehicle has then crashed into another vehicle, with the woman fleeing the scene on foot. (Ros Weatherall, WA Police Media, 4 November 2005 as cited in Ritz 2018, p. 150)

(4) I looked over my shoulder, he's standing right behind me. He's walked in, y'know the doors that separate the classrooms, he's come in the one behind me, they all started laughing. (triple j radio, Sydney, 28 February 2000 as cited in Ritz 2018, p. 145)

As can be seen in (3), we do not expect a car to be stolen nor do we expect it to crash into another vehicle. The use of the present perfect helps to 'describe salient events, perhaps to make them more vivid to the reader as police are often appealing to potential witnesses', explains Ritz (2018, p. 149). Similarly, the anecdote in (4) tells the story of a school student (the speaker) who was caught in the act of impersonating his teacher – there is an undeniable element of surprise in this narrative.

Further disgruntlement with the conclusion that the present perfect is not really a narrative tense comes from Walker (2011), who proposes that indeed a variant of the 'hot news' present perfect is functioning precisely as a kind of narrative, after all. Sifting through stories told by British football players, he argues that a fifth function of the present perfect is on the loose: the 'narrative present perfect', though he admits he is not the first to coin the term, citing Lowrey (2009, p. 231). The narrative present perfect seems a lot like an incoming narrative tense. For one, footballers are using the present perfect to develop the main story line; in other words, developing the progression of events (classic narration if there ever was one), and for another, the restriction of temporal adverbials referencing the (recent) past seems to have been relaxed.

Yet there are differences between this use and what is happening in other Indo-European languages too. Walker's data contains what looks like a random mix of simple past and present perfect tenses in the same story; not (yet?) a dominant invasion led by the present perfect against the simple past. Here is an example (2011, p. 78):

(5) I don't think it was a red card. Mark may have caught their player but he was right next to me and it didn't look a booking. It was on the halfway line and we had players chasing back but the referee has made a decision and there's nothing we can do about it. (Derek Young, manager Aberdeen, *Daily Record* (Scotland), 30 November 2009)

Walker explains the shifting between one tense and another as follows. Footballers (or their team managers) in his interviews would start out their stories with simple past tense forms, but as they began to relive these events again, they tended to shift into the present perfect as a means of placing themselves inside the narrative, as active participants or observers. In other words, the tense choice is not (just) for the benefit of the hearer, but also effective in aiding the speaker relive past events of personal significance.

Walker (2011) goes on to claim that, while the present perfect and the simple past tense may look like distinct entities, they share a great deal of 'grey area' between them. So whence this 'tense shifting'? According to Walker, speakers from various regions around Britain seem to change between simple past and present perfect quite freely. He concludes that the strict dichotomy between the simple past and present perfect tense in English is artificially generated by prescriptive norms imposed by standard written language and not reflective of the reality of spoken English.

Wrapping up

The present perfect in English raises a number of questions. Here is a construction which starts out firmly as a grammatical device and yet, its function spills beyond the scope of grammar, reaching into pragmatic and rhetorical depths. Given its varying uses, it remains difficult to capture the exact role of the construction or even its essence (is it a kind of 'tense' or a kind of 'aspect'?). It also remains unclear how far English is following in the historical footsteps of other related languages, with respect to development of the present perfect as the 'soon-to-be' narrative tense of choice, displacing the simple past tense. Its very relationship with the simple past seems uncertain.

But the story of the English present perfect is one which figures genre (police language), medium (spoken/written) and variety (American/British/Australian/New Zealand) effects, all of which appear to be influencing its use and function. And despite the questions it raises, or perhaps precisely because of these, the present perfect is a fitting example to illustrate that English grammar is indeed very much alive and kicking!

What should I read?

Marie-Eve Ritz has written amply on the topic and her 2018 article is a detailed up-to-date introduction to the latest uses of the 'hot news' present perfect. Her 2012 chapter in the *Oxford handbook of tense and aspect* gives a technical treatment of the inner workings of tense and aspect in relation to the present perfect for true die-hard enthusiasts. Jim Walker's (2011) article makes for an informative read too; he also fills in various background details useful for readers interested in the context surrounding this topic. Finally, the 2016 De Gruyter volume: *Re-assessing the present perfect* contains recent research about the 'hot news' present perfect from an empirical perspective (the introduction is definitely worth a look for those interested in this topic).

References

Biber, Douglas, Stig Johansson, Geoffrey Leech, Susan Conrad & Edward Finegan 1999. *Longman grammar of spoken and written English*. Harlow: Longman.

Bybee, Joan, Revere Perkins & William Pagliuca 1994. *The evolution of grammar: Tense, aspect and modality in languages of the world*. Chicago: University of Chicago Press.

Cox, Rebecca 2005. *Preterite uses of the present perfect in New Zealand English narratives: A case study*. MA Dissertation, University of Canterbury.

Elsness, Joan 2009. The present perfect and the preterite. In Günter Rohdenburg & Julia Schlüter (eds), *One language, two grammars? Differences between British and American English*, 228–245. Cambridge: Cambridge University Press.

Everett, Daniel 2005. Cultural constraints on grammar and cognition in Pirahã: Another look at the design features of human language. *Current Anthropology* 46(4): 621–646. doi:10.1086/431525

Fournier, Jean-Marie 2004. Crise de langue et conscience linguistique: la question de la règle des 24 heures. *Dix-septième siècle* 223: 251–264. doi:10.3917/dss.042.0251

Haiman, John 1980. The iconicity of grammar: Isomorphism and motivation. *Language* 59(4): 515–540. doi:10.2307/414448

Howe, Chad 2013. *The Spanish perfects: Pathways of emergent meaning*. Basingstoke: Palgrave. doi:10.1057/9781137029812

Hübler, Axel 1998. *The expressivity of grammar: Grammatical devices expressing emotion across time*. Berlin: Mouton de Gruyter. doi:10.1515/9783110800173

Hundt, Marianne & Nicholas Smith 2009. The present perfect in British and American English: Has there been any change, recently? *ICAME Journal* 33: 45–63.

Klein, Wolfgang 1992. The present perfect puzzle. *Language* 68(3): 525–552. doi:10.2307/415793

Lowrey, Brian 2009. La directionnalité et la nature non-téléologique de l'évolution linguistique. *Anglophonia* 26: 231–246. doi:10.4000/anglophonia.907

McCawley, James D. 1971. Tense and time reference. In Charles Fillmore and Terence Langendoen (eds), *Studies in linguistic semantics*, 96–113. New York: Holt, Rinehart and Winston.

Michaelis, Laura 1998. The ambiguity of the English present perfect. *Journal of English Linguistics* 30(1): 111–157. doi:10.1017/S0022226700016200

Palmer, Frank 2014. *The English verb*. 3rd edition. Abingdon: Routledge.

Pullum, Geoffrey & Rodney Huddleston 2002. *The Cambridge grammar of the English language*. Cambridge: Cambridge University Press.

Quirk, Randolph, Sidney Greenbaum, Geoffrey Leech & Jan Svartvik 1985. *A comprehensive grammar of the English language*. London: Longman.

Ritz, Marie-Eve 2010. The perfect crime? Illicit uses of the present perfect in Australian police media releases. *Journal of Pragmatics* 42: 3400–3417. doi:10.1016/j.pragma.2010.05.003

Ritz, Marie-Eve 2012. Perfect tense and aspect. In Robert I. Binnick (ed.), *The Oxford handbook of tense and aspect*, 881–907. Oxford: Oxford University Press. doi:10.1093/oxfordhb/9780195381979.001.0001

Ritz, Marie-Eve 2018. "Hot news" and perfect change: Mirativity and the semantics/pragmatics interface. *Catalan Journal of Linguistics* 17: 135–155. doi:10.5565/rev/catjl.245

Ritz, Marie-Eve & Dulcie M. Engel 2008. "Vivid narrative use" and the meaning of the present perfect in spoken Australian English. *Linguistics* 46(1): 131–160. doi:10.1515/LING.2008.005

Schwenter, Scott 1994. 'Hot news' and the grammaticalization of perfects. *Linguistics* 32(6): 995–1028. doi:10.1515/ling.1994.32.6.995

Schwenter, Scott & Rena Torres Cacoullos 2008. Defaults and indeterminacy in temporal grammaticalization: The 'perfect' road to perfective. *Language Variation and Change* 20(1): 1–39. doi:10.1017/S0954394508000057

Walker, Jim 2011. The emergence of the narrative present perfect in British English: Reality or illusion? *GAGL: Groninger Arbeiten zur germanistischen Linguistik* 53(2): 71–87.

Werner, Valentin, Elena Seoane & Cristina Suárez-Gómez 2016. Introduction: The present perfect – A re-assessment. In Valentin Werner, Elena Seoana & Cristina Suárez-Gómez (eds), *Re-assessing the present perfect: Corpus studies and beyond*, 1–20. Amsterdam: De Gruyter. doi:10.1515/9783110443530

Yao, Xinyue 2016. The evolution of the "hot news" perfect in English. *Journal of Historical Pragmatics* 17(1): 129–151. doi:10.1075/jhp.17.1.06yao

8 *An even more interestinger topic*

Comparatives and superlatives

Laurie

Setting the scene

We like things to be simple. If someone asks us why a particular state of affairs should exist, we like to be able to give a single reason: the tides go in and out because of the influence of the moon; I feel sick because I ate too much trifle. But some things are not that simple. In fact, we might suspect that nothing is that simple if we look at it closely. If we ask why the political party we happen to favour lost the last election, there may be any number of reasons (depending on the country in which we live and the recent history of what has been going on). Some possibilities are that the party had been in power for some time and the voters wanted a change, that the leader of the party had lost the support of a large number of people for any one of a number of reasons, that your party was perceived as being likely to affect the economic status of too many voters in a bad way, that there was outside influence in the polls, that voters had believed some false rumours that had been circulated about one side or the other, that the weather had kept most voters at home on the day, and so on. We may not know which of these factors is the most important, and they may all be true at once.

Similarly, complex situations frequently arise when we try to explain patterns of linguistic behaviour. This makes the behaviour difficult to understand, difficult to predict and difficult to explain. We are not good at sorting out the influence of multiple factors at once; even complex statistics cannot always give us useful explanations of what is going on, because statistics can only discuss the influences we can observe and measure. One such linguistic example is the marking of comparison.

Some adjectives denote a single point or an extreme on a scale that you cannot go beyond. *Atomic*, for example, does not occur in expressions like **rather atomic*, **very atomic*, because there is no scale to atomicness. *Colossal* is so big, that you are unlikely to talk about things being *very colossal* or *rather colossal*, *colossal* on its own says it all. Adjectives like *pretty* are different. Someone or something can be *rather pretty* or *very pretty*, there are degrees of prettiness, you can put pretty things on a scale of prettiness. Adjectives that work like *pretty* in this way are called 'gradable' adjectives, and one of the ways in which they show

DOI: 10.4324/9781003148999-8

their gradability is that they have forms showing degrees of application: *prettier* and *prettiest.* In grammatical terms, this is called 'degree' or 'comparison'.

Although adverbs like *soon* can compare as well (*She arrived sooner than I had expected*; *I'd like to see him soonest* – this is now rare), in this chapter I shall limit my attention to adjectives – even though this may be falsifying the situation to some extent.

Gradable adjectives have three forms: the base form (like *big*), the comparative form (like *bigger*) and superlative form (like *biggest*). Usually, -with short, common adjectives like *big,* these forms are made by adding *-er* and *-est* (with some adjustment of the base when necessary, like the double g in *bigger*). Forms like *deeper* and *deepest, smaller* and *smallest, taller* and *tallest, wider* and *widest* and so on are familiar. We will call these the 'synthetic forms' or the 'suffixed forms'. Some very common adjectives have irregular forms: we have *better* rather than **gooder, worst* rather than **baddest* (unless we are very small children, or in the case of *bad,* slang-using people for whom *bad* means 'good' or 'attractive'). There are not many of these forms, and they are relatively boring – even if they are a nuisance for foreign learners: once you've said they are irregular, there is not much more to say about them. With long and rare adjectives we do not use the suffixes, but use *more* and *most* in their place, so that we say *more inconsolable, most prescriptive, more vituperative* and so on, rather than using forms in *-er* and *-est.* We will call these the 'periphrastic forms'. This gives rise to one of the least soluble mysteries of English grammar: how do speakers know when to use *-er* and *-est* and when to use *more* and *most*? And if we cannot answer that one, then there is another. How can we teach English comparison to speakers of other languages? Is *commoner* more common than *more common* or is *more common* commoner?

Actually, even if it were not for this huge mystery, comparison would give us plenty to think about. Here are some questions that we might have considered, but will not consider just now.

How do we know whether an adjective is gradable or not? Lots of people say that one thing is *more unique* than another, while others find such statements abominable, because, they say, *unique* is an extreme and cannot be compared. Clearly there is a difference of opinion on gradability for some reason. You might think that dead is dead, an extreme, but Dickens (in *A Christmas carol,* 1843) speculates that 'a coffin-nail [might be] the deadest piece of ironmongery in the trade'. So is *dead* gradable or not?

If one tree is tall (*tall* is an adjective), but another is taller (*taller* is also an adjective), why do we say that yet another is *the tallest* (where the word *the* implies that *tallest* is a noun)?

If there are many people in a room, and some are reliable and *reliable* is a gradable adjective, then some of these people must be more reliable than others. But if more of the people are reliable than otherwise, we can say that *we have more reliable people in the room*, and our statement is ambiguous: are there more people or are they more reliable? How often are we really in doubt?

If we have many men in a room, we might decide that one of them is clearly the handsomest man in the room. But one of the others might be said, without contradiction, to be *most handsome. Most handsome* can be the superlative of *handsome*, but it can also mean 'extremely handsome'. How can we tell which kind of *most* we are dealing with?

If we return to our three trees, the one that we called *taller* is obviously less tall than the tree that we called *the tallest*. Is the one that we started by calling *tall* now the least tall? Are *less* and *least* negative counterparts to *more* and *most*, and just how do they work?

If we have two puddles of different depths, then one of them is deeper than the other, and the other is less deep. But is the one that is *less deep* also *shallower*? If it is, is it still *shallower* if both puddles are over two metres deep? There may be a difference between what logic tells you and how you feel.

If you see two women, and you call one of them *an older woman* and the other *an old woman*, which is the older?

In this chapter, we leave all these questions to one side, however interesting they may be on their own right, and concentrate on matters of form.

The double comparative

We can begin by looking at a construction which is common in spoken English, but which is no longer common in formal written English: the double comparative. In a double comparative, the problem of whether to use *-er* or *more*, *-est* or *most*, is avoided, because both are used. We end up with examples like the classic ones in (1a, b) – both from Shakespeare, and more modern ones like (1c).

(1) a. The Duke of Milan / and his more braver daughter could controul thee. (*The Tempest* I.ii)
 b. This was the most unkindest cut of all. (*Julius Caesar* III.ii)
 c. I think he's probably one of the most unluckiest people in the world. (Quigley, Sheila 2011. *Nowhere man.* Houghton-le-Spring: Burgess Books, p. 199.)

The rule with double comparatives, like the rule with double negatives (see Chapter 4, on double negatives), seems to be that that you mark the grammatical category as often as you can, to make sure it is not ignored. If we were to repeat (1b) in current standard English, we would say *This is the unkindest cut of all*, and the omission of *most* would not make any difference to the meaning. Prescriptivists tend to deplore the double comparative, presumably because it is redundant, but the use of the construction in non-standard varieties worldwide is probably a remnant that goes back 400 years or more. Examples like (2) sound slightly odd because they include an irregular form, but they are not, in principle, any different from the Shakespearean examples.

(2) …so much more worse… (RNZ National, Checkpoint, 25 February 2020)

Simple adjectives

When dealing with single comparatives (i.e. not double comparatives), it is difficult to know where to begin: different scholars work with different categories. A sort of blanket statement that is often found is that monosyllabic adjectives (those that are only one syllable long) take *-er* and *-est* (Fowler 1968). As a descriptive statement this is wrong. But it's not completely wrong, so we can use it as a starting point.

At the start of this chapter, I used examples with *big, deep, tall, wide* to illustrate the use of *-er* and *-est* suffixation. This is because such adjectives are frequently found with the suffixed form. But what are 'such adjectives'? If we look at them linguistically, we note a couple of things about them: most of them are monosyllabic (but not all), most of them are Germanic in origin (but not all), most of them (but not all) are morphologically simple (they do not have prefixes or suffixes). Some authorities (e.g. Fowler 1968, p. 163) give lists of relevant adjectives, but that is not really fair, because if you come across a new adjective that you have never met before, *smalt* for example, you will still know whether to use *-er* or *more*, so there must be a generalization in there somewhere. Nevertheless, we can make a list of a few adjectives which seem to behave in the expected way, and a few which do not, as in (3).

(3)

Monosyllabic		*Disyllabic*	
Regularly allow *-er*	Do not often use *-er*	Regularly allow *-er*	Do not often use *-er*
big	cross	clever	bitter
deep	real	shallow	concise
tall	right	silly	foreign
wide	wrong	simple	silent

As an aside, the word *wrong* is interesting in this regard. First, there is no obvious reason why we should prefer *more wrong* to *wronger*, although we seem to. But some people do say *wronger* on occasion. The interest is in how it is then pronounced. We would expect it to rhyme with *longer* and *stronger*, but it doesn't, despite the fact that these are the only fully parallel forms in English (we could add *younger* as another relevant form, though it does not rhyme with the others). *Wronger* does not rhyme with *longer* ('more long'), it rhymes with *longer* ('one who longs'). There is a [g] sound in *longer* ('more long') and *stronger*, missing in *wronger* and *longer* ('one who longs') – unless you come from a place like Birmingham or Liverpool, England where the [g] sound is always pronounced. Given that *wronger* is rare anyway (so we do not have much experience of hearing it), and that the obvious parallels go the other way, it is not clear why it should be pronounced in this way so regularly. Here is a minor mystery in the middle of a much bigger one.

To return to the examples in (3), there is one pattern not illustrated there, but which is fairly consistent. Although past participles can act as adjectives, monosyllabic past participles do not take the *-er*, *-est* suffixes when they are compared:

bent, burnt, hurt, marked, spoilt, stuck can take *more* and *most*, but rarely *er* or *est*. *Drunk* ('intoxicated') can take *-er* and *-est*, but its meaning is not quite right for a participle.

Even adjectives which can take *-er* and *-est*, though, take *more* and *most* on some occasions. In particular, although synthetic forms are possible with expressions like *He is more mad than bad* (*He is madder than he is bad*) and *He is more brave than I/me* (*He is braver than I/me*), the periphrastic forms seem more natural most of the time. In other words, the syntactic structure in which such forms occur has an influence as well as the particular adjective involved, its etymological origin, or its morphological structure.

Long adjectives

There is general agreement in the literature that long adjectives are those with three or more syllables (see e.g. Bauer et al. 2013, p. 111), and that they take *more* and *most*, not *-er* and *-est*. This is truer (or should that be 'more true'?) than the corresponding statement about monosyllabic adjectives, but still not entirely true. It is true that we are more likely to say that someone is *more intelligent* than someone else rather than *intelligenter*, that we are more likely to talk about the *most beautiful* girl in the room than about the *beautifullest* girl, but synthetic forms are still found occasionally.

The most famous case is *curiouser*, especially in the phrase *curiouser and curiouser*. This is a quotation from Lewis Carroll's *Alice's adventures in Wonderland*, and it is a joke (although the joke has been lost over the years). The original is given in (4), and occurs just after Alice has eaten a cake which has made her grow.

(4) 'Curiouser and curiouser!' cried Alice (she was so much surprised that for the moment she quite forgot how to speak good English)... (Carroll, Lewis 1865. *Alice's adventures in Wonderland*. London: Macmillan, Ch 2)

The lack of 'good English' is precisely because *curious* should not normally take the *-er* form. Example (4) is an instance of what Fowler (1968, p. 164) calls 'novelty hunting', the use of an unexpected synthetic form to shock the reader or listener. A recent example is given in (5).

(5) 'A substantial sum?'
'The substantialler the better.' (Burrowes, Grace 2017. *Too Scot to handle*. New York and Boston: Forever, p. 156.)

There is one place, though, where the three-syllable rule is regularly breached. It is where the prefix *un-* is added to an adjective which could normally take a synthetic form. Even if the adjective then has three syllables, it can maintain the suffix, as in the examples from the British National Corpus (BNC) (Davies 2004–) in (6).

(6) a. the real world is always much untidier than the world of the textbook.
b. seeking to control unrulier elements in their own jurisdiction.
c. The Black Friar is one of London's unlikelier pubs [...]
d. Litigation can pay off even in the unlikeliest circumstances.
e. He accounted himself the unluckiest man alive.
f. To me it's the unhappiest house I've ever been to.
g. she had the uncanniest feeling [...]

Disyllabic adjectives

The real problem, though, comes with disyllabic adjectives (ones that are two syllables long). We have seen that sometimes they behave like monosyllabic adjectives and take the synthetic form, and sometimes, like *common* and *handsome*, they can take either the synthetic or the periphrastic form. Some of them can also take only the periphrastic form (see (7)). This means that the behaviour of disyllabic adjectives is particularly unpredictable.

(7)

Regularly allow *-er*	Allow either *-er* or *more*	Do not usually allow *-er*
clever	common	cheerful
happy	handsome	civil
narrow	likely	festive
silly	polite	timid

There are some guidelines to keep the different types apart, although they do not always work.

- As with monosyllabic adjectives, past participles do not take synthetic comparison: *most driven, more shaken, more spotted, most surprised, more wounded.*
- In the same way, forms with an *-ing* suffix do not take synthetic comparison: *most binding, most boring, more fitting, most stunning, more tiring, more wearing*. There are minor exceptions here: Perkins (1967) has *the diggingest dog*, and American English allows *the winningest team.*
- Possibly part of the same overall pattern, adjectives that end in *-able, -al, -(i)an, -ar, -ful, -ic, -ish, -ive, -less, -ous, -some* and some other rare suffixes tend to avoid synthetic forms, though occasional novelty-hunting forms are found, as in (8).
- The list of affixes in the last point notably omits *-y* and *-ly*. Both of these allow the suffixed form, though there is some evidence that there is change occurring in English, and that most words with *-ly* now are more usual with *more/most* (Bauer 1994).
- Many of the examples already given are equivalent to saying that adjectives which come from Greek, Latin and Romance are less likely to use the synthetic form. There are counter-examples like *grand, great, noble, stupid,* but

there seems to be a tendency in this direction, although it must be recalled that many such adjectives are long adjectives, and so are covered by a different set of generalizations.

- Where there is a choice, it also seems that recent use of *more* is likely to lead to further use of *more* (Chua 2019).
- American English seems to use rather more periphrastic forms than British English (Bauer et al. 2013).
- Despite all the generalizations, choice is also influenced by the individual word involved. The suffix *-some* may, in general, be found more often with *more*, but *handsome* is found more often with *-er*/*-est*.

(8) a. You're already rich and famous, [...] and you're going to be richer and famouser. (Block, Lawrence 2003. *Small town*. London: Orion, p. 335)

b. 'I've been up for three hours, nervouser than a nun at a penguin shoot,' she said. (Sandford, John 2007. *Golden prey*. New York: Putnam, p. 19)

c. ...she's very patient, much patienter than I am. (Kelly, Susan 2003. *Cold blood*. London: Allison & Busby, p. 45)

The trouble with all these guidelines is that they do not add up to a definite answer in any particular case. We can say that some forms are more likely (or likelier) in some contexts than others, that some forms are commoner (or more common) than others, but we cannot say either that one form is definitely right and another definitely wrong (even in a particular environment), or that we know why a given form has arisen.

There are some factors which make any form of prediction even more complicated:

- It tends to be assumed that what is true for the comparative form is true for the superlative form. We know this is not entirely true. *Winningest* may be found, but *winninger* is not (Bauer et al. 2013, p. 113) or is much rarer. Even a single example of this kind raises the possibility of further such examples, even if we do not have proof of them.
- It tends to be assumed that all meanings of any given adjective work the same way. Consider the adjective *remote*. My own intuition about this is that I would easily say *I haven't the remotest idea*, but that I would have to say *That is the most remote island in Britain*. Even if my intuition actually reflects my own usage, I have to accept that not everyone's use is the same, because corpus studies do not show any such pattern. But if we look at *faint* in the BNC, *fainter* never occurs with *idea* while *faintest* occurs with *idea* more often than in any other use (and that is even if we do not count similar forms like *faintest notion*, *faintest clue*, *faintest suspicion*), so comparative and superlative forms do not always have similar distributions.

- The examples here (and the examples used by most commentators) have come mainly from written English. D'Arcy (2014) provides evidence from New Zealand and British varieties of English that the variation between *-er* and *more* is found more often in written English than in spoken English. In spoken English it is far more likely to be true that monosyllabic adjectives take the synthetic form and trisyllabic adjectives take the periphrastic form. This at least makes it easier to know what to teach foreign learners of English, although disyllabic adjectives may still be problematic.

Wrapping up

The expected default for paradigms like cases in nouns or person in verbs is that the marking for the category concerned is totally predictable. Speakers have to be able to create appropriate inflected forms very quickly, and use them without fear of being misunderstood. Having multiple forms to fill various slots in the paradigm is thus unusual. However, recent scholarship has thrown up quite a number of instances of overabundance of this type (see e.g. Thornton 2012). It is still unusual for such overabundance to be found in such a large portion of the inflected words, and it is even more unusual for the factors affecting the choice to be so complex and seemingly incomputable. This means that there is a mystery here on multiple levels. Not only do we want to know how speakers manipulate such a case (and manipulate it even in a time when the system seems to be changing), we want to know how we can at least model actual usage so that we can teach foreign learners how to use English comparison. At the moment, both remain obscure: the English comparative is a challenge to our understanding of how languages work, and we can give learners of English only a rough idea of how to compare adjectives. A possible silver lining in all of this is that it may be that the amount of variability in this area means that we don't notice incompetence, because even competent usage is unpredictable.

What should I read?

A summary of research in this area can be found in Bauer et al. (2013). The fullest discussion is to be found in Mondorf (2009), and related papers. Another good discussion, but a more compact one, can be found in Hilpert (2008). There are many other discussions of some parts of the area, and most English grammars provide an introduction to the topic.

References

Bauer, Laurie 1994. *Watching English change*. London and New York: Longman. doi:10.4324/9781315844169

Bauer, Laurie, Rochelle Lieber & Ingo Plag 2013. *The Oxford reference guide to English morphology*. Oxford: Oxford University Press. doi:10.1093/acprof:oso/9780198747062.0001.0001

Chua, Deborah 2019. Comparative alternation in y-adjectives: Insights from self-paced reading. *Language and Cognition* 11(3): 373–402. doi:10.1017/langcog.2019.22

D'Arcy, Alexandra 2014. Functional partitioning and functional limits of variability: A view of adjective comparison from the vernacular. *Journal of English Linguistics* 42: 218–244. doi:10.1177/0075424214539702

Davies, Mark 2004. *British National Corpus* (from Oxford University Press). Available online at https://www.english-corpora.org/bnc/.

Dickens, Charles 1843. *A Christmas carol*. London: Chapman and Hall.

Fowler, H.W. 1968. *A dictionary of modern English usage*. 2nd edition revised by Sir Ernest Gowers, corrected. London: Oxford University Press.

Hilpert, Martin 2008. The English comparative – language structure and language use. *English Language and Linguistics* 12(3): 395–417. doi:10.1017/S1360674308002694

Mondorf, Britta 2009. *More support for more-support: The role of processing constraints on the choice between synthetic an analytic comparative forms*. Amsterdam: Benjamins. doi:10.1075/silv.4

Perkins, Al 1967. *The digging-est dog*. London: HarperCollins.

Thornton, Anna M. 2012. Reduction and maintenance of overabundance. A case study on Italian verb paradigms. *Word Structure* 5: 183–207. doi:10.3366/word.2012.0026

9 *I'm lovin' it*

The progressive

Andreea

Setting the scene

You don't need to be a McDonald's fan to be aware of their slogan advert showcasing Ronald McDonald declaring *I'm lovin' it!* Ever since 2004, this slogan has been buzzing on our television screens and ringing in our ears, and some of us are most certainly not loving it, though undeniably, we are not forgetting it either. Dubbed McEnglish and stigmatized as 'marketing speak', the phrase continues to increase in use and visibility (Freund 2016, p. 50). So why is this expression so memorable and can we pin more on the McDonald's empire than just questionable dietary options?

What's wrong with *I'm lovin' it!*?

Few things give a grammarian more pleasure than deconstructing language examples and trying to figure out how and why certain phrases were put together the way they were. Examples such as *I'm lovin' it!* provide an interesting puzzle (at least a dozen linguistics articles have the actual phrase in their title!) because they lie in the no-man's land between perfectly acceptable by some, and utterly ungrammatical by others, with the tide ever-changing. Pushing grammatical boundaries in this way is part of what makes the phrase *I'm lovin' it!* more memorable.

So, let's look at the parts. *I'm lovin' it!* is formed by a subject pronoun (*I*), the contracted auxiliary form of the verb *be* (*'m*), the verb *love* with the suffix *-ing* (actually it is *-in'* in this case which is a colloquial version of the full *-ing* used to mimic the spoken version of the word) and the direct object *it*. Of most interest here is the combination of *be* plus the suffix *-ing* (the phonological substitution is not relevant to the discussion at hand). *Be* does not contribute any meaning, it just helps to form what learners of English call the 'present continuous' and what (most) grammarians label the 'progressive aspect'. Confusingly, some grammar texts use the labels 'progressive' and 'continuous' interchangeably (Quirk et al. 1985), while others see a difference in their meanings (Mair 2012). But that is not important here either.

The theory goes that verbs (action words) like *swim*, *write* and *monitor* can be felicitously used with *-ing* to express the event described as unfolding over

DOI: 10.4324/9781003148999-9

a certain period of time, and often referencing the 'here and now', at the time of speaking or writing. My own English teacher once described it to me like this: you could only say *John is drinking his hot chocolate* if you could see a little dribble on his chin and smell the cocoa flavour invading your nostrils.

As I am writing this chapter (note the progressive form of the verb here too), the world is dealing with the rapid and worrying spread of the Covid-19 virus, and our own university has this message at the top of all its web pages:

(1) The University is closely monitoring the Coronavirus situation. (University of Waikato website, 3 February 2020)

The use of the progressive is meant to reassure everyone that the University is constantly and tirelessly watching updates on news sites and the World Health Organization guidelines in order to keep us all safe. This is not just a 'here and now' situation but an ongoing, in-progress state of affairs. If you compare that with the non-progressive equivalent *The University closely monitors the Coronavirus situation* – this does not have quite the same implied sense of duration and *ongoing-ness* about it. So, a barely noticeable suffix (*-ing*) is charged with carrying a rather important message.

Yet here is the issue at hand: the progressive form is not available to all verbs in the language, because some verbs have built-in meanings which preclude them from being interpreted as unfolding over a period of time. Consider the jarring sentences below:

(2) ?We are owning a house in the country. (Quirk et al. 1985, p. 198)
(3) ?She is believing in God. (Leech et al. 2009, p. 129)
(4) ?The flag is being red. (Huddleston & Pullum 2002, p. 119)

These types of verbs prototypically denote states, such as *own, be, know, understand*, though there are other types of verbs which also clash with the progressive. They describe ongoing static situations, which by definition, do not change. When an event is understood as unchanging, it becomes incompatible with readings that emphasize its open-ended nature, which leads to a contradiction between the meaning of the verb and the grammar used with it. This then leads to the clenching of editorial pens and furrowing of editorial eyebrows. *Love* is precisely such a verb, and so, according to grammars, Huddleston & Pullum (2002), Quirk et al. (1985), and various usage guidebooks (Swan 1984, Willis 1992), it is (or should be!) barred from occurring in constructions of the sort *I'm lovin' it!*

And yet *I'm lovin' it!* is gaining traction. Over time, grammar guides have relaxed their criteria from denying that stative verbs are ever used with the progressive (Swan 1984), to tolerating their presence in colloquial English (Folley & Hall 2012), and even going as far as formulating explanations of how they might be appropriately used with *-ing* after all (Biber et al. 1999, Hewings 2013). The trouble is that linguists are still at a loss in pinpointing exactly what the progressive is doing in constructions involving stative verbs. The picture is messy. In an effort to explain how and why *-ing* marking could be used with stative verbs, linguistic theory has led us to question whether we even understand its function, with any verbs, stative or not.

Aspect: a look inside verbs and verbing

When it comes to expressing events such as *swim, write* or *sing,* the words used can provide information beyond the details of the actual event. The essence of what is happening is captured by the inner semantics of the verb; *write* involves using a pen or keyboard to produce markings on a piece of paper or screen which carry meaning, blinking involves rapid movement of one's eyelids. But, according to many scholars and most famously noted by the philosopher Zeno Vendler (1957), the semantic core of verbs specifies more than that: it also carries information about the internal structure of the event.

An event like writing can easily be deconstructed in a number of distinct sub-events. If you were watching me write this chapter for instance, you might witness the movement of my fingers on a keyboard over a given period of time, with small pauses between movements, followed by more finger strokes, uncountable coffee cups being sipped – yes, it would be very much like watching paint dry. But if you were watching me blink, well there would be even less excitement and not much to say about that at all. We see people blinking all the time without even being aware of it; as the saying goes, it all happens in the blink of an eye. Not being an eye specialist, I doubt I could even describe what blinking really involves, other than eyelids.

Aside from the duration of an event, there is also its boundedness. That has to do with whether or not the event has a natural endpoint. Writing – in my case, this chapter – will hopefully have an endpoint, after sufficient thinking, sweating, editing, and re-writing has taken place. If you had asked my teenage self, idle gossiping has no particular endpoint as it really could go on for hours. And it often does.

On the basis of these observations, Vendler and other linguists like him categorized verbs into three (or four, depending on how detailed you want to be) groupings:

- Verbs like *write*, also called accomplishment verbs, which are perceived to have duration and a natural endpoint.
- Verbs like *blink*, also called achievement verbs, which are perceived to have no duration because of their instantaneous change but they do have a natural endpoint.
- Verbs like *love*, also called stative verbs, which are said to have no duration because of their stativity and permanence and no endpoint.
- Verbs like *gossip*, also called activity verbs, which have duration but no endpoint.

So the very word used to refer to an event carries built-in expectations of its progression through time. Relatively speaking, some events have duration, others do not. Linguists refer to the relative duration of an event with the somewhat opaque label of 'lexical aspect'. Lexical aspect is so tightly bundled in with the meaning of the verb that speakers do not even notice its presence, yet it's there.

You might want to ask: once enough gossiping, writing, blinking and loving is done and all the verbs have neatly been arranged in their respective cubby-holes, are we that much wiser about how language works than before? Actually, yes, because as alluded to earlier, the baggage that verbs bring with them as they pop out of the dictionary (lexical aspect) interacts with what linguists term 'grammatical aspect', which is the toolkit provided by the language to facilitate clearer signalling of the message intended.

Certain languages (though not all) have further resources to signal aspectual information which do not come part-and-parcel of the verb. Special marking can be used to signal distinctions of duration; in English we use the [*be* + verb + *-ing*] marking pattern (the progressive aspect).

The way English grammatical aspect works is relatively straightforward, it is either there or it is not. Of course, there is no need for a simple binary distinction of grammatical aspect, or even any grammatical distinction for aspect at all. For instance, Wuvulu, an Oceanic language spoken on a small island north of New Guinea has a four-way aspectual distinction. Wuvulu speakers have grammatical markers available to specify whether the event in question is completed (perfective aspect), a recurring event (habitual aspect), simultaneously taking place as another event, or not yet taken place (Hafford 2014, p. 93). Standard German, Dutch, Swedish and Norwegian on the other hand, do not have grammatical means for signalling aspect at all (Bylund et al. 2013). This is not to say that speakers of those languages cannot express the meanings of completed and ongoing events, but they do so in other ways, such as through specific words (adverbs and prepositional phrases), rather than grammatical machinery.

While it is easy to describe how the grammar marks aspect in English, figuring out what the progressive really *means* is another matter. Suffice it to say that initial linguistic analyses and many grammar books (still) claim that progressive marking is associated with an in-progress interpretation. There are at least two types of situations where this kind of detail is useful.

Progressive marking can be handy for discussing events which happen at the same time: *I was writing while the phone rang*. With the help of *be* and *-ing*, the writing process is expressed as unfolding over a period of time which includes and intersects with the ringing of the phone. Grammar allows us to focus on the internal makeup of a given event perceived as being stretched out over time. If you think about it, writing need not necessarily take a long time, in fact, it probably takes very little time to write a short text message on your mobile phone. But it can be a lengthy process too; I have been writing this chapter for a considerable length of time and I am still not done (see my use of *-ing* again). This latter example shows another useful function of grammatical aspect: speakers use it to emphasize the length or duration of an event. My perception is that writing this chapter is taking a long time, so the progressive marking can help signal that explicitly, above and beyond the lexical baggage that the verb *write* brings from its own core meaning.

It turns out that grammatical aspect is not blind, or rather that the language system is not blind to what is going on with the lexical content of words. And so it is that stative verbs, like *love*, are incompatible with progressive marking because – the theory goes – such marking conflicts with their implied permanence. It seems superfluous to signal with grammatical tools something that is already implied to be the case by the semantics of a word, such as *I love coffee* and *I hate sprouts.* Unless it changes, of course. Before considering that possibility, let us consider how the progressive first began to occur with stative verbs.

Stative verbs with progressive aspect – an unlikely romance

Like many a long-term relationship, it is difficult to remember how and when it all started. What we do know is that stative verbs have been making an appearance together with progressive marking since at least the 1800s, as documented by Denison (1999). And while many believe that perhaps the Americanization of English has created a shift in grammatical use (and not just in diets!), see for instance, Smith (2005), we cannot pin this one on McDonald's alone, as the first reported usage dates long before 2004.

We can find examples from British English in the prose of Jane Austen, who used the construction in her novel *Emma* (written in 1816), as well as the letters written by the Romantic poet John Keats (dated 1819 – in Forman 1952) (Denison 1999, pp. 146–7):

(6) I ought to have paid my respects to her if possible. It was being very deficient. (Austen, Jane 1816. *Emma.* London: John Murray)
(7) You will be glad to hear...how diligent I have been, and am being. (John Keats, 1819)

It is also worth noting that the initial use of the progressive with stative verbs may not have been as shocking or as noteworthy as it first appears because progressive marking was itself on the rise with all verbs during the nineteenth century, regardless of their type (Collins 2008, Leech et al. 2009, Aarts et al. 2010 and many others). So the new use of a grammatical pattern with stative verbs, which was well on its way to rising fame already may have simply fallen under the radar of speakers and writers at the time.

Alternatively, the spread of the progressive with stative verbs may have not been a small, unnoticed accident, but a very deliberate linguistic act; an act of linguistic extravagance. Language presents us with a paradox: on the one hand, we want to talk like others talk, in order to make ourselves understood, and on the other, we want to talk shockingly differently, in order to stand out. Push too far in either direction and it all goes wrong, you either sound repetitive, or you sound so strange that people can no longer understand you (or relate to you). Inspired by other linguists, Peter Petré (2017) coined the term 'extravagant progressive' to refer to examples of progressive where it does not fit, namely with stative verbs. He suspected that this use developed as a pure act of linguistic rebellion and devised ingenious ways to study retrospectively how this process unfolded, in order to prove his idea that extravagance of this kind can bring about language change (2017, p. 247).

Regardless of how the *-ing* form ultimately came to be used with stative verbs, there is widespread agreement that the progressive has been spreading in English for some time and that this spread continues at present, with a particularly steep increase in American English. Where disagreements appear is in regard to what the progressive is doing with stative verbs and to what extent it is doing it.

Why might stative verbs be used with the progressive?

Typical ways of explaining what the progressive is doing in sentences like *I'm lovin' it!* involve tweaking our understanding of either what it means for a verb to be stative, or what it means for a verb to be used with the progressive (or both sometimes).

One way around the prohibition of progressive marking with stative verbs is to relax our definition of stativity. Maybe stativity is not a black-and-white matter, in other words, not a binary property (stative/non-stative), but a gradable distinction. Taking this view, Mufwene (1984) arranged verbs on a cline from highly stative (*contain, belong to, need, consist of*), to intermediately stative (*depend, want, intend, wish, love, hate*), to low-stative, (*kick, reach, die, break, hit*), as cited by Aarts et al. (2010, p. 163). Repackaging stativity into a more flexible notion allows various verbs to occur with *-ing* marking without breaking the rules. So what is the function of *-ing* in these cases?

Quirk et al. (1985, pp. 198–9) comment that while stative verbs tend to refer to ongoing, unbounded affairs, they can also be used to express temporariness rather than permanence. Not very stative you might think. Yet, according to Dictionary .com, the meaning of *stative* is given as '(of a verb) expressing a state or condition, as *like*, *want* or *believe*, and usually used in simple, not progressive, tenses' (note the explicit mention of its incompatibility with the progressive here). This definition shows that we might be able to tease apart two different subtle components of stativity: on the one hand, there is the idea of a condition, on the other hand, there is the idea of temporality – conditions can change. So *I'm lovin' it!* really means: I may love it now but I may well hate it later. I am guessing not likely what the advertisers had in mind with the McDonald's slogan.

Another way to explain [stative verb + *-ing*] is by recourse to intensity. It's not that *I'm loving' it!* now (for a limited time) and may hate it later, but rather, that my emotional involvement is heightened to an extremely arresting feeling – you can see the strength of my enjoyment consuming me, it's *that* intense. This appears more in line with the McDonald's slogan. But such an intense interpretation is not for everyone!

The slogan *I'm lovin' it!* has caused problems not just for linguists, but also for advertising bodies from more than 100 cultures around the world, who faced having to translate it into their language (Waliński 2018). Some were indeed able to translate it using an equivalent of the verb love in their respective language, for instance, in French it is *c'est tout ce que j'aime* ('it's everything that I love'), though slightly different in Canadian French: *c'est ça que j'm*, in Turkish it is *işte bunu seviyorum* ('this is what I love'), in Latvian *man tas patīk* ('I like it') – for a comprehensive list see the *Language Log* blog post on this (https://languagelog.ldc.upenn.edu/nll/?p=1954). German initially used *ich liebe es* ('I love it') but immediately switched to the English-language version (Kelly-Holmes 2010, p. 484).

The main problem arising in the translations was not so much from the progressive aspect but from the fact that a verb like *love* brings with it an intensity that, in some languages, is reserved for romantic or other such powerful emotional connections, and cannot be applied to watered-down versions of enjoyment, like dietary pleasures. In an interesting study, Polish speaking philology students from the University of Łódź with excellent knowledge of English were asked to offer suitable equivalent translations for the McDonald's slogan in Polish (Waliński 2018). Waliński (2018, pp. 524–6) found a great number of variant translations proposed, ranging from to *jest pyszne* ('this is delicious'), to *niebo w gębie* ('literally: heaven in the mouth'), *jedz, pij, kochaj* ('eat, drink, love') and *rozpływam się* ('I am melting'). Crucially, there was a distinct lack of the Polish equivalent verb *miłość* for 'love' which did not make an appearance in any of the translations offered, confirming that language is not merely a package for capturing reality as we see it, but it is a culturally constructed lens through which each society conceptualizes its own view of reality.

A third explanation proposed for dealing with the combination of progressive marking and stative verbs has to do with tentativeness and politeness (Quirk et al. 1985, Mair 2012, Kranich 2013). The use of *-ing* with pragmatic overtones of this type does not apply to the McDonald's slogan, but it certainly makes sense in explaining how the following sentences are to be interpreted:

(8) I was wondering if you could help me. (Quirk et al. 1985, p. 210)
(9) I was hoping you will be around. (Kranich 2013, p. 5)

These sentences seem natural in some way because wordiness constitutes a key strategy for signalling politeness in English; the more linguistic fuss and lexical fumbling around is shown, the more polite the utterance. But compare them with their non-progressive counterparts: *I wonder if you could help me* and *I hope you will be around.* There is a clear shift in nuance and tone between these pairs, and especially the latter example (with *hope*) seems not just less polite than the progressive form but could in fact be more threatening, depending on the intonation and eye gaze used.

Even more puzzling, when used with some stative verbs, the progressive can express hidden negative evaluations. Subtle covert linguistic ways of expressing stance constitute one of the more nifty tricks that language offers because it allows us to communicate uncomfortable opinions and cutting judgements completely off the record. Interestingly, and for no good reason at all (as far as we can tell), the adverb *always* appears in [stative verb + *-ing*] carrying speaker's negative stance:

(10) Look at him he is always sitting there doing nothing. (Mazzon 2013, p. 32)
(11) They are always being desperate and tragic. (Mazzon 2013, p. 33)
(12) Michael is always taking cigarette breaks. (Kranich 2013, p. 5)

Why the progressive turns up in the expression of both politeness and disapproval remains a bit of a mystery. Yet it does, and the good news is that proficient speakers of the language have no trouble identifying the appropriate contexts for each use.

But maybe stativity is not the answer to the problem here. A completely different tack in explaining progressive marking with stative verbs involves tweaking not what we understand by stativity, but rather, what we think signals the stative meaning in the first place. Arguing that stativity is not a property of the verb, à la Vendler, some researchers claim that stativity is bigger than the verb and resides across the whole construction, and sometimes, the entire sentence (Granath & Wherritt 2014). When the (larger) construction does not conjure a stative interpretation, the (bare) verb can change its interpretation away from stativity *per se*. Similarly, Huddleston and Pullum (2002, p. 292) argue that when *-ing* is added to *love* it yields an activity reading, equivalent to dynamic *enjoy*. Does that mean we have two different verbs for 'love'? Not exactly. Just that the meaning of *love* is not specified in full until rest of the construction is added to fill in the blanks.

Compare another example with the verb *write*: *Stephen King writes tirelessly* vs. *Stephen King is writing tirelessly*. Both might be factually true, but they are nevertheless subtly different. The first sentence seems to make a statement about Stephen King as a general fact: it is more descriptive in nature than eventful, characterising him as someone who writes tirelessly. The second sentence focuses the attention on the event of writing as a happening rather than on the person as a prolific writer. Note also that the second sentence seems to function as a more natural answer to the question *What's happening?* than the first sentence. In other words, a dynamic reading is privileged over a stative reading, depending on what else is going on in the sentence.

Wrapping up

While all these proposals seem to explain parts of the problem, there are two general issues which remain unsolved for linguistic theory. The first is a general dissatisfaction that we do not have straightforward explanations for what speakers and writers do with the *-ing* construction. There are many potential readings that *could* be intended (temporariness, tentativeness, politeness, intensity and so on), but a set of objective criteria for identifying which one of these *actually* applies in any individual example is still missing (Granath & Wherritt 2014).

Secondly, these examples question our understanding of the progressive construction. What might be a unified and consistent way of conceptualizing the function of (*be*+) *-ing*? Some go as far as to argue that there is no core meaning of the progressive, and that its function is split into an aspectual and non-aspectual use, with the latter being itself made up of various possibilities, but there is even disagreement as to what these other possibilities might be (see discussion in Granath & Wherritt 2014, p. 9). It is not satisfying to have a theory which splits the function of the progressive across different verb types, with no coherent story for how these uses are disentangled by speakers or how they arose in the first place.

What should I read?

Aarts et al. (2010) and Mair (2012) offer gentle introductions to work on the progressive in a condensed form. For a longer and more in-depth treatment of the progressive as a topic of research, see Smith's (2005) dissertation or Kranich's (2010) book on the subject. Waliński (2018) offers a nice cultural linguistics perspective of the (im)possibility of translating *I'm lovin' it!* which is extremely readable.

References

Aarts, Bas, Joane Close & Sean Wallis 2010. Recent changes in the use of the progressive construction in English. In Bert Capelle & Naoaki Wada (eds), *Distinctions in English grammar*, 148–167. Tokyo: Kaitakusha.

Biber, Douglas, Stig Johansson, Geoffrey Leech, Susan Conrad & Edward Finegan 1999. *Longman grammar of spoken and written English.* Harlow: Longman.

Bylund, Emanuel, Panos Athanasopoulos & Marcelyn Oostendorp 2013. Motion event cognition and grammatical aspect: Evidence from Afrikaans. *Linguistics* 51(5): 929–955. doi:10.1515/ling-2013-0033

Collins, Peter 2008. The progressive aspect in World Englishes: A corpus-based study. *Australian Journal of Linguistics* 28(2): 225–249. doi:10.1080/07268600802308782

Denison, David 1999. Syntax. In Suzanne Romaine (ed.), *The Cambridge history of the English language*, 92–329. Cambridge: Cambridge University Press. doi:10.1017/CHOL9780521264778

Folley, Mark & Diane Hall 2012. *My grammar lab (Intermediate B1/B2)*. Edinburgh: Pearson.

Forman, M.B. 1952. *The letters of John Keats*. 4th edition, London: Oxford University Press.

Freund, Nina 2016. Recent changes in the use of stative verbs in the progressive form in British English: I'm loving it. *University of Reading Language Studies Working Papers* 7: 50–51.

Granath, Solveig & Michael Wherritt 2014. 'I'm loving you – And knowing it too': Aspect and so-called stative verbs. *Rhesis: International Journal of Linguistics, Philology and Literature* 4(1): 2–22.

Hafford, James 2014. *Wuvulu grammar and vocabulary*. Doctoral dissertation. University of Hawai'i, Mānoa, Hawai'i.

Hewings, Martin 2013. *Cambridge advanced grammar in use*. 3rd edition. Cambridge: Cambridge University Press.

Huddleston, Rodney & Geoffrey K. Pullum (eds) 2002. *The Cambridge grammar of the English language*. Cambridge: Cambridge University Press. doi:10.1017/9781316423530

Kelly-Holmes, Helen 2010. Languages and global marketing. In Nicholas Coupland (ed.), *The handbook of language and globalization*, 475–492. Oxford: Wiley-Blackwell.

Kranich, Svenja 2010. *The progressive in Modern English: A corpus-based study of grammaticalization and related changes*. Amsterdam: Brill Rodopi.

Kranich, Svenja 2013. Functional layering and the English progressive. *Linguistics* 51(1): 1–32. doi:10.1515/ling-2013-0001

Leech, Geoffrey, Marianne Hundt Christian Mair & Nichaolar Smith 2009. *Change in contemporary English: A grammatical study*. Cambridge: Cambridge University Press. doi:10.1017/CBO9780511642210

Mair, Christian 2012. Progressive and continuous aspect. In Robert I Binnick (ed.), *The Oxford handbook of tense and aspect*, 803–827. Oxford: Oxford University Press. doi:10.1093/oxfordhb/9780195381979.001.0001

Mazzon, Gabriella 2013. ALWAYS-progressives in early American English. *Rhesis: International Journal of Linguistics, Philology and Literature* 4(1): 23–39.

Mufwene, Salikoko 1984. *Stativity and the progressive*. Bloomington: Indiana Linguistics Club.

Petré, Peter 2017. The extravagant progressive: An experimental corpus study on the history of the emphatic [be Ving]. *English Language and Linguistics* 21(2): 227–250. doi:10.1017/S1360674317000107

Quirk, Randolph, Sidney Greenbaum, Geoffrey Leech & Jan Svartvik 1985. *A comprehensive grammar of the English language*. London: Longman.

Smith, Nicholas 2005. *A corpus-based investigation of recent change in the use of the progressive in British English*. Doctoral dissertation. Lancaster: Lancaster University.

Swan, Michael 1984. *Basic English usage*. Oxford: Oxford University Press.

Vendler, Zeno 1957. Verbs and times. *The Philosophical Review* 66(2): 143–160.

Waliński, Jacek Tadeusz 2018. The cross-cultural conceptualization of 'I'm loving it' between English and Polish. *Kwartalnik Neofilologiczny* LXV: 517–530. doi:10.24425/kn.2018.125001

Willis, Dave 1992. *Collins COBUILD students' grammar*. London: Harper Collins.

10 *The good, the bad and the ugly*

Adjectives

Laurie

Setting the scene

We spend a lot of our lives classifying things. Many of us have problems in seeing chicken's feet and snails as food, while others are happy with the classification. We disagree as to which books should be classified as obscene, or which films should be permitted viewing for adults only. There is shock value in wearing something which is not classified as formal dress to an event which calls for formality. And the borderline between music and just noise has caused divisions in many families. Not all classifications are necessarily as contentious as these, but if you argue about whether a potato is a vegetable, whether electric scooters count as vehicles, or whether a website in the cloud is an opportunity for the user or a marketing ploy, you are, in effect, having problems with classification. Given the ubiquity of classification, it is not surprising that it should also affect the way we view language, and sometimes cause disputes there as well.

Word classes (or parts of speech) like noun and verb are sets of words which share some linguistic features. The features may be formal or functional or semantic. For instance, verbs allow a third person singular *-s* on the end, so that we get the difference between *(to) infer* and *(she) infers*; that's a formal way of recognizing a verb. Nouns may be used (as the most important word) in the subject or the direct object in a sentence, so that we can find both *Whales are endangered* and *I watch whales off the coast*. This is a functional feature of nouns, and shows *whales* to be a noun in these sentences. Or we could say, in the way of traditional grammar, that verbs are 'doing words', that is their meaning, and that because running, screaming, sneezing, talking and so on are things you do, *run*, *scream*, *sneeze* and *talk* are verbs. In this view, defining a noun, for example, is a matter of finding a set of features, of whichever kind, which between them are sufficient to distinguish nouns from other word classes. This is sometimes referred to as an Aristotelian classification, or a classification in terms of necessary and sufficient criteria (see also Chapter 3, on prepositions).

There is an alternative view, introduced by the psychologist Eleanor Rosch, which says that people do not classify the world in such a manner. Rather than having a set of boxes and a set of criteria for putting *whale* in the noun box and

DOI: 10.4324/9781003148999-10

infer in the verb box, Rosch suggests that our categories are rather like targets in archery. There is a bull's eye, when what you find fits your criteria perfectly, and then there are other examples which are still on the target, but don't fit the criteria nearly as well. Rosch illustrates her idea with the category of birds. Some birds are very birdy birds – robins, blackbirds, thrushes. They are relatively small, relatively good singers, build nests in trees, lay fairly small eggs and fly about in our gardens. Gulls are clearly birds, but they are slightly less birdy birds, because they have raucous voices and can be rather large. Ostriches and penguins are very unlike our fundamental idea of birds. Ostriches do not fly; penguins, if they fly, fly under water; neither of them make nests in trees, they do not sing and their eggs are too large to be normal eggs. On the other hand, they do not fit the criteria for being lizards or mammals or fish, and they are bipedal and they do have wings and feathers, so they are sort of birds by default. Rosch talks of birds like American robins or European thrushes as being prototypical birds, and ostriches being birds that are a long way from the prototype. The term 'prototype' seems unfortunate: prototypical birds are not prototypes of birds in any other usage, they are stereotypical. The term has become standard, though, and will be used here. If you give people a piece of paper and a pencil and ask them to write down as many different kinds of birds as they can in a minute, you will find that people tend to choose the most prototypical birds first, and more of them will list the most prototypical birds. At the same time, prototypes may be culturally determined: New Zealanders might put the kiwi (a very odd bird, with a huge egg, no wings and a burrow) closer to the prototype than most other people, and emus might be closer to the prototype for Australians than for others.

Some scholars accept the general idea of some bird being closer to the target than others, but object to the notion that anyone has just one ideal bird that they can name. They prefer to say that there are birds which fit more criteria for being a bird, and birds which meet fewer criteria for being birds. Birds that meet all the criteria are canonical birds, birds which meet just a few are less canonical birds. This is the terminology that will be used here.

As for birds, so for nouns (and other word classes). *Woman* is a good noun because it denotes not only a concrete entity, but a person, as well as meeting relevant functional criteria such as being used in the subject and the object in sentences. *Infidelity* has to be a noun, but it is far less canonical than *woman* is: you cannot touch infidelity or point to it, but our language forces us to treat it in the same way as we treat *woman*, and it can appear as the direct object of a verb, and so on, as in *She hates infidelity*.

Although this introduction has been in terms of noun and verbs, in the bulk of this chapter I shall deal with adjectives. That is because adjectives are particularly problematic, and they bring the difficulties of classification into focus. They are also fun to think about, because they are so diverse. And in English, as opposed to what happens in many other Indo-European languages like French, German, Italian, Latin, Russian, they are not easily defined formally because they do not, in English, agree with nouns for gender, number or case.

The function of adjectives

Adjectives are generally agreed to have a number of functions. The first of these, and probably the most important, is that are used to tell us more about nouns, and when they do they appear immediately in front of the noun. Examples of this attributive usage are in (1). In each of the examples in (1), the last word in the phrase is the noun, and the preceding word is an adjective used attributively.

(1) a. This red car.
  b. A beautiful painting.
  c. Another theatrical performance.
  d. Shallow waters.

The second function of adjectives is that they can form part of a predicate, where they describe the subject of the sentence. The verb is one of a limited number of verbs called 'copular' verbs, because they link the subject to the predicate. This use is called the 'predicative' use of the adjective, and is illustrated in (2).

(2) a. My car is red.
  b. The painting seems beautiful.
  c. This performance was very theatrical.
  d. The water is growing shallow.

The form of adjectives

Adjectives can be compared using the suffixes *-er* and *-est* or the words *more* and *most*, as in *shallow/shallower/shallowest, important/more important/most important*. These adjectives are called 'gradable' adjectives, and can also be used with *rather, so, very* and the like: *The water is rather shallow, He is very important* (see also Chapter 8, on comparison). Many adjectives have suffixes which mark them as adjectives. For example, the words *beautiful, hopeless, lucky, normal, pedantic, predictable, republican, statuesque, waspish* all have such suffixes, and the list given here is not exhaustive. Many adjectives can give rise to adverbs if *-ly* is added to them, as in *comfortable/comfortably*.

The meanings of adjectives

With the most basic adjectives, the meaning is intersective with the meaning of the noun. So if we take a phrase like *pretty flower*, it denotes the set of things that are both pretty and a flower. Such adjectives are called 'ascriptive' adjectives, their meaning is ascribed to the noun they modify. But other adjectives do not do the same thing. An expression like *canine tooth*, for instance, or *parental control*, does not indicate the intersection of the set of canine things and teeth (the set of parental things and controls); rather it tells us that the tooth is associated in some way with dogs (that the control is associated with parents). Such adjectives are called 'associative' adjectives, because their meaning is associated with the meaning of the related noun.

Criticizing these definitional features

All of these things that are supposed to be typical of adjectives and provide a set of criteria for establishing canonical adjectives are difficult to deal with.

The trouble with the criteria of attributive and predicative usage is that we find other word classes that are also used attributively and predicatively. Consider the examples in (3) which illustrate attributive usage of things that are not usually thought of as adjectives, and (4) for predicative usage of things which are not usually considered adjectives:

(3) a. The then Prime Minister.
  b. The down train.
  c. The downstairs bathroom.
  d. The above example.
  e. A silver service.

(4) a. My father is the president.
  b. My mother is away.
  c. My flatmate is up.

Either we have to find reasons why the elements illustrated in (3) and (4) are not adjectives (they have the wrong form, for example), or we have to suggest that the relevant words belong to two word classes (adjective and something else), or we have to argue that these things become adjectives when used in these ways. None of these positions is necessarily untenable, but the definition of a class of adjectives is weakened because of such instances.

Furthermore, there are some things that we might think of as adjectives which can be used attributively but not predicatively or vice versa. The words in (5) can be used attributively but not predicatively, those in (6) can be used predicatively but not attributively (neither list is exhaustive).

(5) former, future, late (in the sense of 'dead'), main, mere, outright, previous, rightful, scant, urban, virtual.

(6) afraid, alone, asleep (and many other adjectives beginning with *a-*), bereft, broke, glad, late (in the sense of 'not on time'), rife, well ('healthy').

Adjectives which have prepositional phrases attached to them can also only be used predicatively: *bound for*, *dear to*, *fond of*, *inclined to* and so on. That is, we can say *I have a nephew who is dear to me*, but not **I have a dear-to-me nephew*. English differs from some other European languages in this regard.

There are also some adjectives which are used postpositively; that is, immediately following the noun which they modify. Examples include *accounts payable*, *attorney general*, *lie direct*, *times past*, *whisky galore*. In some cases postpositive use gives a meaning which is different from attributive usage – sometimes subtly so, sometimes quite dramatically so, depending on the modified noun. Consider the examples in (7).

(7) a. The only navigable river in the county.
b. The only river navigable in the county.
c. I am looking for the responsible person.
d. I am looking for the person responsible.
e. She is a concerned party in this matter.
f. She is the person concerned.

Some words have different meanings when used attributively and predicatively. Consider the examples in (8).

(8) a. My old friend has arrived.
b. My friend, who is old, has arrived.
c. The present Prime Minister is to speak.
d. The Prime Minister is present.

Determining which adjectives count as gradable is sometimes a matter of opinion. The most obvious problematic adjective is *unique*, which prescriptivists say cannot be graded because it means 'one of a kind', while many speakers, assuming it to mean 'very rare', have no trouble in grading it. But even adjectives like *French*, which we might assume is not gradable, are frequently used as though they are, and we hear things like *She is more French than the French.* And even though we frequently say that someone cannot be a little bit pregnant, pregnant women are sometimes described as being *very pregnant* when the pregnancy is very obvious. Finally, a word like *dramatic* means one thing in a context like *dramatic society*, where it is not gradable, and another in *dramatic entrance*, where it is gradable.

Suffixes which mark words as being adjectives are sometimes problematic, too. Some affixes mark both adjectives and some other part of speech: the suffix *-ly* marks an adjective in *friendly*, but an adverb in *immediately*; the suffix *-ful* marks an adjective in *hopeful*, but a noun in *spoonful*. This is made more complicated by the fact that some adjectives are used as nouns: *intellectual* is an adjective, but we can talk about *an intellectual*; *Russian* can be an adjective describing things from Russia or a noun denoting a native of Russia.

All in all, because there are criteria which do not apply to some putative adjectives and because not all the things which fit the criteria are generally thought of as adjectives, and because it is not always clear whether we should treat a given form as a single word or two related words, it is often difficult to know how to classify adjectives, and even to be sure when something is or is not an adjective. There are two particular cases where the last problem arises: the borderline between nouns and adjectives and the borderline between adjectives and adverbs. I will deal with each in turn.

Adjectives and nouns: *the rich* live behind *stone walls*

As was stated above, sometimes adjectives are used as nouns. The example given above was *intellectual*. A word like *intellectual*, seems to have become a fully fledged noun. It can be made plural (*Intellectuals are weird*), it can take adjectives of its own (*Chinese intellectuals object to this characterization*), it can take a range of determiners (*This intellectual/This country's intellectuals/Many intellectuals…*), it can be post-modified (*An intellectual of some standing*). But this is not the case for all adjectives. We can have nouns like *Catholic*, *native* or *ritual*, but not like *grateful*, *Jewish* or *timid*.

There is a different construction which has much wider application. This is the construction (or possibly constructions) illustrated in (9).

(9) a. The rich are not like you and me: they have more money.
b. The improbable we do at once, the impossible takes a little longer.

Here we have an adjective (*rich*, *improbable*), which is plural if it refers to people (*the rich are*) but singular if it does not refer to people (*the improbable takes*). Unlike examples like *intellectual*, it demands the determiner *the* and cannot be marked as plural: we cannot have *A rich is* or *Some riches are* (meaning 'rich people'). We can put something between the determiner and the word we are discussing, but sometimes it makes it seem that *rich*/*improbable* is an adjective, and sometimes it makes it seem as though it is a noun. In the examples in (10), *very* in (10a) would normally precede an adjective, while *virtuous* in (10b) would normally precede a noun.

(10) a. The very rich are not like you and me.
b. The virtuous rich are not like you and me.

Most adjectives can be freely used in this kind of way, including those like *intellectual* which can also be used in the more noun-y way. Many linguists think that this is a matter of syntax, while the *intellectual* class is a matter of word formation (not syntax), but there are exceptions here, too, although it is not clear how frequent they are. It seems that we do not say the things in (11):

(11) a. *The important is that we should be believed.
b. *The important have a way of standing which shows their status.

Regardless of whether these formations belong to word formation or to syntax, they have the same function of treating adjectives as nouns, which seems to imply that there is an unclear boundary between the two.

The lack of clarity also goes the other way. Many nouns are used in attributive position, and some authorities seem to presume that attributive position is the domain of adjectives. This raises the question of whether *house* in *house guest*, *floor* in *floor covering* and *car* in *car park* are adjectives. The question really has no answer. There are opinions in both directions, and very little solid evidence to decide the issue. There is not even any guarantee that a single answer will fit all examples.

Take, for instance, the situation where you have a noun and then something in attributive position telling you what it is made of. This gives you expressions like *earthen pot, wooden fence* and *woollen blanket* (with adjectives) and also expressions like *iron bar*, *silk dress* and *sugar cube* (with nouns). The instances with nouns are commoner (most adjective endings mean 'resembling X' rather than 'made of X', and even *golden* and *silken* tend to mean 'looking a though made with gold/silk': we tend to say *gold ring* but *golden light*). So the fact that we say *silk dress* may simply be a result of the fact that we have no suitable adjective from *silk*. Does this mean that *silk* is an adjective in *silk dress*? Some authorities think so (e.g. Giegerich 2015). Personally, I am less convinced: *silk* does not fit most of the criteria (even for a non-gradable, associative adjective), except that it can be used both attributively and predicatively (unlike so many adjectives). But despite my own predilections, here, this is one of the examples that is most often seen as illustrating nouns functioning as adjectives. It is also an area where lexicographers get confused: Gove (1966) lists *crocodile* in *crocodile clip* as an adjective, but *alligator* in *alligator clip* (meaning the same thing) as a noun, for reasons which escape me. Nonetheless, lexicographers do seem to be relatively consistent.

Just in case you think I am being too dismissive, let me point out that there are at least two other possible analyses of things like *iron bar* and *alligator clip*. The first is that they are compounds like *paperclip*, *windmill* and *wolfhound*. I have chosen examples where the two nouns are written together to illustrate compounds, and examples where they are written separately to illustrate potential adjectives, but English is inconsistent in the way it spells such items, and *coffee pot*, *coffee-pot* and *coffeepot* (and many other similar examples) can all be found listed in standard dictionaries. Note that I sneaked in *sugar cube* above which is written as two words but pronounced with initial stress, as though it could be one.

The third possible analysis is that these constructions could just illustrate nouns used attributively, exactly as they appear. This might be a piece of syntax or a piece of word formation. Just because the prejudice goes in favour of adjectives modifying nouns and not other nouns modifying nouns, that is not evidence that nouns cannot be attributive modifiers, too. All three of these analyses are discussed in the literature; a fourth analysis could be that the same answer does not fit all examples, and that some examples could be compounds, some nouns and some adjectives (or choose just two of these options). Just do not expect much agreement on which of these is right. Which is what makes it a mystery. Again, though, if linguistics cannot definitively determine which of these analyses is correct, it suggests that the borderline between nouns and adjectives is not always clear-cut.

Adjectives and adverbs: *a real difficult problem*

A question which raises its head from time to time is whether adjectives and adverbs are different word classes (parts of speech) or the same word class. The fundamental difference between them is that adjectives modify nouns, while adverbs modify verbs (and everything else). Perhaps this is enough to make them separate word classes, but perhaps all it indicates is that we have a single class of modifier, and we add an *-ly* on the end when a modifier modifies a verb or an adjective so that we can distinguish between the two sentences in (12).

(12) a. I left the house quiet.
b. I left the house quietly.

(In (12a) the house is quiet, in (12b) it is the leaving which is quiet.) If you really care about such things, then in the two-word-class solution, *-ly* is a derivational ending which creates a new word of a new word class (i.e. it creates an adverb), while in the one-word-class solution, *-ly* is an inflectional ending which just signals the word's syntactic position. If you think that this sounds like one of those questions which is unlikely to worry your average sixteen-year-old speaker of English, you are quite right. It is a technical linguistic question, and answers to it (on either side) involve technical linguistic notions. But one of the pieces of evidence that the linguists may want to use to support their points of view, is which way speakers treat them in their actual speech. Do speakers act as though they have two different types of word, or as if they have just one? It will probably not surprise you to learn that the jury is out.

First, we should note that there are some adverbs that look just the same as adjectives. We can tell which of the two we have only by the way they function. That means that we get pairs like those in (13) where a single form has double function, and pairs like those in (14) where different forms function the same way.

	Adjectival use	*Adverbial use*
(13)	This car is fast.	The jogger ran fast.
	My wife is late.	We are working late.
	Your ring looks cheap.	We buy cheap and make big margins.
	The house was big.	He talks big, but doesn't act.
(14)	She spoke slow.	She spoke slowly.
	He told me loud and clear.	He told me loudly and clearly.
	He showed up quick.	He showed up quickly.

What this means is that there are some cases where the adverb and adjective have the same form, and they are often frequent words. Because they sometimes share a form it makes it harder to perceive a distinction between them.

One place where we often do not distinguish is with words modifying adjectives which indicate an extreme degree. Because they modify adjectives, we expect adverbs; what we find is examples like those in (15).

(15) bloody stupid (and other potentially offensive forms), cold sober, dead serious, jolly glad, plain silly, pretty expensive, real difficult

Sometimes, the adverbial forms (with final *-ly*) are also possible, but they do not always mean the same thing: *really difficult* is the same as *real difficult* (and may be preferred by prescriptive commentators), but *plainly silly* is not the same as *plain silly*. It is not clear whether we should call *bloody, jolly, plain, real* and so on 'adverbs' in this construction, or whether we should call them 'adjectives'. It may not matter. What we have is a situation where the distinction between an adjective and an adverb is not clear.

There can also be problems with adjectives that end in *-ly*. There are several kinds of these: (a) adjectives that happen to end in *-ly* but the *-ly* is not meaningful (*jolly, silly*); (b) adjectives that end in *-ly* where the final *-y* is meaningful (*oily, pearly*); (c) adjectives that end in *-ly* where the *-ly* is meaningful, and is added to a word for a human (*friendly, saintly*) or to something which is not a noun (*likely*); and (d) adjectives that end in *-ly* where the *-ly* is meaningful, and is added to a word for a period of time (*daily, hourly*). If you look in dictionaries, especially British dictionaries, you will probably find adverbs that come from groups (a) and (b): *sillily, oilily*. People do not like using them, though. Adjectives in group (c) can also be used as adverbs, especially by American speakers: *She smiled friendly*. Adjectives in group (d) never get an extra *-ly*, but can be used as adverbs: *New stock arriving daily*. Again, what this means is that there is a set of words, this time ending in *-ly*, which are sometimes adjectives and sometimes adverbs, and again the distinction is not necessarily clear.

The examples above are cases which are widely used, even in writing, though not in all varieties of English. Now we turn to cases which are less well accepted. Consider first the examples in (16), which are from the British National Corpus (BNC) (Davies 2004–), and which show what are normatively seen as adjectival forms in adverbial positions.

(16) a. They didn't do bad did they? No, they did very well.
b. before we go too deep into the issue
c. In an exclusive and wide-ranging survey we have delved deep into the minds of 13 to 17-year-old girls and boys.
d. He's doing fine thank you.
e. He takes out a coin, spins it high, catches it
f. I was laid low

These particular examples are from speakers whose origins we do not know. But we find similar examples from various dialect areas in Britain. Beal (2008, p. 381) cites examples such as those in (17) as ones where northern English has adjectival forms for adverbials.

(17) a. I told thee confidential.
b. A high technical job.

Anderwald (2008, p. 455), in the same volume, cites examples like those in (18) from the South East of England.

(18) a. They fussed him up terrible.
  b. That use to last you a week easy.

In a more detailed study, Tagliamonte & Ito (2002) show that forms with no *-ly* go back to the Middle English period or before, so that most such forms today can be thought of as remnants, rather than innovations. Such forms are regularly used by authors as disparate as Shakespeare and Mark Twain. However, because of standardization and prescriptivism in the nineteenth century, the forms with no *-ly* came to be seen as non-standard, dialectal or lower-class forms. Tagliamonte & Ito find that *real* is extremely different from other examples. We might want to treat it as an adverb in its own right when it is used to intensify in this way. How to deal with the other cases, is more awkward. We might want to say that the list of forms which can be either adjectives or adverbs is longer than we first thought, though Tagliamonte & Ito have examples which suggest that there is no fixed list at all (consider *confidential* in (17)). We might want to conclude that speakers of English do not have a firm idea of the difference between adverbs and adjectives, and that the two are members of the same word class. There is some hint in Tagliamonte & Ito's study that the two forms are starting to be used slightly differently, but if that is the case, it is not yet an absolute distinction. At the moment, we can add this to the evidence that the boundary of the class of adjectives is rather fuzzy at times.

Wrapping up

Although we might be very clear that *shallow* in the sentences in (19) is an adjective, there are lots of cases where we can be in real doubt as to what is or is not an adjective.

(19) a. The shallow water tickled my ankles.
  b. The water round my ankles was shallow.
  c. The water here is shallower than on the other side of the bay.

We come back to the notion of adjective being a prototypical category, or perhaps rather better, a canonical category. This means that while central members of the class are not in doubt, round the periphery of the class, we have to be careful about any decisions we make. And we have to accept that an opinion which differs from our own might well be justified, even if ours is also well justified. That's a hard position to live with, but assuming extreme answers must be correct will land us in greater trouble.

What should I read?

On ascriptive and associative adjectives see, among other sources, Giegerich (2015). There is discussion of the difference between adjectives like *intellectual* and those like *rich* in Bauer et al. (2013). For differing analyses of things like *iron bar* and *alligator clip* see Bauer (1998, 2017), Payne & Huddleston (2002) and

Giegerich (2015). For the question of whether adjectives and adverbs are or not members of the same class, see the contrasting views but forward in Payne et al. (2010) and Giegerich (2012): these are the latest exchanges in a discussion which goes back a long way, and are quite technical.

References

Anderwald, Liselotte 2008. The varieties of English spoken in the Southeast of England: Morphology and syntax. In Berndt Kortmann & Clive Upton (eds), *Varieties of English: The British Isles*, 440–462. Berlin: Mouton de Gruyter. doi:10.1515/9783110208399.2.440

Bauer, Laurie 1998. When is a sequence of two nouns a compound in English? *English Language and Linguistics* 2(1): 65–86. doi:10.1017/S1360674300000691

Bauer, Laurie 2017. *Compounds and compounding*. Cambridge: Cambridge University Press. doi:10.1017/9781108235679

Bauer, Laurie, Rochelle Lieber & Ingo Plag 2013. *The Oxford reference guide to English morphology*. Oxford: Oxford University Press. doi:10.1093/acprof:oso/9780198747062.001.0001

Beal, Joan 2008. English dialects in the North of England: Morphology and syntax. In Berndt Kortmann & Clive Upton (eds), *Varieties of English: The British Isles*, 373–403. Berlin: Mouton de Gruyter. doi:10.1515/9783110208399.2.373

Davies, Mark 2004. *British National Corpus* (from Oxford University Press). Available online at https://www.english-corpora.org/bnc/.

Giegerich, Heinz 2012. The morphology of *-ly* and the categorial status of 'adverbs' in English. *English Language and Linguistics* 16(3): 341–359. doi:10.1017/S1360674312000147

Giegerich, Heinz 2015. *Lexical structures: Compounds and the modules of grammar*. Edinburgh: Edinburgh University Press. doi:10.1017/S1360674315000453.

Gove, Philip (ed.) 1966. *Webster's third new international dictionary*. Springfield, MA: Merriam.

Payne, John & Rodney Huddleston 2002. Nouns and noun phrases. In Rodney Huddleston & Geoffrey K. Pullum (eds), *The Cambridge grammar of the English language*, 323–524. Cambridge: Cambridge University Press. doi:10.1017/CBO9781139166003.007

Payne, John, Rodney Huddleston & Geoffrey K. Pullum 2010. The distribution and category status of adjectives and adverbs. *Word Structure* 3(1): 31–81. doi:10.3366/E1750124510000486

Tagliamonte, Sali & Rika Ito 2002. Think really different: Continuity and specialization in the English dual form adverbs. *Journal of Sociolinguistics* 6(2): 236–266. doi:10.1111/1467-9481.00186.

11 *What it is is a nonstandard feature*

Double *be* construction

Andreea

Setting the scene

If grammar were personified in a Hollywood movie, it would be more likely to appear as a pedantic Sherlock Holmes character than a free-spirited Robin Hood type; restricting and dominating behaviour, rather than enabling social good. This is because grammar is stereotypically understood to be that set of rules which limits, constrains and 'corrects' what people say or write (typically, write, but let's not go there), holding them to a higher standard, and if you are of a certain persuasion, to a 'better' standard.

But there is another side to grammar, which is less often discussed or emphasized. Languages have structures which function specifically to facilitate clearer and more efficient communication not by merely doing things the way we have always done them, but by allowing speakers and writers to specify what is newsworthy or unexpected in their message. This helps the listener (or reader) to pick out the most important element to focus their attention on. For example, if you were to say *John moved Jane's cheese to the cupboard*, it is impossible to determine, in the absence of any other information, the most noteworthy part of the message: is it that John moved the cheese, is it the fact that it was Jane's cheese that was moved, or is it its relocation to the cupboard?

A tool of grammar: the cleft construction

Grammar can help with that. Here are some alternative formulations, which differ only in the grammatical arrangement used, and which help to focus attention on the intended part of the sentence:

(1) What John moved to the cupboard was her cheese.
(2) It was John who moved her cheese to the cupboard.
(3) It was to the cupboard that John moved her cheese.
(4) All that John did was move her cheese to the cupboard.

Linguists call examples such as those in (1) through to (4) 'clefts'. Clefts arise from 'business as usual' structures like *John moved her cheese to the cupboard* by

DOI: 10.4324/9781003148999-11

means of a cleaving process which splits sentences in what is assumed or presupposed (termed the 'cleft clause') and what is important, new or contrastive (called the 'cleft constituent'). So if we were to look into the nuts and bolts of the cleft in (1), we would see the cleft clause *what John moved to the cupboard* encoding what is known, the assumed no-surprises-here bit, followed by the verb *was* (the verb *be* is used as a linker or copula to join the two parts), and last of all, by the cleft constituent, *her cheese*, this being the newsworthy part that the reader's attention is directed towards.

The beauty of English grammar is that, as far as native speakers are concerned, no overt knowledge of cleft constituents or cleft clauses is necessary to parse the message or to glean that *her cheese* constitutes the important part of the message in example (1). In fact, if all goes well, the cleft structure flies by completely unnoticed. It's when we start noticing things that problems arise.

Other languages have clefts too, but English just cannot get enough of them. All sentences in (5) are clefts, each involving a specific formula with slots for the cleft clause and the cleft constituent and signature components, be they specific words, like *it* or *all*, or types of words, *wh*-words (*what*, *where*, *why*), and often the copula verb *be* (in its various forms, including *is*, *are, am, was, were*).

(5)
a. It was a cleft that I wrote my thesis on. [it-cleft]
b. That is what I wanted to do. [demonstrative cleft]
c. Where I want to go this summer is Spain. [pseudo-cleft]
d. All I want for Christmas is you. [all-cleft]
e. There's the money to think about too. [there-cleft]
f. It's not that I don't trust him, I just don't like him. [inferential cleft]

It is an unfortunate accident of linguistic history that cleft types are unimaginatively named following their respective signature elements in English. Problems arise in the cleft literature when we go looking for *it* or *all* in other languages, rendering the terms '*it*-cleft' and '*all*-cleft' of zero value outside English. The reasonable thing to do then is to look for counterparts of *it, all* and so on in other languages and identify equivalent constructions that way, see some examples in (6a-c). But even when the equivalent of *it* is found in say, Romanian, does it make sense to talk about an '*it*-cleft' in Romanian or are we better discussing '*ceea ce* clefts'?

(6)
a. Romanian (my own example)
Nu îmi plăcea engleza. Ceea ce mi-a plăcut mai mult era franceza.
'I didn't like English. What I liked more was French'.
b. German (from Miller 1996, ex. 9, p. 116)
Es ist aber nicht Fiona, die uns damit hilft, sondern Kirsty.
'It's not Fiona who's helping us but Kirsty'.
c. Māori (from Herd et al. 2011, ex. 9, p. 1255 citing Orbell 1992, p. 27)
Ko ngā kupu ēnei a taua manu i karanga haere atu ai...
'These are the words the bird kept calling...'

A problematic cleft: double *be*

Clefts present more problems than mere terminological quibbles. Consider the following examples from known and prominent American public figures.

(7) Wh-when Governor Romney talks about this board, for example unelected board that we've created what this is, is a group of health care experts, doctors, et cetera to figure out how can we reduce the cost of care in the system overall. (Barrack Obama, cited in Language Log)
(8) You are right, this is not just a Trump phenomenon, it is clearly an international phenomenon. And I think that what it is is that the world is changing very, very rapidly. (Bernie Sanders, quoted in *Boston Review* (podcast), 4 April 2017)

What makes the examples in (7) in (8) remarkable is the repeated use of *is* – *what this is is*. Now, if we rearrange the cleft structure in (7) to its 'business as usual' equivalent, we find that the main verb is *be*: *a group of healthcare experts is this [board we have created]*. This rearrangement shows why we have two copies of *is*: the first is the verb *is* from the original sentence, and the second *is* makes up the cleft formula, linking the cleft clause with the cleft constituent. The repetition of *be* has earned the construction its label of 'double *be*'.

Yet, stylistically, repetition is disliked, not just because it can jar but also because it is often superfluous. For instance, in sentences like *Bart wants to buy ice-cream*, the person doing the wanting (the subject of *wants*) is Bart, and the person doing the buying (the subject of *buy*) is also Bart, and because the referent is exactly the same, English deletes the would-be repeated referent (instead of *Bart wants Bart to buy ice-cream*, we have *Bart wants* ~~Bart~~ *to buy ice-cream*). German does the same. This avoidance of repetition (linguists have a term for it, 'equi-NP deletion', it's *that* frequent) appeals to the human desire to simplify and eliminate unnecessary detail. In general, we often talk about someone wanting to do X, so we agree that we delete the subject of X and avoid repetition.

But what about (8)? The problem with (8) is that it is not clear what the 'original' non-cleft version of the sentence should be. And because there is no good version of (8) which is not a cleft, it seems odd to impose a cleft structure here.

Will a comma help?

You might even think, I can live with the repetition of *is* as long as there is at least a comma after the first *is*, like in (7) – the lack of comma making (8) that much harder to process. And in this, you are not alone. It turns out that on the Internet, most double *be* examples do occur with a comma (70% of the time, according to Andersen 2002, p. 56); but here is the weird twist, in these examples, the comma does not mark a pause; 'a more plausible explanation may be that the writer uses the comma as a way of preventing the erroneous interpretation that the double copula is a spelling mistake' according to Andersen (2002, p. 56). So in online writing, the comma exists to confirm the author's intention to produce a double *is is*: *yes, I really mean to use is is, it's not a typo.*

If (7) and (8) make you uncomfortable, again, you are not alone; such examples have been making some linguists rather uncomfortable, ever since at least 1987, when linguist Dwight Bolinger published the first article on this use. But possibly not for the same reasons; I will come to these reasons shortly. Repetition of *is* has had the prescriptive public in a real tizzy it seems. In 2011, it made the top seven Huffington Post 'readers' pick of seven really annoying language blunders' (https://www.huffpost.com/entry/grammar-pet-peeves_1_n_778486), and it figures as a regular linguistic curiosity on the Language Log blogging site which discusses linguistic topics for a wide audience.

Barack Obama's *is-is* has been duly noted too, on more than one occasion (see particularly Ben Zimmer's posts on the Language Log), showing that the former US president has been making a name for himself not just in political spheres, but also in linguistic circles.

But before you dismiss (7) and (8) as Americanisms, let's be clear that British English is not immune from double *be*, nor are other English varieties, for example Australian English (McConvell 1988).

Double *be* is not just a disfluency

Tempting as it is to relegate double *be* constructions to the realm of 'bad grammar', 'speech errors' or 'disfluencies' (Cochrane 2004, as cited in Massam 2017, p. 124), linguistic research suggests otherwise. Tuggy (1996, p. 743) allows the possibility that double *be* may have started out as a hesitation, disfluency or stutter, which through repeated use has achieved grammatical status – this is precisely one of the aspects that make the construction interesting to linguistic theory. But more recent research makes a stronger case against double *be* as a disfluency.

Coppock et al. (2006) analysed the spoken data with acoustic analysis software to investigate just what speakers are up to when they use double *be* sentences. Their working assumption was that for double *be* to constitute a disfluency, the structure would either be used as a smoothing technique to buy thinking time (with a pause between the two *be*s, equivalent to a comma in writing), or that it would be used as a linguistic repair device for delaying the next utterance to fix some mistake (lengthening the second *be* and adding a time-buying pause after it).

Results showed that double *be* behaved acoustically nothing like typical known disfluencies. Coppock and her team found that there was rarely a pause or intonational break between the first *be* and the second *be* (no commas needed here!), or between the second *be* and the bit that follows it (the clausal complement), and what is more, the first *be* tended to be more heavily accented and longer in duration than the second *be*.

So, given that the acoustic properties of double *be* make it distinct from typical speech disfluencies, and that speakers of many English varieties use it recurrently, double *be* could no longer be dismissed as an error. Any comprehensive theory of English grammar had to roll up its sleeves and take note of its existence. And take note it did!

Some problems with double *be*

There is little agreement as to what to call double *be* which provides the first clue that there are some problems with it. Like many grammatical and linguistic phenomena, the *is-is* use can be found under various other terms in the literature, including 'extra BE' (Massam 2017), the 'ISIS construction' (Coppock et al. 2006), 'intrusive BE' (Massam 2013), 'double copula' (Bolinger 1987, McConvell 1988), '*thing-is*' (Massam 1999, though this refers to a specific subtype, namely *the thing is is X*), 'reduplicative be' (Shapiro & Haley 2002) or '2-*be*' (Tuggy 1996).

The second clue that we are dealing with a possible grammatical mystery is the fact that traditional grammar books (such as those mentioned in the Introduction, Huddleston & Pullum 2002 and Quirk et al. 1985), are conspicuously silent about it. Like a secret society, the double *be* construction lurks in those dark grammatical corners where only the most adventurous grammarians dare to look, namely, in spontaneous, spoken English (and truth be told, in the spontaneous, spoken versions of a number of other languages too, see Massam 2017, p. 147). So what makes the double *be* such a difficult construction to handle?

Why do we have the two *be*s in the first place?

The first mystery to sort out in relation to double *be* is how we end up with two *be*s in the first place. In some cases, it makes perfectly good sense to have two *be*s (Shapiro & Haley 2002, pp. 307–8), so long as we can live with the repetition.

(9) Dostoevsky is a murder witness.
(10) What Dostoevsky is is a murder witness.

But in other cases, like (11), the two *be*s are harder to explain. Here we do not have a *be* in the 'original' sentence (*I have said he is an idiot*), so it is unclear why we end up with two *be*s in the clefted version.

(11) What I have said is is that he is an idiot.

Various theories have been proposed to explain what is going on here, but none seems to cover all the relevant points. One explanation claims that double *be* is essentially a cleft-gone-wrong, what Shapiro & Haley (2002, p. 308) described as a 'misfired cleft'. The claim is that in an attempt to produce a cleft, speakers get confused, and wrongly assume the verb of the cleft clause is a *be* verb, presumably because they are already anticipating the *be* required to form a cleft, and this leads to a doubling up of *be*.

Put another way, were the verb of the simple (non-cleft) sentence not *be*, then we would not be facing a doubling of *be* in the cleft version, unless we suffered from 'cleft misfire' (their prescriptive hand is unmistakable here). Shapiro and Haley claim that speakers misanalyse structures of the type: [[*What* X verb] *is* Y], as though they were of the type: [[What X is] is Y]. But surely, if that were the case, we would end up with a different type of double *be*:

(12) I have said that he is an idiot. → What I have is is that he is an idiot.

where the verb *said* is left out altogether. However, that is not what we find.

Interestingly, anticipation of this type is not unexpected in linguistics research. Phonologists are well aware that when producing certain words, speakers engage their articulators in position earlier than necessary, in anticipation of upcoming sounds, thus ending up with a modified original form of the word. This is why *good night* sounds more like *gon night* in connected speech, i.e. because the /d/ sound becomes more like the upcoming /n/ sound; speakers are just fantastic forward planners. This phenomenon – progressive assimilation – is commonplace in phonology. Such zealous forward planning in syntax is not as common, and in our case, – the suggestion goes – it ends up causing a doubling up of *be* – a kind of progressive syntactic assimilation.

Returning to the analysis put forward by Shapiro & Haley (2002), matters get more complicated by the fact that double *be* seems to have spread out to other constructions too, rather than remaining confined to (what look like) clefts. Here is an example from Massam (2017, p. 122):

(13) One of the realities is, is that we have hit the wall with respect to spending.

Now this example does not look like a (typical) cleft; instead of a cleft clause we have a good old-fashioned noun phrase (*the thing*, *the problem*, *one of the realities*). So what are speakers doing here? Shapiro and Haley cannot argue for a 'cleft misfire' because the sentence neither begins like a cleft, nor does it end up as a cleft. Their solution is that speakers suffer from an additional problem while producing such structures: more syntactic amnesia. Speakers start out with a given structure in mind, and then change their mind mid-utterance, while also suffering from cleft-misfire (forgetting what the main verb of the original sentence was).

Even more troubling are examples such as (14), from McConvell (1988, p. 287), where it is unclear why we even have a second *is* in the first place. The original, uncleaved sentence would be something like *I am thinking (that) I may need a Research Assistant*, and thus the main verb of the sentence is *think* (not *is*). So why have *is-is* in (14)?

(14) What I'm thinking is is that I may need a Research Assistant. (University teacher)

Tuggy (1996) and Curzan (2012) argue that the first *is* links the cleft clause *What I'm thinking is* with *that I may need a Research Assistant* and that *what I'm thinking is* comes as a ready-made chunk (a bit like *by and large* and other relics of former versions of English).

However, this explanation runs into problems too because the assumed frozen structure appears to be more flexible than first thought. In other words, a frozen [cleft clause + *is*] does not account for all the uses identified because we find examples such as *The cruel facts of life are, is that not every person who teaches Art is a good artist himself* (McConvell 1988, p. 290), and *the bottom line being is*... (Bolinger 1987, p. 39) and even *the problem being is there is*... (Bolinger 1987, p. 39). These sentences show that the [cleft clause + *is*] is more flexible than Tuggy (1996) and Curzan (2012) first assumed. In case you are thinking that *the bottom line* and *the problem* are not quite the same type of examples as the earlier ones, keep reading (you are also right, but they are close enough and they share a doubling of *be*). Interestingly, the second *is* remains in this singular, present tense form throughout and for whatever reason, it seems immutable.

One of the latest proposals accounting for double *be* comes from Massam (2017). She offers some solutions to (among other things) Shapiro & Haley's (2002) problem in accounting for the spread of double *be* to other constructions beyond clefts. Massam noticed that the nouns which occur at the start of double *be* constructions, in what she terms 'the setup' portion of the construction (*what the problem is, what the issue is, where the question is at*) are not just any old nouns. They are what linguists have come to term 'shell nouns' (Schmid 2000). Shell nouns denote abstract, vague entities like *thing, problem, fact, issue* and *question*, which are handy because their reference is open to being interpreted in the context of their use, but useless if you are playing a game of Pictionary and have to draw them.

Using this observation, Massam proposed that double *be* is really, no different from single *be* in shell-noun constructions (she terms these 'shared shell-noun constructions'). They are all the same type of construction, after all. In an ironic twist of linguistic-theory fate, 'single *be*' only comes into being as a term in order to contrast with double *be*. What is the regular, the normal, the default construction (single *be*) only appears as such by virtue of the presence of the second *be* (double *be*). The difference between single *be* and double *be*, according to Massam (2017), comes from the fact that the setup verb (the first *is* in *What the problem is is that he cannot be trusted*) happens to be another *be* verb, hence the doubling up of *be*. Whether this happens for 'good reason' in Shapiro and Haley's terms (like in the Dostoevsky-as-murder-witness example), or because of some overextension (their 'misfired cleft' which adds *be* for no 'good reason') does not figure in Massam's article; the main point is that single or double, it's still the same *be* verb.

There is a certain elegance to this parsimonious view that double *be* is merely a specific instantiation of single *be*, and not a separate construction in its own right.

First, we don't have to worry about speakers changing structures mid-utterance because it no longer matters whether speakers were aiming to produce a cleft or not. Clefts and shell-noun constructions behave in similar ways in this respect. Secondly, there is no need to explain the similarity in form and function of double *be* to the regular (single *be*) construction; everything that applies to regular, single *be* will similarly apply to double *be*, with minor differences. Finally, the analysis does not require new types of grammatical concepts or operations in order to explain the structure of double *be*, which makes good practical and theoretical sense.

Nevertheless, we still do not quite know how to explain examples like (15). And in case you are thinking that surely, no sensible English speaker would say something like that; well, they do.

(15) The fact remains is that people's living standards are being cut. (Bolinger 1987, as cited in Massam 2017, p. 128)

Massam (2017) suggests that in order to produce the sentence in (15), speakers start out with something like that in (16) – though it is not entirely clear why this particular sentence is their starting point:

(16) The fact remains the fact is that people's living standards are being cut.

and then delete the superfluous *the fact*:

(17) The fact remains ~~the fact~~ is that people's living standards are being cut.

However, it is still unclear why speakers go on to delete the superfluous noun phrase *the fact*, but keep the equally superfluous verb *is*, which would render the well-attested and non-prescriptive-eyebrow-raising structure *the fact remains that* X.

Despite the plethora of theories, we still do not have one which answers all our questions, even though there is general agreement regarding the overarching function of the double *be* construction. Double *be* constructions are 'routinized resources for speakers to organize talk' (Curzan 2012, p. 218). The second *is* thus functions as a focus marker or topic particle, and its meaning is akin to phrases like *Hey! Pay attention to this!* (Tuggy 1996, p. 726). This is in keeping with the aim of cleft structures more generally.

Wrapping up

Far from being constrained to the discourse of politicians like Barack Obama or to the speech of the misguided or uneducated, the use of double *be* persists in the discourse of English speakers. It continues to puzzle linguists and the wider public alike, despite some decades of research on the topic. Although the linguistics community seems in agreement that sentences like *What the problem is is that we need to know more* or *What it is is that we still don't know what's going on yet* are not deformed disfluencies, there is still little agreement beyond the general consensus of their function as discourse management devices. The lack of agreement among linguists, however, does not prevent agreement among speakers that double *be* is here to stay. The fact remains that (or even 'the fact remains is that') neither their source, nor their structure are completely transparent to us. But if it's good enough for Charles Darwin (who used it in a letter, no less: 'My excuse and reason is, is the different way all the Wedgewoods view the subject from what you and my sister do' – cited in Bolinger 1987, p. 39), then it's good enough for me.

What should I read?

Bolinger's (1987) article is a great initiation into the topic because it provides a number of examples of the double *be* construction. He makes a good case that its use is prevalent and worth investigating further. Ben Zimmer's posts on the Language Log are also good introductions ('Obama's "is is"', https://languagelog.ldc.upenn.edu/nll/?p=4269 and 'Obama's "is is" redux', https://languagelog.ldc.upenn.edu/nll/?p=4593). Massam's (2017) article gives a thorough background for the more advanced reader.

References

Andersen, Gisle 2002. The best part is, is that you get to shoot your opponent: Corpora and the double copula. In Leiv Egil Breivik & Angela Hasselgren (eds), *From the COLT's mouth... and others': Language corpora studies: In honour of Anna-Brita Stenstrom*, 43–58. Amsterdam: Brill Rodopi.

Bolinger, Dwight 1987. The remarkable double IS. *English Today* 3(1): 39–40. doi:10.1017/S0266078400002728

Cochrane, James 2004. *Between you and I: A little book of bad English.* Naperville, IL: Sourcebooks.

Coppock, Elizabeth, Jason Brenier, Laura Staum & Laura Michaelis 2006. ISIS: It's not disfluent, but how do we know that? In Zhenya Antić, Charles B. Chang, Emily Cibelli, Jisup Hong, Michael J. Houser, Clare S. Sandy, Maziar Toosarvandani & Yao Yao (eds), *Proceedings of the 32nd annual meeting of the Berkeley Linguistics Society*, Berkeley, CA.

Curzan, Anne 2012. Revisiting the reduplicative copula with corpus-based evidence. In Terttu Nevalainen & Elizabeth Closs Traugott (eds), *The Oxford handbook of the history of English*, 211–221. Oxford: Oxford University Press. DOI: 10.1093/oxfordhb/9780199922765.013.0020.

Herd, Jonathan, Catherine Macdonald & Diane Massam 2011. Genitive subjects in relative constructions in Polynesian languages. *Lingua* 121(7): 1252–1264.

Language Log. Accessible from: https://languagelog.ldc.upenn.edu.

Massam, Diane 1999. Thing is constructions: The thing is, is what's the right analysis? *English Language and Linguistics* 3(2): 335–352. doi:10.1017/S136067439900026X

Massam, Diane 2013. Intrusive be constructions in (spoken) English: Apposition and beyond. In *Proceedings of the 2012 annual conference of the Canadian Linguistic*

Association. Online from http://homes.chass.utoronto.ca/~cla-acl/actes2013/Massam-2013.pdf.

Massam, Diane 2017. Extra *BE*: The syntax of share shell-noun constructions in English. *Language* 93(1): 121–152.

McConvell, Patrick 1988. To be or double be? Current changes in the English copula. *Australian Journal of Linguistics* 8(2): 287–305.

Miller, Jim 1996. Clefts, particles and word order in languages of Europe. *Language Sciences* 18(1–2): 111–125.

Orbell, Margaret 1992. *Traditional Māori stories*. Auckland: Reed Books.

Pullum, Geoffrey K. & Rodney Huddleston 2002. *The Cambridge grammar of the English language*. Cambridge: Cambridge University Press.

Quirk, Randolph, Sidney Greenbaum, Geoffrey Leech & Jan Svartvik 1985. *A comprehensive grammar of the English language*. London: Longman.

Schmid, Hans-Jörg 2000. *English abstract nouns as conceptual shells: From corpus to cognition*. Amsterdam: Walter de Gruyter.

Shapiro, Michael & Michael Haley 2002. The reduplicative copula *is is*. *American Speech* 77(3): 304–312.

Tuggy, David 1996. The thing is is that people talk that way. The question is Why? In Eugene H. Casad (ed), *Cognitive linguistics in the redwoods: the expansion of a new paradigm in linguistics*, 713–752. New York: Mouton de Gruyter.

12 Human dogs and inhuman people

Gender and related matters

Laurie

Setting the scene

If you go by the way we talk about them, you would think that blondes and brunettes were very different types of people. Gentlemen, apparently, prefer blondes, blondes have more fun, and we tell any number of blondist jokes. Yet, although languages like English have words to describe these people as differing from each other, I know of no language that has built that division into its grammatical system. That is, there is (assuming I am right) no language that forces you to say whether you were told something by a blonde or a brunette, what the hair colour of your interlocutor was, or obliges you to introduce yourself by means of your hair colour. Perhaps this is odd. Languages force us to provide information on so many things, from whether you know something because you have perceived it yourself or whether you know it because someone told you to whether it happens to a group of exactly three entities or more than three (see Chapter 2, on norm). And the lack of obligatory marking for hair colour is presumably not because of people with pink hair or blue rinses, which I take to be relatively recent phenomena. A bigger problem is that if you have such marking, how are you to describe King Charles spaniels, Friesian cows and tortoiseshell (calico) cats? You either become inaccurate, or you have to multiply your categories and complicate the system (and all for rather little reward).

Sex, though, is a far more fruitful category to use. Not only do our societies traditionally divide up roles according to sex (even those that are not biologically based), but sex has economic importance too in that female cows give milk, female hens give eggs and so on. We might not care much, from an economic point of view, whether the cat that catches mice is male or female, but the distinction can be useful when it comes to the production of kittens. Sex, then, is not only socially important, it appears at first glance to be simple to apply. That turns out not to be entirely true.

When languages have classes of noun which, among other things, distinguish entities based on their sex, we talk of 'gender classes'. French is a language which has two gender classes: masculine and feminine nouns. Nouns denoting males are typically masculine, for example *homme* 'man', *père* 'father' and *prêtre* 'priest'. Nouns denoting females are typically feminine, for example *bonne* 'maid', *fille*

DOI: 10.4324/9781003148999-12

'daughter', *tante* 'aunt'. The system gets confused over time. The word *sentinelle* 'sentinel' is feminine, although most sentinels through history have been men. As professors and judges are more and more often female, it becomes difficult to make the language change to keep up with society, though adjustments have been made in recent years. Most seriously, in a language like French, all nouns have gender, whether or not they refer to entities that can be said to show sex. The French word *lune* 'moon' is feminine, and *soleil* 'sun' is masculine. Such marking is deeply entrenched in the language, but in semantic terms is fundamentally arbitrary. In German, *Sonne* 'sun' is feminine and *Mond* 'moon' is masculine.

English has gender, too, originally of the same type as that found in French and German, but it works differently in modern English. We have things that we can refer to as *she* (mainly females), things we can refer to as *he* (mainly males) and things that we must refer to as *it* (things which are perceived as neither male nor female – we can call this the 'neuter' pronoun). This system is sometimes referred to as 'natural gender'. In English we can refer to a maid as *she*, to a professor as *he* or *she* depending on whether the professor is seen as a man or a woman, but the *sun* and the *moon* and a *basket* must, in normal, non-poetic discourse, be referred to as *it*.

Although it is not strictly a matter of gender as such, English also has another phenomenon that involves pronouns referring back to nouns of different types. This shows up in relative clauses – clauses which go with the nouns they follow and tell us more about them. Here the difference is not between masculine, feminine and neuter, but is at base a difference between human and non-human. In (1) we might not need to determine whether the professor is male or female, but by using *who* (and the same would apply to *whom*, *whoever*, *whomsoever*) we implicitly claim that they are human. In (2), on the other hand, by using *which*, we implicitly claim that the sun is not human.

(1) The professor who marked my essay did not seem to be impressed by my learning.
(2) The sun, which is a relatively small star, still has a surface temperature of millions of degrees Celsius.

I have said that the difference is basically a difference between human and non-human, although we will see that the division is not always strictly maintained. But given that we would use *who* of God and the devil, who are not human, some other label, such as 'rational' might be preferred. If we met an extraterrestrial traveller from a flying saucer, we would probably use *who* rather than *which* of him/her/it.

In this chapter, I discuss ways in which English speakers seem to diverge from this basic usage. Two brief notes are appropriate before we proceed, though.

First, despite many attempts (see the summary in Baron 1986), there has been no generally accepted way of avoiding the binary choice between *he* and *she*. Although many proposals have been put forward for an epicene or gender-neutral pronoun – forms ranging from *en* and *thon* to *hizer* and *heesh* – the best we have is *they*, which can be used where sex is unknown or unknowable, as in (3), a usage which goes back at least as far as Shakespeare.

(3) Whoever your professor is, they will not appreciate you handing in essays late.

While *they* might also be used to cover people who do not identify as either male or female, it is very difficult to change the grammatical structure of any language for social or political reasons, and there is as yet no way to capture grammatically anything outside the binary division.

Second, in the above I have distinguished between 'sex' as a natural category and 'gender' as a grammatical category (which may or may not reflect nature accurately). Others (West & Zimmerman 1987, Eckert & McConnel-Ginet 2003) use 'gender' in a rather different way, for the way in which roles are socially constructed. That will not be relevant here.

Who's she?

Although *he* and *she* are, as described above, typically used of entities which are male and female sex respectively, there are well-known exceptions. The most obvious of these is the use of *she* (and *her* and so on) to refer to ships. The origins of this usage are much debated, and give rise to a great deal of sexist speculation, but it is established at least since the eighteenth century, and is entirely standard. How far this usage is extended is far more problematic. Certainly, it was widely used of cars (though it is not clear how far that usage persists). Beyond that, *she* in such usages is restricted to very informal usage, and seems to be used more by men than by women. I once overheard a male student say, 'She's a great crash helmet', but that was in New Zealand (which may be relevant).

Australian vernacular English has a wider usage of *she*, which can be traced back to seventeenth century England (Pawley 2008). In this kind of Australian English, the use of *she* certainly extends to tools and machines, as in the examples in (4), from Pawley, but occasionally has wider usage still, as in (5).

(4) a. The modern way is to take your computer 'nd set 'er up in the village.
b. She's a good tape measure. Er… thanks for oilin 'er.

(5) a. I've given up me morning job. […] I gave 'er away.
b. She's a rough sea today.

This informal Australian variety also uses *he*, notably for plants and for animals of unknown sex. Examples from Pawley are in (6).

(6) a. I had a Golden Snail and he climbed all over the place.
b. This one here, this avocado – he ran wild and I cut the top off 'im.

Australian and New Zealand varieties of English also have the phrase *She'll be right!* where the *she* does not refer to anything at all; the phrase is equivalent to something like *Things will sort themselves out*. Such usages have parallels in older standard British English. Jespersen (1949, p. 214) reports various examples with *he* referring to articles as varied as a turnip, a bullet or a necklace. Some items (Jespersen mentions a watch) may be referred to as either *he* or *she*. Either seems to indicate a certain amount of emotional attachment. Such examples seem rarer today, at least in standard English.

There is also a common objection to the use of *she*, without any other indication of who is involved, which seems to be considered a matter of politeness, rather than a matter of grammar. *She* alone is not supposed to give sufficient acknowledgement of which woman is involved. The challenge *Who's she? The cat's mother?* is intended to provoke a more adequate description. Strangely, there is no corresponding phrase pertaining to men: it seems perfectly acceptable to say *He told me so* without specifying directly who *he* is.

Babies and pets

Babies provide a particular problem. Their parents know perfectly well which sex they are, but strangers may not be able to tell, or may be in a situation where the sex of the baby is irrelevant. So we sometimes hear *it* used to refer to babies, though rarely by people who are emotionally attached to the baby.

The emotional attachment seems to extend to pets. Although there appear to be some people who refer to any unknown cat as *she*, pet owners care about their own pets, and usually refer to them as *he* or *she* as appropriate. In fact, pets are often treated as though they are human – or rational. So we find examples like (7), spoken in the aftermath of the Australian bushfires.

(7) He's been worrying about the family pets, who he says are really struggling. (RNZ National, Checkpoint, 20 February 2020)

Although this could be a matter of personification – treating non-human things as though they are human – it is so widespread as to be virtually the norm. So whether or not you believe that your dog understands every word you say, you are likely to treat your dog grammatically as though it (sorry!) is human. Personification is, of course, much wider. We tend to say things like *The weather smiled upon us* without even recognizing the personification; whether we would call the weather *she* or *he* is less clear.

Countries are regularly personified, and are referred to with *she*: *France has increased her exports again*. Even if Germans call their country the Fatherland, *Germany* would be female in such contexts in English.

Groups of individuals or single entities?

A committee or a team can either be considered to be a unity in itself or can be considered to be a group of individuals. Correspondingly, we can say either (8a), with singular concord with the verb, or (8b), with plural concord with the verb (see further in Chapter 14, on number agreement).

(8) a. The committee has decided to deny the application.
b. The committee have decided to deny the application.

One or the other may be preferred, depending upon the dialect of the writer or speaker, and written and spoken English may not show the same preferences, but there is variation here which is never entirely predictable, even though there are some places where the concord is not open to variation, as in (9), where (9a) indicates a large number of people and (9b) indicates a number of large people.

(9) a. The audience was enormous.
b. The audience were enormous.

What is of interest here is that the choice of number agreement also affects the choice of relative pronoun. Consider the instances in (10) (see Quirk et al. 1972, p. 361).

(10) a. The audience, which was enormous, listened with bated breath.
b. The audience, who were enormous, were uncomfortable in their seats.

In other words, a noun like *audience* (*committee*, *orchestra*, *staff*, *team*, etc.) is viewed as non-human when it is singular, and human when it is plural and we are seeing it as being made up of human individuals.

What's the problem, then?

Although there are fuzzy edges, where usage cannot be predicted, the real problem lies in just a few types of usage which seem to fly in the face of what is expected, and where it is not clear why this should be. The most obvious of these is the use of *which* to refer to humans, as in (11).

(11) a. [...] for the taxpayer, which is going to pick up the tab. (Senior politician, interviewed on RNZ National, Checkpoint, 18 February 2020)
b. The result was that those First National customers which had borrowed most heavily [...] were forced under. (Cited in Bauer 1994, p. 78)
c. We have two people who live on the grounds, one of which has a dog. (Cited in Bauer 1994, p. 78)
d. New Zealand is full of athletes which are hugely talented. (NZ Prime Minister, John Key, interviewed on RNZ National, 11 June 2010)

Presumably, the taxpayer is human; and although we might be talking about a generic taxpayer, this is not really a group, which might merit the *which*. Perhaps politicians do not view taxpayers as human.

This kind of usage seems odd, given our general understanding of the way the grammar works here, but it may be less odd than it seems. Earlier English regularly allowed *which* with humans: remember the version of the Lord's Prayer which began *Our father, which art in heaven* [...]. It seems entirely plausible that the use of *which* in the examples in (11) is a left-over from that period, although *which* is no longer as current as it once was.

There is another reason why *which* may be gaining ground with humans, too. It has to do with the gradual loss of *whom*. *Whom* has been on the way out for a long time, and its use in questions can sometimes sound pedantic. *Who did you see?* is normal, *Whom did you see?* sounds as if someone is making a grammatical point. One of the last refuges of *whom* was (or is) immediately following a preposition, as in *To whom it may concern*. But even that usage is weakening, as we see in the examples in (12) from the British National Corpus (BNC) (Davies 2004–).

(12) a. There are about 1 billion Indians, about half of who were at Madras airport [...]
b. you can come in and not know which baby belongs to who [...]
c. You vote for who you want.
d. Sad indeed, but for who?

In the examples in (12), *whom* has been replaced by *who*, a usage which is very common. But sometimes that doesn't sound right, and people prefer to replace *whom* by *which*. Examples from the BNC are given in (13), and another example is in (14).

(13) a. ICI employs about 26000 people of which 27.5 per cent (just over 7000) are women.
b. she ensures that she does nothing to cross the 'important' people on which she is dependent.
c. the people with which he was dealing, ...
d. there are enough women from which to choose [...]
e. the girls with which he filled his mind [...]

(14) It's made up of Corrections officers and supervisors, the identities of which are confidential. (Cornwell, Patricia 1993. *Cruel and unusual*, London: TimeWarner, p. 55)

Examples like these suggest that Quirk et al.'s (1972, p. 215) observation that '*Whom* is the obligatory relative pronoun as complement immediately following a preposition' no longer holds true.

If the use of *which* for humans (or rational beings) is explicable, the use of *who* for non-humans is rather less so. Yet we find that, too. In most cases, the use of *who* is justified by the fact that people are involved, even if the noun to which the *who* refers does not denote a person. Examples from the BNC are given in (15).

(15) a. There were grocery shops who blended tea [...]
b. modules from the 1989/90 Catalogue will continue to be available in 1991/92 for centres who have successfully sought approval from SCOTVEC.

c. Our picture shows the Torness Financial Department, one of the sections who have taken part in the process [...]

Shop is not a human noun, but the shop is run by people, and they are the ones who actually blended the tea, and so on. Examples like these provide a middle ground where the use of *who* is justified semantically, though not strictly grammatically. The examples in (16), on the other hand, have no such justification beyond rampant personification. We seem happy to class lurchers (dogs) and horses as rational beings; hedgehogs are surely a little further out, but plants as rational beings seem to suggest a different grammatical system – as do the bugs in (17).

(16) a. strong-growing 'weed' appears to intimidate those plants who were previously growing there.
b. This is just one of hundreds of hedgehogs who owe their lives to the Vale Wildlife Rescue Centre in Evesham.
c. feeding the rest of the steak to the shaggy lurchers who ringed the table [...]
d. Foals who have learnt to evade bot-flies in such a way, will continue to do so.
e. glorious MUD! It's not just hippos who benefit from wallowing in it, you know.

(17) It was twilight and half a dozen bats were snarfing up the random bugs who had been on a variety of important errands until rudely interrupted by death. (Dobyns, Stephen 1994. *Saratoga backtalk*. New York and London: Norton, p. 150)

Two possible misconceptions

There are two places where some people seem to have invented new rules which are not historically justified. The result may be a change in the way English is used, but if that is the eventual outcome, we are somewhere along the way towards adopting the change, and both the old and the new versions are currently common. Under such circumstances, it is potentially misleading to say that either version is wrong, we just have to say that we have two competing versions, and the grammar has not yet sorted itself out.

The first of these concerns the relative pronoun *that*, meaning the kind of *that* found in (18). Notice that, for most people, most of the time, this word is pronounced as if it were *thit* or *th't*. I'll call it 'reduced *that*'. It does not rhyme with *cat*, unlike the word spelt the same way in (19), which performs different functions. Reduced *that* is occasionally pronounced to rhyme with *cat* in reading aloud, in very clear or very slow speech, but mostly has the form discussed here.

(18) The picture that he painted looks very messy to me.

(19) a. That is the car I want to buy.
b. That car is the one I want to buy.

Many people seem to feel that you cannot use reduced *that* to refer back to a human. They have a rule that *who* refers to people and *that* refers to things. They feel very uncomfortable with the examples in (20), all of which come from the BNC.

(20) a. we had this man that used to come from India [...]
b. I became the kind of woman that my friends, mother, sisters and other friends warned them about.
c. The Flight-Lieutenant became suddenly petulant, like a child that has lost its toy.
d. Events that happen previously show us that Atticus is a person that we can put our trust in.
e. After about ten minutes Mr Morris, the violin teacher that visits the school, came in [...]
f. The driver was given directions to take her to the doctor that Julius had contacted.

Such examples are common and have a long history. Recall the nursery rhyme about the house that Jack built (date uncertain, but before the mid-eighteenth century), a few lines of which are reproduced in (21):

(21) This is the priest all shaven and shorn
That married the man all tattered and torn
That kissed the maiden all forlorn
That milked the cow with the crumpled horn [...].

Indeed, it is the *who* form which is the usurper here. Baugh (1959, p. 206) dates the arrival of *who* in relative clauses to the sixteenth century; before that, the use of *that* (or its predecessor) was the norm everywhere. The change going on here has been a very slow one, taking several hundred years, and it still has not reached an obvious endpoint.

The second problematic form is *whose*. Because it is clearly related to *who*, some people feel that it should be used only with a human antecedent. That is, while they think (22a) is fine, they find (22b) odd.

(22) a. The woman whose daughter works in the Post Office.
b. The house whose roof is leaking.

The problem with (22b) is that there is no easy alternative. *The house that's roof is leaking* is impossible for most speakers outside of Scotland, and that leaves the rather clumsy *The house of which the roof is leaking*. Accordingly, we find the examples in (23) – again from the BNC, which show precisely the usage that such people object to.

(23) a. The oxalis, whose leaves are often mistaken for shamrock, [...]
b. Equal rights for disabled workers is an ideal and idea whose time has come.

c. Tom told us of one horse whose molars on one side of the mouth were excessively short.
d. the Georgian town house style hotel whose lounge boasts two public telephones [...]

Such examples are sanctioned by usage, though they may eventually die out if an alternative becomes normal.

Sexist use of gender

Because English demands that we mark the gender of a person when we refer to them with a pronoun, we get into trouble when the gender of the person being referred to is either unknown, unknowable or irrelevant. Look at (24):

(24) The person who wrote the complaint said that he/she was complaining on behalf of a friend.

We may not know the sex of the person who wrote the complaint (perhaps the complaint was signed 'A. Smith', for instance) and even if we do, it is not relevant for the message. Nevertheless, we have to choose, and choosing is problematic. In old-fashioned, formal English the solution was to choose *he*, and to some extent, this persists, even though it has not worked well for a long time. If we choose *she*, the implication seems to be that we know that the person was female, which at the very least shows that *he* and *she* are not used in comparable ways. But *he or she* sounds clumsy, and *(s)he* (or *s/he*) works only in writing, not in speech. Very often, and increasingly, we use *they*, in an attempt to avoid the issue, despite the fact that *they* is usually plural. Although this is a modern solution, it has roots going back over 400 years, and is not as contrived as some opponents seem to believe.

They may not be a perfect solution, but it is often far better than using either *he* or *she*. People who have studied this area of language use have found some really astounding instances where writers have got themselves into a real mess, either by using *he* where the sex of the person referred to is not clearly male, or by trying to use *man* in the sense of 'human being', and getting apparent nonsense. Examples like this may be rare, but they are symptomatic of a greater malaise, and less extreme examples were frequent not all that long ago, and still persist today. Places where writers or speakers have got into real trouble with such matters, and with the use of man to mean 'humankind' can be quite overwhelming. Consider the examples in (25), cited from the relevant literature.

(25) a. Man has been civilized for centuries. He no longer needs to hunt for food for his women and children. (Cited by Holmes 2013, p. 328).
b. During his life, the average American consumes 26 million gallons of water... (Cited by Key 1975, p. 100)
c. He believes that the artist is a man of his time, his society, of a particular culture and social class. (Widely quoted.)

d. The Masculine Person answers to the general Name, which comprises both Male and Female, as Any Person, who knows what he says. (1746; cited by Bodine 1975).

While examples like those in (25) certainly show usage which may rightfully be called sexist, we need to raise the question of whether it is the usage or the language which encourages sexism. As far as I am aware, there is no evidence that languages which do not distinguish between words meaning 'he' and 'she', and which have a single word which can be translated by either, depending on the context, (like Chinese, Finnish and Persian) are associated with cultures which are measurably less sexist than the cultures associated with English or languages like it, with separate words. The fact that English has not inherited a pronoun which allows an automatic avoidance of the issue means that we have to work harder to sidestep the linguistic expression of sexist assumptions, but it can nearly always be done when we have time to edit our words. In rapid conversation, such avoidance may be harder.

There are plenty of other places where usage is often sexist. Suffixes like *-ess* in *poetess* or *-ette* in *usherette* are often perceived as trivializing and demeaning, even if they are not intended to be. The fact that we would talk about a *lady* or *woman doctor* but not about a *gentleman* or *man doctor*, and about a *male nurse* but not about a *female nurse* says much about (often outdated) expectations, and is often not necessary for successful communication. Such expressions can be avoided, just like the offending pronoun usages, and show that it is people who perpetuate sexist usage, not the language itself. In order to avoid sexism, users have to be aware of the potential for such usage to affect others in several ways and take positive action if they want to avoid this.

Wrapping up

What sounds like a fairly simple idea of gender and related matters of referring back to particular nouns ends up being grammatically complicated for two reasons. First, the language is changing. Some parts of it change fast, some parts change extremely slowly. We still have remnants of a system where *he* and *she* do not refer solely to male and female creatures – rather like the way that gender works in French and German. But it has taken over 600 years for that old system to wear away, and it is still not entirely gone. The loss of *whom* is more recent, but the system is still settling down from that, and some speakers still have traces of *whom* – especially in their written language.

The other major cause of confusion is the distinction between what the grammar seems to require and what the sense of the sentence seems to require. A team might not be human, but it is made up of humans, and sometimes its humanness is more important to us than its inherent unity. Because we are human, humans are important in our world, and we want to show human participation where it makes sense to do so.

The result of these two factors is that the system is not entirely predictable. We can say *the team is* or *the team are*, and if we use *is* we see the team as non-human, if we use *are* we see it as essentially human. Either view is permitted by our language, but you would have a hard time telling a computer how to replicate the way we use that language.

What should I read?

Most grammars of English will have sections on the uses of *he* and *she* and on the uses of relative pronouns (e.g. *who*, *which*). The basic grammars seldom go into the kind of detail that I have given here, although the more comprehensive grammars do indicate that there is variation. There is discussion in some of the recent grammars as to whether *that* is a relative pronoun or something else, but I have not mentioned this dispute, since it seems too academic and tangential an argument to require consideration in this book. For those that are interested, there is a good introduction to the topic in Huddleston, Pullum & Peterson (2002, pp. 1056–7).

There are other issues that I have avoided here: the difference between restrictive and non-restrictive relative clauses, for instance. They make a difference as to whether *who* or *that* can be used. Because I have avoided this issue, I have also avoided differences between British and American English in the use of *that*. I have also avoided the earlier history of the development of relative clauses in English. Baugh (1959) gives a good brief summary, and fuller histories of English will provide more detail.

On sexism in language, see Key (1975), Baron (1986), Holmes (2013). Baron is particularly good on epicene pronouns like *thon*.

References

Baron, Dennis 1986. *Grammar and gender*. New Haven: Yale University Press.

Bauer, Laurie 1994. *Watching English change*. London: Longman. doi:10.4324/9781315844169

Baugh, Albert C. 1959. *A history of the English language*. 2nd edition. London: Routledge & Kegan Paul.

Bodine, Ann 1975. Androcentrism in prescriptive grammar: Singular 'they', sex-indefinite 'he', and 'he or she'. *Language in Society* 4: 129–146. doi:10/1017/S0047404500004607

Davies, Mark 2004. *British National Corpus* (from Oxford University Press). Available online at https://www.english-corpora.org/bnc/.

Eckert, Penelope & Sally McConnel-Ginet 2003. *Language and gender*. Cambridge: Cambridge University Press. doi:10.1017/CBO9781139245883

Holmes, Janet 2013. *An introduction to sociolinguistics*. 4th edition. Harlow: Pearson.

Huddleston, Rodney, Geoffrey K. Pullum & Peter Peterson 2002. Relative constructions and unbounded dependencies. In Rodney Huddleston & Geoffrey K. Pullum (eds), *The Cambridge grammar of the English language*, 1031–1096. Cambridge: Cambridge University Press. doi:10.1017/9781316423530.013

Jespersen, Otto 1949. *A modern English grammar on historical principles*. London: Allen & Unwin.

Key, Mary Ritchie 1975. *Male/female language*. Metuchen: Scarecrow.

Pawley, Andrew 2008. Australian vernacular English: Some grammatical characteristics. In Kate Burridge & Bernd Kortmannn (eds), *Varieties of English 3: The Pacific and Australasia*, 362–397. Berlin: Mouton de Gruyter. doi:10.1515/9783110208412.2.362

Quirk, Randolph, Sidney Greenbaum, Geoffrey Leech & Jan Svartvik 1972. *A grammar of contemporary English*. London: Longman.

West, Candace & Don H. Zimmerman 1987. Doing gender. *Gender & Society* 1(2): 125–151. doi:10.1177/0891243287001002002

13 *The chapter that I put too many pronouns in it*

Shadow pronouns

Andreea

Setting the scene

As a celebrated Victorian novelist, Anthony Trollope is probably best known for his *Chronicles of Barsetshire* novels, a set of six stories set in the made-up English county of Barsetshire, written between 1855 and 1867. But for certain grammarians, he is equally well-known for producing one of the earliest attested examples of shadow pronouns, a type of pronoun which remains elusive to linguists on account of its unexplained use. In the third of his Barsetshire novels, Trollope presents the reader with the following passage:

(1) If he does not marry money, he is lost. Good Heavens! A doctor's niece! A girl that nobody knows where she comes from! (Trollope, Anthony 1858. *Chronicles of Barsetshire.* London: Longmans, p. 144).

The passage expresses the dismissal of a romantic relationship between a doctor's niece, whose background is unknown and social status (assumed) low and a young man in need of a wealthy marriage arrangement. Putting the scandalous affair aside, of most interest in the passage is the use of the clause *that nobody knows where she comes from* to refer back to *a girl*, and in turn, to *the doctor's niece*. These clauses are termed 'relative clauses', following Latin terminology meaning 'to carry back', because they relate information back to previously mentioned entities (nouns). More specifically, what is troublesome in the above relative clause is the pronoun *she*. *She* is called a 'shadow pronoun' or 'resumptive pronoun'. Both terms capture different aspects of how the pronoun is understood: 'shadow pronoun' captures the fact that the pronoun is casting a shadow of the noun it denotes inside the relative clause; 'resumptive' captures the fact that the pronoun takes up again (resumes) the reference of a previously mentioned entity. The point is that whichever way you look at it, such shadowing or resuming is not part of standard English grammar use (Biber et al. 1999, p. 622, Huddleston & Pullum 2002, p. 1091).

Keith Brown and Jim Miller discuss this particular (in their own words) 'pleasing example' from Trollope in their *Critical account of English syntax* and explain that a 'classical' version of the relative clause in (1) might be 'whose origins

DOI: 10.4324/9781003148999-13

nobody knows' or 'whose parentage nobody knows' (Brown & Miller 2016, p. 193). The 'pleasing' example would have endeared itself to grammarians like Jim Miller because it shows long-standing use of what would be a grammatical thorn in any prescriptivist's eyes, normally relegated to a mere error of absent-minded or uneducated speech.

Shadow pronouns cast a rather long shadow

Writing for the *Language Log*, a linguistics-related blog, American linguist Mark Liberman draws attention to an example of a shadow pronoun extracted from an article in the *Washington Post* (Language Log, 'Resumptive Pronoun of the Week', 11 February 2017). The quote from Chaffetz published in the *Washington Post* related the awkward situation in which the Trump administration officials were having to investigate the dealings of business run by the president's family.

(2) 'His being both the landlord and the tenant is something that we're curious what the GSA's opinion of that is,' Chaffetz said. (*Washington Post*, 10 February 2017)

Jim Miller would have probably found it equally pleasing to learn that this quote has indeed proved popular and as a result, it has appeared in a number of other sources, though sadly, not owing to its value to linguistic debates.

Here is another example from the *Kent Online* news site which British linguist Peter Sells (1984) would have labelled 'intrusive pronoun'.

(3) 'I am the sort of person that I need to see it to believe it.' (*Kent Online*, 31 October 2016)

Despite the negative press they receive, these pronouns are prevalent and persistent, particularly in speech, and occasionally in written language too (though admittedly, their appearance in writing is usually to relate direct speech). The mystery troubling linguists is this: why do speakers use what appear to be unnecessary shadow pronouns given their negative evaluation and the extra effort required in uttering them (after all, this non-standard use cannot be reduced to lazy grammar)?

Asking speakers why they use shadow pronouns turns out to be unhelpful because most speakers either deny ever using them, or else deem them to be speech errors arising from poor (grammatical) planning. We know the first assertion is untrue because shadow pronouns turn up sufficiently frequently in speech. Jim Miller used to delight in sharing with his students examples of various shadow pronoun sentences which he had overheard uttered by senior linguistics professors, who would later go on to deny ever uttering them. He even collected emails containing these pronouns which would later show up analysed in linguistics journals (see his 2006 book with Keith Brown for such examples).

In other words, even speakers with access to high levels of formal education produce shadow pronouns, despite their claims to the contrary (Miller & Weinert 1998).

As regards the second point, that shadow pronouns are mistakes, for those grammarians concerned with understanding what speakers actually do (since intuitions may not be reliable, see Chapter 1, Introduction), the question still necessitates an answer. Could it be that shadow pronouns actually help speakers in formulating their discourse or listeners in understanding it?

Inside a relative clause: minding the gap and resolving island constraints

In order to consider the advantages of shadow pronouns, it is useful to probe the structure of relative clauses more closely. Relative clauses provide additional information about a particular entity (a noun). This noun sits outside the clause itself, but has a grammatical role to play inside it.

Let us begin with *the movie that I saw last night*, and focus on the relative clause, *that I saw last night*. An alternative version of this clause, one that could stand alone, is *I saw the movie last night*. But if we compare it to the version with the relative clause, *the movie* has disappeared from inside the relative clause, probably because we have mentioned *the movie* already. Such a pattern is common in many languages including English, French and Italian. In other languages, like Hebrew, Irish and certain varieties of Arabic, *the movie* does not disappear from the relative clause, instead it leaves a pronoun in its place, becoming something like *the movie that I saw it last night*. This pronoun (*it* in the example sentence) is a shadow pronoun, and depending on the languages in question, such a shadow pronoun may be optionally allowed or actually required by the standard grammar of the language.

Crucially – and here is the rub – in English, such resumption, shadowing or intrusiveness is not part of the grammar of standard varieties. Instead, in standard English relative clauses, the noun (*movie*) leaves a gap (indicated by ___): *the movie that I saw ___ last night;* which the listener fills by using the context (the word 'gap' used here is widely employed by linguists to refer to the site where something is missing). In other words, English speakers have a bit more inferencing to do in order to interpret relative clauses than, say, Hebrew speakers.

In some sentences, the gap is closer to the noun while in others, it is further away from it. Here are some examples from Nomi Erteschick-Shir's work (1992), which illustrate the incredible distance that the grammar of English allows between nouns and their gaps inside relative clauses:

(4) This is the girl that Peter gave some cakes to ___.
(5) This is the girl that Peter said that John gave some cakes to ___.
(6) This is the girl that Peter said that John thinks that his mother had given some cakes to ___.

Despite the fact that such long gaps are allowed by the grammar system, speakers know it is just not sensible to leave long gaps because they make interpretation too difficult (which may also explain why these very same examples can be found cited in so many linguistics articles on shadow pronouns; it takes quite a bit of tinkering to put together such spectacular sentences).

And there are further problems which English speakers face in interpreting relative clauses. If you found the sentences in (5) and (6) taxing, take a look at the next one.

(7) I'd like to meet the linguist that Peter knows a psychologist that works for ___.

With (7), it is not immediately obvious how to best rephrase it; it certainly sounds odd, but it is difficult to know how to improve it. Alleviating the oddness requires a complete overhaul of the sentence; it means starting again (something like 'I'd like to meet the linguist that employs the psychologist that Peter knows').

The problem with (7) is not one of distance between noun and its gap, but rather, the problem relates to the position of the noun inside the relative clause. If we think of nouns as starting out in the relative clause and moving out into the main clause (as some theories of grammar propose), then one could say that the noun in (7) just doesn't like being moved – it simply resists it. This has come to be known as a type of 'island constraint', the terminology first introduced by John Robert Ross in the 1960s (Ross, 1967). Owing perhaps to his interest in poetry, Ross coined this metaphorical term to capture the fact that some words are constrained and cannot move freely around the sentence, forming 'syntactic islands' – places on which they appear to be marooned without the possibility of escape. Ross has spent a great part of his linguistic career studying syntactic islands and has documented many other grammatical structures, besides relative clauses, which are subject to island constraints.

Fifty shades of shadow pronouns

Even though grammaticality is generally conceived by speakers as a black-and-white matter, so that an expression is either grammatical or it isn't, the reality is that there are grey areas in grammaticality too.

Although shadow pronouns are generally not accepted as part of standard English grammar, some types of relative clauses containing shadow pronouns seem less 'bad' than others. Compare (8) and (9). They both use shadow pronouns, but most speakers find (8) a bit worse than (9). Why?

(8) John saw the French movie that it had that old French actor in it.
(9) John saw a French movie, which he didn't like it much.

One difference between the two relatives is the fact that the clause in (8), *that it has that old French actor in it* helps to pick out the noun in question (the correct movie) from a set of possibilities (it could be any movie, but in this case, it is the one that had the old French actor in it). In contrast, the clause in (9), *which he didn't like it much*, does not delimit, it simply elaborates on what is known about the noun. We call this latter type of relative a 'non-restrictive' (or 'appositive') relative clause, and the former a 'restrictive' relative clause.

For some (yet to be fully understood) reason it turns out that non-restrictive relative clauses will more comfortably allow shadow pronouns than restrictive relative clauses (Loss & Wicklund 2020). This matter is further complicated by the fact that the most frequent type of non-restrictive clause also happens to be one of the most versatile type too, namely the *which*-clause.

Work on *which* has shown that in different varieties of English, *which* is not only used to introduce a relative clause, but can also function as a general discourse marker linking one chunk of language to another, in a much looser and unconstrained manner (Burke 2017) – see also Chapter 15, on insubordination.

Given that so many non-restrictive clauses are introduced by *which*, and that *which* seems to have other grammatical roles to play, it is impossible to test reliably why a sentence like (8) is worse than one like (9): is it that non-restrictive clauses allow shadow pronouns more readily (and if so, why?) or is it that *which*-clauses allow shadow pronouns more readily (and again, why?) or is it something else entirely (Loss & Wicklund 2020)?

Do shadow pronouns actually fill gaps and rescue islands?

Putting the difficult *which*es aside, let us return to the reason why a shadow pronoun might arise in the first place. Thinking in terms of processing, it might be that shadow pronouns help speakers put together complex relative clauses off the cuff and with little planning time, or that they help to remind listeners which noun is being referenced in the relative clause (or both).

If we take the previous examples and rephrase them to contain shadow pronouns, we find that the sentence in (10) seems a bit strained and the shadow pronoun perhaps unnecessary.

(10) This is the girl that Peter gave her some cakes.

However, (11) and (12) are easier to interpret, and so is (13).

(11) This is the girl that Peter said that John gave some cakes to her.
(12) This is the girl that Peter said that John thinks that his mother had given some cakes to her.
(13) I'd like to meet the linguist that Peter knows a psychologist that works for him.

So there we have it: theories of grammar have come up with an elegant and plausible explanation for the use of shadow pronouns: they can alleviate the processing pressures caused by long distances between nouns and their gaps, and marooned nouns by allowing them to have a pronoun re-establish a potentially lost link.

But can we be sure that this is indeed the true motivation for shadow pronouns? Enter psycholinguistic experiments. The last ten years have seen a flurry of experimental studies which have tried to find support for what grammarians think is driving the use of shadow pronouns. Despite this effort, their findings remain mixed and not entirely conclusive.

How do speakers feel about shadow pronouns? Well, they are certainly not in favour of them. But perhaps if they consider the alternative, a gapped relative clause, they might concede that shadow pronouns are not that bad after all.

Surprisingly, bringing native English speakers into a lab and asking them to rate how good a particular sentence sounds, does not lead to higher ratings of shadow pronouns, even when they have the explicit gapped equivalents as a comparison (Polinski et al. 2011, Alexpoupoulu & Keller 2007). In fact, this exercise only leads to low ratings of both linguistic constructions because speakers dislike shadow pronouns just as much as gapped relative clauses, especially where distances are large (between nouns and gaps or shadow pronouns), and where island constraints are present. However, a lot seems to ride on details of how the experiments are conducted and how the results are interpreted. A small tweak in the questions being asked can apparently lead to rather different conclusions.

One research team wittily lead participants to produce sentences with shadow pronouns and then asked the same people to judge the acceptability of (essentially) the language they have had just been manipulated into producing (Ferreira & Swets 2005). Speakers remained undeterred in their aversion of shadow pronouns (though they had not been asked to compare these directly with gapped versions of the same sentences). So even if we use a particular linguistic structure ourselves, it does not mean we find it acceptable. It also goes some way towards explaining why people who judge sentences which they themselves use as ungrammatical, then go on to deny using them in the first place. Presumably, the denial is an attempt to maintain consistency between the speakers' intuitive sense of 'correct' grammar and their language use.

The same study also found that time pressure did not predispose speakers to increase their use of shadow pronouns, which seemed to contradict the idea of poor (grammatical) planning being responsible for shadow pronouns.

Granted, shadow pronouns may not be a great deal of help to speakers trying to produce language off the cuff, but perhaps they are helpful to listeners, in increasing comprehension. One criticism of early experiments asking participants to rate acceptability of various constructions was that *acceptability* is essentially a synonym of prestige and grammaticality. Higher prestige is attached to standard grammar regardless of whether the standard form is actually efficient in facilitating successful communication.

With these observations in mind, new experiments were conducted to check the effect of shadow pronouns on comprehension. So in order to study comprehension effects, it became important to steer participants away from attitudinal judgements of aesthetics and prestige. Betrama & Xiang (2016) conducted a study in which they asked participants to rate both acceptability and comprehension, but crucially, they separated out the two notions. They found that indeed, shadow pronouns were judged to increase comprehension, especially in sentences like (14) (example from Bertrama & Xiang 2016, 12).

(14) This is the boy that the newspaper reports that the cop who beat him up was leading the operation.

Distance between a noun and its gap seemed to be relevant to some extent but not as much as first predicted. Other analysts proposed that the distance of their test sentences was not nearly taxing enough to see a real benefit of shadow pronouns (if indeed these would aptly provide it). It could be that if the separation of the noun from its corresponding gap were sufficiently great, then the use of the shadow pronoun in the relative clause might be warranted. However, current experiments do not push the human cognitive capacity far enough to engage it and thus be able to detect it in a lab setting (Alexopoulou & Keller 2007). Coming up with good lab data to test is no mean feat!

In spite of all this work, the comprehension advantage is still not fully accepted. This is because of a problem in Betrama and Xiang's study: their measures of comprehension were self-reported and thus deemed insufficiently rigorous (they did not capture eye tracking or record the time it took participants to understand the sentences they were presented with). Put another way, participants may feel like the shadow pronouns help them understand sentences quicker, but do they really?

Just to make matters worse, without going into the full details, more recent work argues precisely the opposite, namely that shadow pronouns could even be detrimental to comprehension (Meltzer-Asscher 2020).

Wrapping up

Studying real language exchanges tells us that shadow pronouns represent a recurring feature of spoken English. What these studies do not (as yet?) show is a conclusive and undisputed explanation as to why a construction uniformly deemed ungrammatical continues to persist. And not only persist but actually spread – those watching language change predict it is likely to emerge as a regular feature of written English (Loss & Wicklund 2020).

In searching for the motivation driving the use of shadow pronouns, we have uncovered that our commitment to preserving the status quo in grammar seems more important than our desire for increased comprehension or efficiency of communication. Speakers remain undeterred in their disapproval of shadow pronouns. The experiments conducted also illustrate how hard it is to obtain solid evidence for any given language form. Speakers do not know why they use a given structure, nor do they even realise that they do in fact use it, they just know they dislike it.

What should I read?

The literature on relative clauses is dense and full of jargon, but the experimental studies are typically easier to follow, despite the fact that they often adopt a formal (generative) and thus highly technical view of relative clauses. Loss & Wicklund (2020) present an up-to-date and thorough review (though their findings section can be daunting to beginners). The chapter on relative clauses in Brown & Miller (2016) is an excellent introduction to the topic of relative clauses, containing many meticulously collected natural examples.

References

Alexopoulou, Theodora & Frank Keller 2007. Locality, cyclicity, and resumption: At the interface between the grammar and the human sentence processor. *Language* 83: 110–160.

Beltrama, Andrea & Ming Xiang 2016. Unacceptable but comprehensible: The facilitation effect of resumptive pronouns. *Glossa* 1(1): 1–24. doi:10.5334/GJGL.24

Biber, Douglas, Stig Johansson, Geoffrey Leech, Susan Conrad & Edward Finegan 1999. *Longman grammar of spoken and written English.* Harlow: Longman.

Brown, Keith & Jim Miller 2016. *A critical account of English syntax: Grammar, meaning and text*. Edinburgh: Edinburgh University Press.

Burke, Isabelle 2017. Wicked *which*: The linking relative in Australian English. *Australian Journal of Linguistics* 37(3): 356–386. doi:10.1080/07268602.2017.1298398

Erteschik-Shir, Nomi 1992. Resumptive pronouns in islands. In Helen Goodluck & Michael Rochemont (eds), *Island constraints*, 89–108. Dordrecht: Springer.

Ferreira, Fernanda & Benjamin Swets 2005. The production and comprehension of resumptive pronouns in relative clause "island" contexts. In Anne Cutler (ed.), *Twenty-first century psycholinguistics: Four cornerstones*, 263–278. Malway: Lawrence Erlbaum.

Huddleston, Rodney & Geoffrey K. Pullum (eds) 2002. *The Cambridge grammar of the English language*. Cambridge: Cambridge University Press. doi:10.1017/9781316423530

Keffala, Bethany 2011. Resumption and gaps in English relative clauses: Relative acceptability creates an illusion of 'saving'. *Annual Meeting of the Berkeley Linguistics Society* 37: 140–154.

Language Log. Accessible from: https://languagelog.ldc.upenn.edu.

Loss, Sara & Mark Wicklund 2020. Is English resumption different in appositive relative clauses? *Canadian Journal of Linguistics/Revue Canadienne de linguistique* 65(1): 25–51. doi:10.1017/cnj.2019.19

Meltzer-Asscher, Aya 2020 Resumptive pronouns in language comprehension and production. *Annual Review of Linguistics* 7: 177–194. doi:10.1146/annurev-linguistics-031320-012726

Miller, James & Regina Weinert 1998. *Spontaneous spoken language: Syntax and discourse*. Oxford: Oxford University Press.

Polinsky, Maria, Lauren Clemens, Adam Milton Morgan, Ming Xiang & Dustin Heestand 2011. Resumption in English. In Jon Sprouse & Norbert Hornstein (eds), *Experimental syntax and island effects*, 341–362. Cambridge: Cambridge University Press.

Ross, John 1967. *Constraints on variables in syntax*. PhD Dissertation. Boston: Massachusetts Institute of Technology.

Sells, Peter 1984. *Syntax and semantics of resumptive pronouns*. PhD Dissertation. Amherst: University of Massachusetts.

14 *There's heaps of money to be won*

Number agreement

Laurie

Setting the scene

If you are trying to dress formally, you might want to ensure that your handbag and your shoes match, or that your tie and your socks match. A match for the sake of fashion in this kind of way is not obligatory: if you don't have a blue handbag to go with blue shoes, you can always carry a black one. The fussy will notice, and in some circles will condemn; but for most occasions, the more important fact is the fact that you have come to the event. In grammar, languages sometimes demand that things match in grammatical terms. If you fail to make the requisite things match, you do not sound like a natural user of the language concerned. Just what has to match depends on the language you are speaking. In many European languages, adjectives have to match the nouns they go with for gender and number, as do articles (words that translate as 'a' and 'the'). English has fewer such categories, but does still have one major one, though it is not always easy to see how the matching works.

Speakers of standard varieties of English, if they heard a foreigner saying something like *My mother make good soup*, would object and correct them to *makes*. It would probably be perfectly clear what our foreigner meant, but standard English demands that extra final *-s*. The matching between the subject of a clause (*My mother* in the example above) and the main verb in the clause (*makes*) is called 'agreement', and because the agreement shows singular or plural, it is more fully termed 'number agreement'. The basic rules of number agreement in English are very simple; the details are very complicated.

The fundamental point is that a singular subject requires a singular verb and a plural subject requires a plural verb. Except with the verb *be*, where there is a difference between *was* and *were* in the past tense, number is shown on verbs only in the present tense, so that it is only with things like *make* versus *makes* that we find the agreement. Singular forms of verbs (as long as they are not modal verbs like *can* and *may*) include *is*, *has*, and verbs with an *-s* ending (*does*, *explodes*, *identifies*, *runs*, *sneezes* and so on). Verbs agreeing with plural subjects have no ending on them and look just like the stem, the form used with *I* or *you* (*are* is a major exception to the first part of this). The examples in (1) show the basic pattern. *Car* and *oak* are singular, *cars* and *oaks* are plural (they have a plural marker, here

DOI: 10.4324/9781003148999-14

the regular -*s* form), *grow* is the same form we would find with *I* or *you* (*I grow tomatoes*, *You grow more handsome every year*).

(1) a. The car is in the garage.
    b. The cars are in the garage.
    c. The oak grows in England.
    d. Oaks grow in England.

There are extra complications with the verb *be*, because here we not only have an *is* form, we also have *am* which goes with the first person singular. Because this is not a matter of singular versus plural, it is not relevant to the discussion in this chapter, and we need not consider it further.

Where we are just dealing with singular and plural, there are some extra points that we should mention, but they are not very difficult.

First, if we conjoin the two different singular things in the subject, then the two together make a plural, and we get plural concord (as in (2)).

(2) The owl and the pussy cat are in the boat.

If the two conjoined words are just different aspects of a single object, then we get singular concord.

(3) My friend and sponsor is Kim.

Because we get a plural noun form when we have, say, *one and a half*, we also get plural concord there, as in (4).

(4) One and a half letters are still visible, painted on the wall.

With measures, even ones expressed with a plural noun, it is often the case that the measure is seen as a single lump, and it then takes singular concord, as in (5).

(5) a. Five miles is a long way to walk.
    b. $1.2m is a lot of money.

Along with these minor problems, there are some major ones, which we consider next.

Is zero singular or plural?

Zero is a relatively recent invention in mathematics, and remains a problematic notion there. Dealing with nothing in language is sometimes just as difficult. The standard answer to whether zero is singular or plural is that *none* means 'not one' and is therefore singular. This would work for the way in which we treat *nothing* and *nobody*, but it does not match the way we treat *none*.

(6) a. Nobody is here.
b. Nothing was said.
c. None of us are perfect. (Wilde, Oscar (1895). *The importance of being earnest,* Act II).

None can be used with countable nouns and with mass nouns (see Chapter 6, on countability). With the latter, the singular is natural, as in (7).

(7) I've ordered some rice, but none has arrived yet.

With countable nouns, despite a prescription for singular usage, plural seems to be more normal, as in (8).

(8) I've ordered some biscuits, but none has/have arrived yet.

Since this is the first place where the point arises, and we will need to discuss it later, we should talk about proximity as a factor in determining verb number. Very often the verb number is not there to match the *none*, but to match the closest noun (or pronoun). Contrast (9) and (10).

(9) None of the milk I've ordered has/*have arrived yet.
(10) None of the books I've ordered *has/have arrived yet.

In (10) the plural verb is chosen because of the proximity of *books* (a plural noun), while in (9) the proximity of *milk* (a singular noun) matches the singular which might be expected from *none*, and they gang up so that the plural becomes impossible. Since number matches countability in (9) and (10), it is hard to distinguish between the two. We will have to return to the grammatical structure of such phrases, but the principle of proximity is an important one.

Is the team singular or are the team plural?

There is a large set of nouns in English which denote collections of people (or, indeed, of other things, but the ones denoting people are of particular importance here). These are often called 'collective' nouns, and they include words like *audience, committee, family, government, opposition, parliament, team* and so on (see also Chapter 17, on possession). The names of countries can be added to the list when they are used metonymically to mean the team representing the country, as in (11).

(11) England won the Rugby World Cup in 2003.

All such collective nouns can take singular or plural concord. We can say (12a) or (12b).

(12) a. The family is on holiday at the moment.
b. The family are on holiday at the moment.

The received wisdom on such instances is that the singular is used when we perceive the collectivity (e.g. the family) as a single entity, and the plural is used when we perceive the collectivity as a set of individuals. According to this rule, a speaker who produces (12a) perceives the family as an undifferentiated body, while the speaker who produces (12b) perceives the family as being made up a lot of people, each of whom is on holiday. Since we cannot predict whether a speaker will perceive a collectivity in one way or the other, subject agreement here is in principle unpredictable.

However, such a view is insufficient. We can start with the fact that Microsoft Word (which I am using to write this chapter) thinks that *are* in (12b) is wrong. That is, the programmers for Word were prepared to predict a unique right answer here. It is not coincidental that the programmers for Word were almost certainly American. Different varieties of English show different tendencies in the way in which subject concord is used here, and that implies that the form used may be more predictable than was suggested above – it's just that you have to predict different concord in different varieties. Traditionally, American English is more likely to use the singular than British English is. But British English is changing in this regard. In an earlier study (Bauer 1994, p. 64), I found that the word *government* was usually used in the plural for the British government but in the singular for foreign governments in editorials from *The Times* of London between 1935 and 1965, but after 1970, the singular was used in both sets of circumstances. Had I had sufficient attestations of the word *team*, particularly if they had been found on the sports pages and not in editorials, I might have found plural concord lasting a lot longer. In other words, regional dialect, formality and meaning may all be factors influencing whether singular or plural concord is used.

There is another factor to be taken into account with collective nouns. Even when singular concord is used on the verb, the plural pronoun may be used. That is, alongside sentences like *The team is getting some practice but it needs more*, we can get sentences like *The team is getting some practice, but they need more*, where *they* and *the team* are the same group. Strangely, perhaps, this only seems to go one way. We do not usually find **The team are getting some practice, but it needs more* where the singular follows the plural. So we can go from grammatical agreement (where a singular pronoun refers back to a noun marked as singular by agreement) to semantic agreement (where a plural pronoun refers back to a noun marked as singular by the agreement), but not from semantic to grammatical. Even when we are apparently breaking rules, there are rules as to how we do it.

There is, there are

A sentence like (13) is grammatically awkward, even if it is perfectly natural.

(13) There is a car in the garage.

The awkwardness is in the grammatical analysis of the sentence. Specifically, what is the subject of the sentence? Remember that the subject agrees with the verb. So what agrees with the verb *is* in (13)? The answer seems to be *a car*. And if we make the change to (14), we see that the verb changes when we make the relevant noun plural.

(14) There are two cars in the garage.

This leaves open the question of what function *there* has (13) and (14). Because of its position, it looks like a subject – compare with (15) from the British National Corpus (BNC – Davies 2004-), where the subject is *A multi-million pound deal*.

(15) A multi-million pound deal…is the icing on the cake […]

If *there* in (13) and (14) were really a pointing *there*, we could call it an adverbial, as in (16), but *there* in (13) and (14) do not point.

(16) Look, there is the Mona Lisa.

An alternative analysis is that the *there* is the subject. This is odd for several reasons, not least that it does not fit the definition of the subject as performing the action of the verb. We will ignore this analysis here (for a justification see Huddleston 2002, pp. 242–3). In either case, it is the bit that immediately follows the *there is/there are* in (13) and (14) which determines the agreement.

There are further complications with the *there is/there are* construction. The first of these is phonetic. In spoken English we have a form of this construction that we do not know how to write. It has an initial element which sounds like *thiz* or *thez* (unless you speak a variety of English where the letter R is pronounced at the end of a word, in which case it sounds like *thrz*). I'll call it 'reduced *there's*'. Specifically, *there* does not rhyme with *care* in this construction. The trouble is that we cannot write this form. We have to write *there's* or *there is* (or, as appropriate, *there're*, *there are*), and these written forms can be spoken as though *there* does rhyme with *care*. Reduced *there's* allows either a singular or a plural to follow it. Since I cannot write this unambiguously, you'll have to imagine it. But often when we see or hear things like (17) – all from the BNC, it's because people are trying to use reduced *there's* or pronouncing the written form as though it were not reduced when it should be. Some speakers find these awkward, because they interpret sentences like those in (17) as breaking the rules of number agreement, even though they may not be.

(17) a. There's people on the pitch.
b. There's things that I want to try that haven't been tried.
c. There's all these bombs keep going off […]
d. There's many girls that could be that much worse […]

Perhaps because of this spoken-language construction, we do find examples with *there is* or *there are* that break the basic rule of agreement. We also find *here is/here are*, *where is/where are*, *there exists/there exist* and other variants. Example (18) looks like one of the unexpected patterns.

(18) Yes, there is supply issues. (Radio New Zealand National, Morning Report, 2 June 2020, with both *there* and *is* clearly pronounced)

It turns out that the longer you have to wait between the verb (*is* or *are*) and the relevant noun, the more likely you are to use *is*, even if purists would want you to use *are*. It seems to be a matter of how far ahead you can look in your planning: talking is not always as easy as it sounds – it takes a lot of mental space (Hay & Schreier 2004).

Proximity redux

Consider the construction illustrated by the expression *a lot of rice*. It takes singular concord, of course, but why? Do we say *A lot of rice has been wasted* because we say *Rice has been wasted* or because we say *A lot has been wasted*? The simple answer is that it might be either; the construction is fundamentally ambiguous. Either *a lot of rice* is like *much rice*, and *rice* is the most important word in the construction, or *a lot of rice* is like *a library full of books*, where *library* is the most important word. In retrospect, we can look back and see which construction must have been intended, but we cannot predict which one a speaker will use on a particular occasion. Well, not entirely. Proximity plays a role. So all other things being equal, we are more likely to say *A lot of rice has been wasted* but *A lot of potatoes have been wasted*, because then we get *rice has* (which looks like a normal piece of verbal concord) and *potatoes have* (ditto). If this is purely a matter of proximity, it shouldn't matter whether we have *a lot* or *lots*, and this seems to be true. *Lots* (or *heaps*, or *loads*, or *stacks…*) *of rice has been wasted*, and *Lots (heaps/loads/stacks) of potatoes have been wasted.*

Unfortunately, the proximity rule is not always followed. Consider, for example, *Pounds of butter have/*has been wasted, Five loaves of bread have/*has been eaten, Several bottles of wine were/*was consumed.* The difference between these examples and those in the previous paragraph seems to be that these are real measures, while the examples in the previous paragraph are just ways of expressing some vague but large amount. While we can have *Lots of rice has been wasted*, we cannot have **Five lots of rice has been wasted*, because *lots* cannot be enumerated in this way. The result is that we probably want to say that the idiomatic structures like *lots of*, *heaps of*, *stacks of* (or whatever you may use in your variety of English) belong in a different grammatical construction from the real measures.

This is fair enough, but most of us are not instant grammarians who might keep track of which kind of noun + *of* + noun structure we are dealing with. Because in cases like *Five loaves of bread have been eaten* we must take the first noun to be the main noun in the construction (and therefore make agreement follow that first noun), we might feel that this should happen in every such case. This would lead us to say (or to write) *A lot of rice has been wasted* and *Lots of rice have been wasted.* This sounds odd with *lots*, but *Tons of rice have been wasted* is fine, perhaps because *tons* can either be a vague expression meaning 'lots' or a specific measure. You can try other expressions: *bags of rice, heaps of rice, loads of rice, mountains of rice, pots of rice*, and so on. With examples like this, you can see that we are not simply dealing with matters of countability here, there are difficulties with the use of agreement with measure terms and proximity is a factor.

While proximity is a factor in these constructions with quantifiers, this is not the only place that proximity plays a role. We also find examples like those in (19).

(19) a. The status of other fixtures are still in doubt. (RNZ National 6pm news, 2 June 2020)
b. The directors believe the effect of the above resolutions are in the best interests of the company. (cited by Payne & Huddleston 2002, p. 500)
c. the far sound / Of their retiring steps in the dense gloom were drowned. (Shelley, cited in Jespersen 1914, p. 180)
d. peer review in our really top journals are not a marker of good science. (RNZ National, Nine to Noon, 17 June 2020)

In these cases, the standard grammatical description is not in doubt: the main noun in the noun phrase is singular, but the closest noun to the agreeing verb is plural. We would expect singular concord, but find plural concord. If we ask *What is in doubt?* with (19a), the answer is *the status*; if we ask *What is the best interests of the company?* with (19b), the answer is *the effect*. We assume that speakers lose track of what is the most important noun because of the effects of processing constraints, and look to the closest noun for a clue. But if that is the case, we would equally expect to find things like *The directors believe that the effects of the resolution is the best interests of the company*, and it is not clear that we do, at least not as frequently. Jespersen (1914, p. 180) cites (20).

(20) The different and contrary reasons of dislike to my plan makes me suspect that it was really the true medium.

The example in (21) goes the other way round, with unexpected plural marking on the verb, but perhaps the speaker thinks of work as including several disparate tasks. To know whether there is an error here or not, you have to be a mind-reader; it is often more sensible to assume that what the speaker says is what they mean and that semantic agreement is more powerful than grammatical agreement.

(21) There's been some work done specifically from Christchurch which have shown [...]. (RNZ National, Saturday Morning, 6 June 2020)

A particular example of attraction comes with the expression *more than one*, which is always singular, whether a verb or a noun follows, as illustrated in (22) with examples from the BNC. The example in (22c) is anomalous, although attested; Curme (1931, p. 59) allows for a plural verb here, which suggests some change has taken place.

(22) a. editors anxious to contain the play, to create a singular text where more than one exists.
b. we could find ourselves in a very enviable position of more than one members wishing to be considered as a candidate for the C E C

Lack of concord

Although there is a lot of variation in the patterns we have seen here, we have been able to pinpoint factors that lead to that variation. We have seen that there are multiple factors pulling towards either singular or plural concord, and that where they come into conflict, the outcome in any individual instance is unpredictable. At some point, though, we seem to come to examples where there is no obvious factor leading to variation, and we still find examples which, from the point of view of standard English, are inexplicable. Consider (23).

(23) the job losses at Millennium and Copthorne Hotels is a concern for whole the industry [sic]. (RNZ National, Midday Report, 27 May 2020).

In (23) both *losses* and *hotels* (the main word in the noun phrase and the closest noun in the noun phrase, respectively) would lead us to expect plural concord, but we find singular. Perhaps the concord was with a following noun phrase (*a concern*), a factor that has not been considered here. All we can say in this particular case, is that we do not know what caused the singular concord.

It could simply be an error. Perhaps the speaker/writer would agree it was wrong, if asked about it, perhaps due to lack of time when writing (just like the error with *whole* in the same sentence), and not something that the grammarian needs to worry about. It could be a matter of the variety of English spoken by the speaker/writer. There are varieties of English which have *-s* on all present-tense verbs (*I says*, *she says*, *they says*) (Kortmann 2008, p. 482). The writer could be a person whose first language is not English. Finally, it might be a sign that change is happening, but this cannot be our first assumption on the basis of a single example. We need to find a regular pattern before we can start to consider this hypothesis. It is not that we cannot find other examples of lack of agreement. Consider the examples in (24). What we need is an environment in which such lack occurs regularly before we can see a pattern emerging.

(24) a. Our international students is a branch of that business. (RNZ National, The Detail, 2 July 2020)

b. The livelihoods of them and their families is a huge concern. (RNZ National, Standing Room Only, 9 August 2020)
c. There are need for improvement. (RNZ National, Checkpoint, 11 August 2020)

Wrapping up

Number agreement in English looks, at first glance, like a simple matter. But there are two kinds of exceptions to this. There are those cases where we cannot predict which pattern of agreement we will find (though we can 'explain' whatever version we happen to get), and there are those cases where rules of number agreement simply seem to fail. In the first case, we have competing principles, and any one of them can predominate at any time. In the latter case, we do not know how to interpret the data. Do we simply have mistakes, and the number of times we find such instances is a result of the number of times that number agreement has to apply in any English text? Or is there something more systematic going on? If the latter, it may be that the variation from competing principles looks to speakers as if number agreement is not a fixed rule at all, and anything goes. If that is the case, we can look forward to finding much more use of the singular than we have been used to.

What should I read?

English grammars, and websites on English grammar aimed at foreign learners, look at the regular rule, and also look at problematic cases such as collective nouns. The extensive grammars, such as Payne & Huddleston (2002), also consider problems raised by proximity. The extent of irregularity here is not really known, because it is so difficult to search for relevant examples in corpora. Problems with *there is/there are*, on the other hand, are well-known, and widely discussed, because they are easy to search for in corpora, but as has been pointed out here, the pronunciation of such cases creates barriers to a good description.

References

Bauer, Laurie 1994. *Watching English change*. London: Longman. doi:10.4324/9781315844169

Curme, George O. 1931. *A grammar of the English language. Vol II: Syntax*. Boston: Heath.

Davies, Mark 2004. *British National Corpus* (from Oxford University Press). Available online at https://www.english-corpora.org/bnc/.

Hay, Jen & Danny Schreier 2004. Reversing the trajectory of language change: Subject-verb agreement with *be* in New Zealand English. *Language Variation and Change* 16(3): 209–235.

Huddleston, Rodney 2002. The clause: Complements. In Rodney Huddleston & Geoffrey K. Pullum (eds), *The Cambridge grammar of the English language*, 213–321. Cambridge: Cambridge University Press. doi:10.1017/9781316423530.005

Jespersen, Otto 1914. *A modern English grammar on historical principles. Vol II.* London: Allen & Unwin. doi:10.4324/9780203715932.

Kortmann, Berndt 2008. Synopsis of morphological and syntactic variation in the British Isles. In Berndt Kortmann & Clive Upton (eds), *Varieties of English 1: The British Isles*, 478–495. Berlin: Mouton de Gruyter. doi:10.1515/9783110208399.2.478

Payne, John & Rodney Huddleston 2002. Nouns and noun phrases. In Rodney Huddleston & Geoffrey K. Pullum (eds), *The Cambridge grammar of the English language*, 323–523. Cambridge: Cambridge University Press. doi:10.1017/9781316423530.006

15 *Because I'm worth it*

Insubordinate clauses

Andreea

Setting the scene

In 1973, L'Oréal coined the slogan *Because I'm worth it!* in response to their competitor, Miss Clairol's *Does she or doesn't she?* But there is more going on here than just an advertising battle over hair colour products. Malcolm Gladwell (1999) commented in the *New Yorker* on the impact of slogans like these, pointing out that 'they lingered long after advertising usually does' and that they 'somehow managed to take on meanings well outside their stated intention'. For social commentators like Gladwell, the story of *Because I'm worth it!* centres around the innovative use of the pronoun *I*, which contrasts with the pronoun *she* in *Does she or doesn't she?* L'Oréal's *I* puts the woman at the centre stage of decision-making, allowing her to overcome the status of a silent object, judged from afar on whether or not she dyes her hair.

But there is another reason why *Because I'm worth it!* is interesting. It exemplifies a peculiar construction of English grammar: the slogan consists of a single clause, which would be analysed traditionally as dependent (or subordinate) to an accompanying main clause. Yet in this example, there is no main clause alongside it and the subordinate clause *Because I'm worth it!* is left hanging. So what has happened to the main clause? This sentence is just one among a range of phenomena at odds with our understanding of main and subordinate clauses.

The distinction between clause types matters because clauses and the process of linking them in texts provide a gateway to building sentences, which in turn leads to the creation of longer texts and the expression of complex meaning. However, in order to understand how linking of clauses happens, it is necessary to know something about the type of clauses we are dealing with.

Main and subordinate clauses

Two key ingredients associated with linking clauses in discourse are recursion and embedding. Embedding allows information to build up incrementally by having clauses nested inside one another in a hierarchical manner. This process is recursive, which is to say that we can do it over and over again, or at least as far as our memory allows us to, and this helps us build sentences.

DOI: 10.4324/9781003148999-15

The clause constitutes an important level in the embedding chain because each clause captures roughly one idea (one proposition). Grammatically speaking, a clause involves a verb phrase and all the other phrases which are directly connected to it, such as the subject (the main protagonist in the event) and any associated objects (the affected parties). In a sentence like *I bought a car last week, since the old one broke down,* there are two clauses: *I bought a car last week* (containing the verb *bought*) and *since the old one broke down* (containing the verb *broke*). Crucially, the two clauses are not equal in either their contribution to meaning or their structural importance. The clause *I bought a car last week* carries the bulk of the meaning and structurally, it can stand on its own. We call this the main clause. The clause *since the old one broke down* expressed additional details of the main message in the sentence; and it is structurally incomplete on its own. For these reasons, it is classified as subordinate to the main clause.

There are various complications which arise in putting clauses together and the issue of subordination has kept some linguists busy their entire research lives. Two almost paradoxical characteristics of subordination speak to its troubling status not just in English, but for grammar more generally. First, with some few exceptions (for example, the Amazonian language of Pirahã, Everett 2005), most human languages have some sort of clauses which are more or less subordinate. Second, it is next to impossible to come up with consistent criteria for identifying subordinate clauses which hold both within a given language and across languages, and problems sometimes arise even within a single language.

Partially insubordinate: somewhat dependent but not entirely so

One difficulty with classifying clauses as either main or subordinate comes from the fact that embedding and importance in discourse do not always go hand in hand. There are clauses which are grammatically embedded inside other clauses and which express the most important part of the message in the sentence. Conversely, some clauses can be grammatically independent but not express an especially salient part of the overall message. New terms have been added to refer to the phenomenon or to clauses which appear to be neither exactly main clause-like nor completely subordinate, such as 'insubordination' (Evans 2007, Evans & Watanabe 2016), 'co-subordination' (Cristofaro 2005), 'unintegration' (Miller & Weinert 1998, Brown & Miller 2016, Guz 2015), 'free clauses' (Vallauri 2004) and 'lone clauses' (Cheshire 2004). A plethora of terms is often a clue that there is no general agreement on what is going on.

Consider the sentence *I think clauses are tricky.* This sentence contains two propositions and thus two clauses. *Clauses are tricky* is one of the clauses. It is tempting to think the other clause is *I think,* but that is not the case. The main clause of the sentence is in fact *I think clauses are tricky,* where the subordinate clause is embedded inside the main clause. This is because the verb *think* tends to require something after it; it cannot be left hanging (unless one is translating the philosopher Descartes's Latin *cogito, ergo sum* into English 'I think, therefore I am' or using the progressive to emphasize one's involvement in thinking: *I am just thinking*). So *think* can be followed be a simple noun phrase (*I think happy thoughts*) or by an elaborate set of clauses (*I think that he will finish the thesis well before the year is up*), or by something in-between, namely a single clause (*I think clauses are tricky*).

However, this classical analysis, whereby *clauses are tricky* is a subordinate clause, runs into problems. Structurally, *clauses are tricky* looks to be embedded inside the higher-up clause (*I think X*) for the reason mentioned above. The first problem is that there is no agreed upon exhaustive list of tests for embeddeness: Green (1976) lists some, but it is not clear that there are no others. Green (1976, p. 394) herself concludes that there may not be 'a simple explanation of which clauses are embedded and which are not' and that 'it may be necessary to examine the phenomena case by case'.

The second problem is that although Green (1976) attempts to give a set of criteria for embeddedness, even she agrees that with sentences like *I think clauses are tricky,* the criteria do not all agree. So we are left unsure whether *clauses are tricky* is really embedded or not.

Even if we agree that *clauses are tricky* is (mostly) structurally dependent on the main clause spanned by *I think*, it is difficult to show that *I think* constitutes the main message. The bulk of the content expressed by the sentence seems to be about clauses being tricky, not about me thinking something. Sentences like *I think X* are not the only cases where the main content resides within (what would be) the subordinate clause.

In a 2002 article, Sandra Thompson argues that three specific types of otherwise subordinate clauses can be identified where the subordinate label does not fit comfortably with their general function in discourse: clauses expressing knowledge or belief (like *I think X, I believe X, I bet X, I hope X, I realise X* and so on), clauses expressing evidence (*It can be said that X, It looks like X, It seems that X*) and clauses expressing evaluation (*I am glad that X, It is incredible that X, I like that X, Too bad that X, I don't give a damn that X*). Thompson suggests that these types of clauses should not be classified as subordinate. Certainly, the start of the would-be main clause can be easily removed without loss of grammaticality (X can always stand on its own without the initial 'I think', 'It can be said that', 'I am glad that', etc.).

The question is, what should they be classified as? If we see them as main clauses, what do we do with the remaining parts of the (would-be) main clause (we could have two main clauses but they would have to have equal status, and it is not clear that the clauses in question do)? And do we really want to posit a special category just for these types of clauses? Conversational data seems to be riddled with these types of clauses so they cannot be cast aside as a mere anomaly.

Because-clauses

In addition to the clauses mentioned above, there are other subordinate clauses which are structurally dependent but semantically salient in the discourse.

Compare the clause starting with *because* in (1) with that in (2) from Huddleston (1994, p. 3856).

(1) I left early because it started to rain.
(2) We must hurry – because didn't you say it started at six?

In (1), *because it started to rain* provides the reason for leaving. The clause is subordinate to the main clause *I left early*, being both semantically and structurally dependent on it. In contrast, the clause *because didn't you say it started at six* is semantically linked to the main clause *We must hurry*, once again, giving a reason for the need to rush. Yet, structurally, it is phrased as a question. Traditional theory assumes that, while a sentence can contain an interrogative main clause which subsumes a declarative subordinate clause, the opposite is not true. So, it is difficult to square off the question raised by the subordinate clause with the declarative main clause accompanying it. In terms of communication, the *because*-clause provides a reason for the assumption that there is a need to rush. In this sense, the subordinate clause appears to be more salient in the discourse than the main clause and speakers do not appear to have trouble in parsing these types of sentences.

The previous examples are at least relatively straightforward to interpret – they come largely from written English. But things get messier when we look at spontaneous conversation (Miller & Weinert 1998, Miller & Calude 2020). Indeed, it is predominantly spoken language that challenges current grammar theories with regard to subordinate clauses. In this genre, the link between main and subordinate clauses is much looser, and sometimes, we do not have any main clauses at all.

Here is an example from spoken New Zealand English, in which it is unclear how the clause *because I'm tall* and the clause *I learnt fast* relate to the rest of the discourse.

(3) when I left um taranaki when <pause> I started playing volleyball and um which was a new sport for me cos um the school didn't facilitate for volleyball itself at um at a very good level so when I got into it the people that that my own age were very good at playing volleyball and because I'm tall um I learnt fast cos I pick things up a a lot easier if I watch and and am involved myself in it so I started playing volleyball and I thought wow I like this cos it was fast um. (Wellington Corpus of Spoken New Zealand English, Holmes et al. 1998)

Grammatically, the structure appears similar to the earlier example *I left early because it started to rain*, whereby *I'm tall* (= subordinate clause) constitutes the reason for *I learnt fast* (= main clause). Semantically, however, it makes little sense to interpret the clausal relationships in this way: why would being tall enable the speaker to learn fast? It seems more likely that being tall is an advantage in playing volleyball and that may have helped the speaker to get good at it faster. This analysis works but the interpretation involves a few inferential steps missing in the language. However, despite being a little roundabout, it appears to work. But following this interpretation gets us into difficulty when we get to the next clause. The clause *cos I pick things up a lot easier if I watch and am involved myself in it* is only loosely connected with the rest of the discourse. It could be that this clause is connected with the earlier one (*I learnt fast*) and that the speaker is saying they got involved with the sport and they learn faster by being involved. If that is the case, then the clause *because I am tall* is left hanging. Alternatively, if it does belong with *I learn fast*, then what is the clause *cos I pick things up a lot easier if I watch and am involved myself in it* attached to? At any rate, the relationship between these clauses is unclear and whichever way we look at it, one of the clauses seems to be left hanging without an associated main clause.

It must be noted that reading through the remainder of the transcript makes it clear that speakers have no trouble understanding what is being said. In any given conversation, speakers are said to be jointly involved in the communication act, so that if a hearer is faced with loosely connected ideas, they keep inferring until appropriate connections are made and the message is successfully parsed. This idea is credited to work by philosopher Grice (1989), in his Maxim of Relevance.

Returning to the use of *because*, more recent analyses have scrutinized cases in which *because* occurs with highly reduced clauses, often single words. This usage is not new but has previously not received much attention. Here is an example from an American English news item, cited in Bergs (2018, p. 43), where the word *famished* appears to be part of a shortened version of the clause meaning loosely 'because I am/was famished'.

(4) Eat veggie burger. Finish this one, but only because famished. (*Chicago Sun-Times*, 'Going for the daily double', 17 June 2005)

Because can thus be followed by a full clause, as we saw in examples (1) and (2), an abbreviated clause (*because yolo* 'you only live once'), a noun (*because language*), an adjective (*because tired*), an interjection or agreement particle (*because nah*), or a pronoun (*because me*). What these uses of *because* have in common is their provision of reasons. The difference between *because* followed by a full clause and *because* followed by a single word is that the latter provides a personal, subjective opinion, compared to the former (Bergs 2018, p. 57).

Which-clauses

Problems also arise with clauses introduced by the subordinating conjunction *which* or sometimes a preposition followed by *which*. Huddleston (1994, p. 3856) cites the following sentence:

(5) I may be a little late, in which case please do start without me.

The clause *in which case please do start without me* is phrased as a suggestion or request, whereas the main clause *I may be a little late* is phrased as a statement. The link between the two clauses is not smooth because the first clause seems to act as a condition to the second, which is the opposite of the semantic interpretation expected of a subordinate and main clause.

Huddleston (1994, p. 3856) terms these cases 'structurally incongruous subordinate clauses', suggesting they are still regarded as subordinate. His terminology appears to privilege grammatical status over communicative role; if it's embedded then it's subordinate, regardless of its importance in the discourse. But it is not clear why grammatical status should be privileged over discourse function.

Let's consider some further troubling *which*-clauses from spoken Australian English, as discussed by Burke (2017, p. 11). In the following excerpt, it is unclear how the subordinate clause *which, we don't mind bein' insured really* fits with the rest of the discourse.

(6) And no one'll...I mean say, for instance with...insurance, I mean you have to be insured...which, we don't mind bein' insured really but it does cost a lot... But you have to comply – there's all sorts of compliance.

On the one hand, the *which*-clause is subordinate because *which* points back to the previous clause *(you have to be insured*), but on the other hand, it is not tightly integrated in the structure of the main clause (it is not clear why *insured* is repeated). Similarly, the clause in (7), *which we've formed a very good relationship of course with the dog* is structurally more like a main clause than a subordinate clause. The prepositional phrase *with the dog* seems similarly unnecessary. The clause might be rephrased in written standard English as *with which /whom we've formed a very good relationship.*

(7) That was rather sad...because we had the joy of the...uh...birth of our daughter...but unfortunately we had to say good-bye to the dog which we've formed a...very good relationship of course with the dog.

But sometimes, rephrasing does not help because it is not clear how to do it:

(8) I guess she's leaving now so she won't really be needing to deal with it. But like, yeah, she's all for, having interviews and stuff which I, I don't know I think interviews are important.

Burke (2017) found that the use of *which* in examples like those above cannot be merely reduced to a speech error; the data is too compelling and recurrent for that to be the case. After carefully analysing many recordings, she concludes that *which* can introduce a subordinate clause but can also function as a discourse marker, with two specific functions: resuming a previous topic or focusing on an important detail. Why would speakers resort to using *which* in this way? According to Burke, this kind of *which* makes a connection between various parts of the discourse, something she terms 'textual coherence'.

Completely insubordinate

Then there are those subordinate clauses which are neither structurally dependent nor semantically less salient than a would-be main clause. The problem with these clauses is that what we might otherwise analyse as a subordinate clause is found in complete isolation from a main clause. These include *if*-clauses, *when*-clauses and *what*-clauses.

If-clauses

In English (Evans & Watanabe 2016, p. 2) and languages like Swedish, Finnish, Italian, German and Japanese (Valauri 2004, Lindström et al. 2016), conditional clauses are sometimes found without an accompanying main clause, despite their subordinate status. Speakers utter the *if* clause but omit the rest. Below are some English examples:

(9) a. If I have to say it one more time. [threat]
b. If I see you loitering around here again. [threat]
(10) a. If I could just take a few minutes of your time. [request]
b. If you could put that desk over there please. [request]
(11) If only I could lose even a few pounds. [wish, hypothesis]
(12) If your mother could only see you now. [praise]
(13) If that's the best you've got. [disapproval]

Such conditional clauses, termed 'free conditionals' or 'independent conditionals', seem to have arisen in contexts where the meaning of the main clause can plausibly be recovered from the context and is thereby not strictly needed. Vallauri (2004, p. 207–8) explains that, with repeated use, these conditionals have become formulaic and their various meanings predictable, so that the semantic content of both main and subordinate clause are absorbed into a single clause (the *if*-clause), allowing this *if*-clause to become free or independent; in other words, main clause-like. As regards the communication act, hearers will keep inferring and hunting for relevance of what is being said, until the meaning is successfully parsed.

When-clauses

Similar issues have also been identified with certain *when* clauses. In the following interview transcript recorded by Jenny Cheshire (2005, p. 90) in Reading (UK), the *when* clause *when I went in hospital* occurs in complete isolation from a main clause.

(14) (the discussion has been about jobs the girls might consider doing when they leave school)

Jenny: you have to do horrible jobs if you're a nurse .. all the bed pans.
All: <laughter>
Jenny: have you ever been in hospital?
Valerie: I have.
Christine: oh yeah I have.
Valerie: I got run over by a car.
Christine: I fell off a gate backwards <laughs> and I was unconscious.
Tommy: oi when I. when I went in hospital just for a little while…
Valerie: sshh.
Tommy: cos my sister and my cousin they bent my arm…they twisted it right round.

The *when* clause in Tommy's second to last turn is used to frame the upcoming narrative within a particular context, almost like a heading (if speech had such things). It also functions as a tool for managing the discourse, to help Tommy hold onto his turn, and signal that more is coming. Cheshire (2005, p. 92–4) writes that such *when*-clauses are formulaic, stored expressions which might be used in conversation as 'story openers' and go some way towards establishing group membership and solidarity among those taking part in the dialogue. In this way, it seems that lone *when*-clauses serve a more important role in organizing the discourse than in specifying informational content.

What-clauses

Another linguistic mechanism functioning as a heading-like story opener consists of what some linguists have labelled 'unintegrated clefts' (Weinert 1996, Miller & Weinert 1998, Calude 2008, Koops & Ross-Hagebaum 2008, Guz 2015, among others). Various types of unintegrated clefts are in current use, but here is one example from a recent BBC article, in which the CEO of the successful company Pandora, Alexander Lacik, is quoted as follows:

(15) What we see, for instance, in places where we have closed down physical retail, my ecommerce retail also goes down. So it's a combination of the two. That seems to be the sweet spot, at least now. (BBC, 'Pandora paying all staff in full through Pandemic', 9 November 2020)

The label is not terribly important; the point is that the *what*-clause (*what we see*) is not followed by a main clause – unless we want to say that the whole rest of the sentence is the main clause, but then we need to explain how structural dependency can go across multiple sentences. Even though the clause could be fixed to look like a typical written sentence by adding 'is that' ('what we see … is that my ecommerce retail also goes down'), this is not what Alexander Lacik actually said. The analysis has to consider what is actually said, not some altered version of it. In sum, the subordinate *what*-clause is only loosely linked structurally and semantically to what follows it. And Alexander Lacik is by no means the only speaker to produce such examples.

Wrapping up

It is clear that the classifications proposed for clauses by traditional theories do not match actual language data, particularly when we look at spoken conversation. While no general consensus has been reached regarding how to alter such theories yet, we do know which clauses are likely to be troublesome and recurrently diverge from classical categories, namely *because*-clauses, *if*-clauses, *which*-clauses, *when*-clauses and certain *what*-clauses. So we have a starting point at least.

But, does it really matter if we cannot always distinguish the various types of clauses we are dealing with or is this simply a linguistic curiosity? These distinctions matter to language learners who may need such information in order to make sense of differences between their native language and that which they are learning. For example, if English speakers learning German are told to place the verb last in subordinate clauses, they will want to know how to identify such clauses. And the distinctions matter to native speakers too. The perception that speakers of English are becoming less and less able to form proper sentences requires us to know what a sentence should be like in the first place.

We take written language – as opposed to spoken language – to be the norm and our definitions and criteria of sentences reflect this. But the two genres are very different! Increasingly, analyses of real interactions show variation from the types of sentences that traditional theories of grammar have led us to expect. Yet despite the variation, speakers have no trouble understanding them. Given that we speak more than we write, it seems important to come up with realistic analyses of clausal structure which reflect what speakers (as opposed to writers!) actually do.

What should I read?

Miller & Brown (2016) offer a gentle introduction to clause structure and to how we verify what is integrated within a clause and what is not, giving plenty of good examples (especially the chapters 'Clause and Text' and 'Clause Structure'). Miller & Calude (2020) discuss main and subordinate clauses in spoken language. Burke (2017) and Guz (2015) are slightly denser texts but both offer good examples of clauses which present difficulties.

References

Bergs, Alexander 2018. Because science! Notes on a variable construction. In Elena Seoane, Carlos Acuña-Fariña & Ignacio Palacios-Martínez (eds), *Subordination in English: Synchronic and diachronic perspectives*, 43–60. Berlin: De Gruyter Mouton. doi:10.1515/9783110583571-201

Brown, Keith & Jim Miller 2016. *A critical account of English syntax*. Edinburgh: Edinburgh University Press.

Burke, Isabelle 2017. Wicked which: The linking relative in Australian English. *Australian Journal of Linguistics* 37(3): 356–386. doi:10.1080/07268602.2017.1298398

Calude, Andreea 2008. Demonstrative clefts and double cleft constructions in spontaneous spoken English. *Studia Linguistica* 61(1): 78–228. doi:10.1111/j.1467-9582.2007.00140.x

Cheshire, Jenny 2004. Syntactic variation and spoken language. In Leonie Cornips & Karen P. Corrigan (eds), *Syntax and variation: Reconciling the biological and the social*, 81–106. Amsterdam: John Benjamins.

Cheshire, Jenny 2005. Syntactic variation and spoken language. In Leonie Cornips & Karen Corrigan (eds), *Syntax and variation: Reconciling the biological and the social*, 81–108. Amsterdam: Benjamins.

Cristofaro, Sonia 2005. *Subordination*. Oxford: Oxford University Press. doi:10.1093/acprof:oso/9780199282005.001.000

Evans, Nicholas 2007. Insubordination and its uses. In Irina Nikolaeva (ed.), *Finiteness: Theoretical and empirical foundations*, 366–431. Oxford: Oxford University Press.

Evans, Nicholas & Honoré Watanabe 2016. *Insubordination*. Amsterdam: Benjamins.

Everett, Daniel 2005. Cultural constraints on grammar and cognition in Pirahã: Another look at the design features of human language. *Current Anthropology* 46(4): 621–646. doi:10.1086/431525

Gladwell, Malcolm 1999. True colors: hair dye and the history of postwar America. *New Yorker* [accessed from https://www.newyorker.com/magazine/1999/03/22/true-colors].

Green, Georgia 1976. Main clause phenomena in subordinate clauses. *Language* 52(2): 382–397.

Grice, H. Paul 1989. *Studies in the way of words*. Cambridge, MA: Harvard University Press.

Guz, Wojciech 2015. The structural non-integration of wh-clefts. *English Language and Linguistics* 19(3): 477–503. doi:10.1017/S1360674315000180

Holmes, Janet, Gary Johnson & Bernadette Vine 1998. *Guide to the Wellington corpus of spoken New Zealand English*. Wellington: School of Linguistics and Applied Language Studies, Vict\oria University of Wellington.

Huddleston, Rodney 1994. Sentence types and clause subordination. In R.E. Asher & J.M.Y. Simpson (eds), *The encyclopedia of language and linguistics*, Volume 7, 3845–3857. Oxford: Pergamon.

Koops, Christian & Sebastian Ross-Hagebaum 2008. Information structure and discourse function of amalgam wh-clefts. *Proceedings of the 37th Annual Meeting of the Berkeley Linguistics Society* 37: 461–472.

Lindström, Jan, Camilla Lindholm & Ritva Laury 2016. The interactional emergence of conditional clauses as directives: Constructions, trajectories and sequences of actions. *Language Sciences* 58: 8–21. doi:10.1016/j.langsci.2016.02.008

Miller, Jim & Andreea Calude 2020. Spoken and written language. In Bas Aarts & April McMahon (eds), *Handbook of English linguistics*, 549–568. 2nd edition. Oxford: Blackwell/Wiley.

Miller, Jim & Regina Weinert 1998. *Spontaneous spoken language: Syntax and discourse*. Oxford: Clarendon Press.

Thompson, Sandra 2002. "Object complements" and conversation towards a realistic account. *Studies in Language* 26(1): 125–164.

Vallauri, Edoardo Lombardi 2004. Grammaticalization of syntactic incompleteness: Free conditionals in Italian and other languages. *SKY Journal of Linguistics* 17: 189–215.

Weinert, Regina & Jim Miller 1996. Cleft constructions in spoken language. *Journal of Pragmatics* 25(2): 173–206. doi:10.1016/0378-2166(94)00079-4

16 *They are cleverer than she and I*

Pronominal case

Laurie

Setting the scene

If we were asked what language is for, we would probably answer that its job is to allow us to communicate thoughts to each other, to convey information. This makes sense if you think of language as being used to provide an answer when you ask the way to the airport, wonder why the moon does not fall out of the sky or want to know how to make a sponge cake. But that is not all that language does. Language can be used to help cooperation, it can be used to woo, it can be used to comfort, it can be used to lie and it can be used to distinguish one group of people from another. This last function has been argued to be vital in evolutionary terms. Sitting in the dark round a fire, you want to be able to share food with the in-group, without having any freeloaders taking any of your scarce resources. Differences in language allow this to happen. That is one of the reasons why a homogeneous language – even if it were possible – does not seem to be suitable for the purposes of humans. We use it to distinguish individuals (you from your same-sex sibling), small groups (teachers from retail workers), large groups (the population of Leeds from that of Bradford, men from women, 16-year-olds from 76-year-olds) and extremely large groups (the French and the Germans). This function of language must never be forgotten.

When Harriet Smith in Jane Austen's *Emma* says the sentence in (1), it is intended to indicate that Harriet is not of the same social class as Emma herself. The message is probably lost on most modern readers.

(1) […] they are quite as educated as me. (Austen, Jane 1816. *Emma*, Ch 4)

The Duke of Sussex, in a press statement on 20 January 2020, made an announcement that included the words in (2), and given who he is and the formality of the situation, we must conclude that what he says is an example of standard English.

(2) […] for my wife and I to step back.

The point at issue in both these examples is a matter of case in pronouns: the difference between *I* and *me*, *she* and *her*, and so on. The use of case in pronouns

DOI: 10.4324/9781003148999-16

has been undergoing variation since before the time of Shakespeare, and has been subject to prescriptive notions of what should be done since at least the eighteenth century. It has still not settled down entirely.

The notion of case

Case is the name given to marking in noun phrases to show who did what to whom and with what. Although some languages have many cases and some have none, and not all languages use case according to the same pattern, we need only concern ourselves with the way in which case used to be used in English, which is fairly typical of the Germanic languages (of which English is one) and the Indo-European languages more generally. Old English worked rather like modern German. In German we find sentences like (3).

(3) Der Sohn des Lehrers gab seinem Vater einen Wagen.
The (nominative) son of the (genitive) teacher (genitive) gave his (dative) father a (accusative) car
'The teacher's son gave his father a car'

In German, the case (nominative, accusative, genitive and dative) is shown mainly on the determiners, words like *the* and *a.* In many other languages it is marked directly on the noun, as it is with *Lehrers* ('teacher's') in (3). In the main we have to deal with the four cases that we find in German. These cases are shown by the use of suffixes, have standard names and are used for standard functions, often across languages (we use the names to denote cases which have those particular jobs).

(4) The nominative case is for the subject of the sentence, and the subject complement (e.g. *president* in *He became the president*).
The accusative case is for the direct object of the verb, and the object of some prepositions, especially those that show direction (e.g. *ball* in *He kicked the ball* and *Mars* in *life on Mars*).
The genitive case is used to show possession and related matters (e.g. *Pat's* in *Pat's picture* and *day's* in *the day's end*).
The dative case is used for the indirect object, and the object of some prepositions, especially those showing location (e.g. *Jane* in *I gave Jane the book*).

In English, nominative, accusative and dative are no longer shown by suffixes on nouns. The genitive (see Chapter 17, on possession), which is often called the 'possessive' these days, is still marked, sometime on the noun (as in (5a)), sometimes on the wider noun phrase (as in (5b)).

(5) a. The woman's ideas were stimulating.
b. The woman I spoke to's ideas were stimulating.

However, we do not need to worry further about case on nouns, because what interests us in this chapter is what happens with pronouns. Do they, or do they not, mark case in English?

Case in English pronouns

We have four sets of relevant pronouns in English (set out in (6)). We will not discuss other types such as relative and reflexive pronouns in detail here.

(6)	*Subject*	*Oblique*	*Possessive*	*Strong possessive*
	I	me	my	mine
	you	you	your	yours
	he	him	his	his
	she	her	her	hers
	it	it	its	its
	we	us	our	ours
	they	them	their	theirs

The difference between the possessive and the strong possessive is that the possessive is used when there is a following noun (as in *It is my book*) and the strong possessive is used when there is no noun (as in *The book is mine*). We shall not need to consider these forms any further. The forms that I have here called 'subject pronouns' and 'oblique pronouns', though, are problematic. The problem arises in choosing which pronoun to use in which function. The particular problems depend on which function is involved, and they will be considered individually in just a moment.

If we look at the way these forms are used in modern English when they are used in isolation, we find that the list does not differ greatly from that set out in (6) for German. Some examples are given in (7).

(7)
a. subject: *I/you/he/she/it/we/they saw the teacher.*
b. direct object: *The teacher saw me/you/him/her/it/us/them.*
c. indirect object: *The teacher gave me/you/him/her/it/us/them a book.*
d. object of a preposition: *The teacher showed the book to me/you/him/her/it/us/them.*

If this were all there was to the matter, there would be nothing to discuss. We would conclude that the case system of English is considerably reduced from that of Old English (or German), but there would be enough commonality of pattern for us to be happy to say that the, fundamentally, the inherited pattern was in place. Unfortunately, there is more.

Subject complements

One of the functions that is missing from (7), and that was present in the corresponding German list in (6), is the function of subject complement. A subject complement, when it is a pronoun or a noun, refers to the same entity as the subject, as in *George was king*, where the *king* is the same person as *George*, and *king* is a subject complement. In German, and, more importantly, in Latin, the subject complement appears in the nominative case, so that we get sentences like those in (8).

(8) a. German: Mein Vater ist der Lehrer.
my father (nominative) is the teacher (nominative)
'My father is the teacher'.
b. Latin: Flavia puella est.
Flavia (nominative) girl (nominative) is
'Flavia is the girl' or 'Flavia is a girl'.

In English, though, (full) nouns are no longer marked for nominative and accusative case, and *the girl* has the same form in (9a) and (9b), even though in German or Latin, it would be nominative in (9a) and accusative in (9b). This difference correlates with the fact that in (a) *Chris* and the *girl* are the same person, while in (b) *Chris* and the *girl* are not the same person.

(9) a. Chris is a girl.
b. Chris saw a girl.

The only place where we might be able to see a difference of case in English is if we have pronouns rather than nouns. If English was like German and Latin, we might expect the forms that are shown in (10).

(10) a. Chris is she.
b. Chris saw her.

The crucial question here is whether English is really like German and Latin in this regard. Perhaps English is like French, where, in the seventeenth century, Louis XIV announced to his parliament:

(11) L'état, c'est moi.
The state, it is me.
'I am the state'.

There is a story, no doubt apocryphal, of a group of people at an event in England being asked by an organizer if anyone spoke French. After an embarrassed silence, one person put up his hand, and said, 'je'. The point of the story is that, although *je* means 'I', anyone who uses *je* in that way immediately indicates that they do not speak French. The French have to use *moi*, which corresponds to English *me*. Louis could not have said **L'état, c'est je* because *je* cannot carry stress in French and must always lean up against a following word (the technical term for such forms is 'clitic'). So is there any good reason why English should follow the German pattern or the Latin pattern rather than the French pattern? Not really; and left to itself it would not. Shakespeare was confused as to what set of pronouns to use under such circumstances, and it was not until the eighteenth century that the idea that English should follow Latin and use pronouns corresponding to the ones used for the subject of the sentence for subject complements. The reason for this was not that the Latin system was, in some obvious way, better, but because Latin, as the language of power and academia and the church was considered to be a language on which English should model itself, to make it an elegant language, capable of expressing subtle thoughts. For example, it was not until the 1960s that Cambridge University stopped demanding a knowledge of Latin from all its undergraduate students.

The result was a prescription for *It is I* rather than *It is me* (although, ironically, both German and Latin speakers would normally say the equivalent of *I am (it/that)*: German *Das bin ich,* Latin *Ego sum*). The prescription sort of worked. In American English, at least in print, it is still found more frequently than in British English, and it has given rise to a feeling, widespread throughout the English-speaking community, that *I* is better than *me*, in some vague and often ill-understood way. The use of *I*, in particular, but also the other subject-pronoun series in subject complement position has certainly led to all kinds of social values being attributed to this construction.

(12) a. 'It's not she,' he said.

'Don't talk like that,' Dino whispered. 'It's not her.'

'It's not she,' Stone said again.

[14 lines]

'And, Stone,' Dino added, 'never say "It's not she" to some guy at the morgue. He'll think you're a jerk.' (Woods, Stuart 1991. *New York dead.* London: HarperCollins, p. 20)

b. If it were I, I thought, I could live without them. (Elkins, Aaron 1991. *A glancing light*. New York: Fawcett, p. 86)

c. It is he you'll have to answer to. (Hamilton, Denise 2003. *The jasmine trade*. London: Orion, p. 256)

d. 'That you, Chris?' 'That's me. Or this is I, as they probably say in Hampstead.' (Fox, Anthony 1999. *Threat warning red.* London: Michael Joseph, p. 85)

Pronouns with adjacent elision

Another place where there has long been confusion between *I* and *me* (and other members of each set) is when some part of a sentence is deleted. One typical case where this happens is after *than*. If we take a sentence like *She is prettier than I am* we can envisage two differing analyses. Either *than* is a conjunction, introducing the clause *I am*, or *than* is a preposition, as it would be in *We drove faster than 100kph*. If we now miss out the *am*, we get *She is prettier than I* (and *I* is the subject of the deleted verb *am*). But if *than* is a preposition, we would expect *She is prettier than me*. We find both.

(13) a. When she looked up again, she had the same maniacal grin as he. (Roberts, Nora 2003. *Birthright*. London: Piatkus, p. 18)
b. 'How is she?' Sam asked.
'In a far better place than you and me.'
'You and I.'
(Hightower, Lynn 1999. *The debt collector*. London: Hodder & Stoughton, p. 41)

As with subject complements, the variation in these constructions was understood in the general population as meaning that *I* was what posh people said for *me*. So we now have two constructions where the difference between *I* and *me* is not seen as being a difference of case, but a difference of formality.

In this particular instance, the kind of English you speak may also make a difference. Note the contrast between the American example in (14) and the British examples (from the BNC: Davies 2004-) in (15).

(14) He looked a bit younger than she, perhaps in his early eighties. (Baldacci, David 2019. *Redemption*. New York: Grand Central, p. 71)

(15) a. Jack Stone was two years younger than her, but he looked ten years older.
b. He's at least five years younger than her and he has an ironic smile [...]
c. She had at least one brother, who was younger than she.
(The last example in (15) is the only example in the BNC that has *younger than she* rather than *younger than her* is this position.)

Who(m) do you love?

Let us now turn to a type we have not yet mentioned, the difference between *who* and *whom*. The final *-m* in *whom* gives a clue to the history: just like *him* and *them*, this was originally a dative marker, and in modern English (at least until the twentieth century) marks the oblique case. In the older pattern, it doesn't matter if *who(m)* occurs in a relative clause (16) or in a question (17).

(16) a. I saw the man who insulted me.
b. I saw the man whom I insulted.

(17) a. Who saw you?
b. Whom did you see?

(16a) is equivalent to *The man insulted me*, with *who* replacing *the man*, and that is the subject of the sentence, so *who* is in the subject case. In (16b), the implication is that *I insulted the man*, *the man* is the direct object, and *whom* (which replaces *the man* in the sentence) is in the oblique case. In the examples in (17), (17a) asks about the subject of the seeing, (17b) asks about the object of the seeing. This system has been breaking down for a long time. The use of *whom* has been weakening, so that people regularly ask things like *Who did you see?* (contrast (17b)). Even in relatively fixed phrases such as *To whom it may concern*, and *Ask not for whom the bell tolls*, *who* can sometimes be heard for *whom* (in (18) we have some less established phrases from the BNC using the same pattern). And occasionally we see things which show that the writer (or the assumed speaker) does not know how *who(m)* works any more, as in (19).

(18) a. Plays for who?
 b. Who would be paired with who?
 c. What we don't know is why and by who.

(19) But the woman he loved, the *women* he loved, they weren't whom they pretended to be. (Kandel, Susan 2004. *I dreamed I married Perry Mason*. New York: Morrow, p. 171)

In (19), we can simplify to *The women pretended to be someone*. The *someone* is the subject complement of the verb *to be*, and, in the old system would be in the subject case (this is equivalent to the *It is I* instances discussed above). Accordingly, *who* would be the normatively required form, as well as the expected colloquial form. The use of *whom* is here because the structure is not easily analysed, and there is an overriding idea that *whom* is the posher form to use (note that this goes against the general pattern, where the subject case has been seen as the posher form). The solution in this instance may be different from the solution that has arisen elsewhere, but it still shows confusion between the case used for the subject and the case required when the noun occurs with a preposition (oblique case).

The perplexing case of coordinated case

We now turn to the most complex part of an already complicated story: what happens when pronouns are coordinated. The general rule with coordination is that two items are joined by *and* to form a larger item of the same kind (I ignore *or* and *but* here, though the basic idea remains the same). We can have *Tom and Dick* (two names), *arrives and departs* (two finite verbs, both third person and present tense), *through thick and thin* (two adjectives) and even *loves climbing mountains and evenings by the fire* (two objects of different types). But we cannot have **Tom and arrives*, **through thick and climbing mountains* and so on. Accordingly, if you are going to combine pronouns, they must form a unit of the same kind, and a subject and a direct object are not of the same kind. So, as long as we assume that *I*, *we* and so on are subject pronouns, we can only coordinate them with other subject pronouns, and oblique pronouns can only coordinate with oblique pronouns. Note the let-out clause in all of this.

Another way of looking at this is to say that if you have two pronouns coordinated they must be of the same type, as set out in (6), and they must both be of the type that would occur if there were no coordination. That is, if you can say *I saw the new movie last night*, and you went with someone else, then the pronoun for the other person must be of the same type as *I* – must be a subject pronoun. So you can have *He and I saw the new movie last night*, or *They and I saw the new movie last night*, but not **I and her saw the new movie last night*. This is still the system used by some speakers of standard English, though it is an increasingly outdated system. Part of the problem in understanding what is going on is that multiple systems coexist at the moment, some people use one, some people another, and others vary between the systems.

There are a couple of things we should get out of the way at this point. First, what is the difference between *he and I* and *I and he*? In the traditional system outlined above, there is none. As a matter of overt politeness, people are often taught not to put themselves first (that is, to say *he and I*) to overcome the overwhelming egocentricity of humans who would otherwise say *I and he*. In this system, though, that is a matter of politeness, not a matter of grammar. In the BNC we find examples like those in (20) which show the less polite form, independent of the grammar used.

(20) a. So me and him struggled to throw the thing out of the window.
b. I and she'd never said a word!

The second point to make is that not all languages use pronouns in the same way as English does or did. We have already seen that French uses the pronouns differently. In French the strength of a pronoun (to do with its position or its stress) is an important factor as well as case.

Strong and weak pronouns also have a role to play in English. Consider the sentence *There goes Mary*. *Mary* is strong. We cannot say **There goes she*, because *she* is weak. The best we can do is to say *There she goes*, where *she* is unstressed because of its position. Pronouns that occur alone in subject position are weak; pronouns that occur in coordinated pairs are strong. This factor has become more important in the innovative system that modern speakers are now using. The system set out in (6) still works for weak pronouns. So we still get *I saw him* and *He saw me*, but *I*, in particular, is also used as a strong form in coordination: *He saw you and I*.

Third, we need a notion of default. A default form is the form you get when there is nothing specific to tell you to use some other form. In English *-ed* is the default past tense form: unless you know that the past tense of, say, *throw*, is *threw*, you will assume that it must be *throwed*. Once you know about *threw*, it overrides the default – it is a specific rule which tells you not to use the default.

And finally, we need to note that it is not true that all pronouns in a single set act in precisely the same way. It might be, for example, that some of the subject pronouns have been slower to change to the new system and tend to be found abiding by the old rules more often. When we find such effects, it is often due to the relative frequency of the relevant forms. Frequent forms change faster than rare forms.

Now we are in a position to look at the new system which is more and more frequently being used with pronouns.

The default pronouns are the oblique pronouns. If someone asks *Who would like more cake?*, you are more likely to answer *me* than *I* (you might add a *please*, of course). Part of the reason is that in your utterance, *Me* or *Me, please*, there is no information as to whether the pronoun is the subject or the object or anything else. We can deduce that this is a form of *I would like some more cake, please*, but in what we actually say, that is missing. Perhaps we meant *Give me a piece, please* or *Please make sure there's some for me*. This is precisely the kind of environment where it makes sense to use the default form. Also, as with the French examples cited earlier, *I* needs something to hang on to. It is weak. Where the pronoun occurs in isolation, it must be stressed, so we need the strong form. The strong form is *me*. So we can get *Me, please* (strong form) or *I would, please* (weak form), but *I, please*, is odd.

What is odd about the form *I* is that it is now used as the second pronoun in a set of coordinated forms. Wherever they arise. So we can have *He and I took the plane across to Paris*, *Sam will give you and I a lift to the airport*, *My uncle paid a visit to my wife and I*. We do not generally find *I* in the first position; that is, we do not find **I and he took the plane across to Paris*, **My uncle paid a visit to I and my wife* and so on (although recall (20)). In such sentences, we need a strong form, and we get *me* (with a rather different social effect): *Me and him took a plane across to Paris*. It is not clear why this pattern should have emerged (our general expectation would be that coordinated pronouns can occur in either order with the same forms). Quinn (2005) suggests that it has to do with the syntactic structure in such instances; we might also suggest that it is a combination of the politeness rule (other people first) and the feeling that *I* is posher than *me* and the frequency of coordination with *I*.

Quinn (2005, p. 383) cites a passage from the Christchurch (New Zealand) broadsheet, *The Press*, over a century ago, which seems to show this (and seems to get confused because the writer puts *I* in the object of a preposition – not the kind of English the writer seems to be proposing. The example shows that the confusion about the original system is of long standing).

(21) When a country cousin remarks that 'Me and Tom' have done so and so, it is necessary for the town cousin, in the interests of polite speech and general gentility, to reply that that the same thing was once done by 'Tom and I'. (*The Press*, 8 October 1887, cited from Quinn)

It should be noted that while *I* has this preferential position in a coordinate structure, the same does not necessarily apply to the other pronouns that used to belong to the subject series, or not to the same extent. Quinn (2005, pp. 198–200) reports that *us* is more likely than *we* in the second conjunct of a coordinated structure. Examples in (22) are again from the BNC, and show *us* where it is prescriptively wrong and where it is prescriptively right.

(22) a. Just them and us, up here in the roof […]
b. There is then no longer them and us […]
c. But an exchange puts both them and us into a geographical funnel towards the meeting point […]

Wrapping up

The problem with English pronouns is that the system is in the process of changing, and it is not completely clear what the final system will look like. In the meantime, at least two systems (possibly more, but it is hard to tell) co-exist. The old system, which prescriptivists love, has not functioned properly for at least four hundred years. This says something about the speed of grammatical change: at the present time, glaciers change a lot faster than some grammar.

Not only is it not clear what the system we are headed for will be like, it is also not clear that what we have in the new system is still a matter of case. And if it is not case, we do not have a good label to apply to it. It may not be case because, although the weak forms still mostly work as though they were case forms, the form that arises elsewhere is no longer a matter of who does what to whom and with what, it is partly a matter of social distinctions and partly a system where coordination is no longer determined by purely grammatical principles (coordinate like form with like form) but determined by some principles which are far more complex, including stress, for example. Certainly, whether it is case or not-case is something of a nerdy-linguist question, which is unlikely to bother the majority of speakers. But it would be really nice to know how to help language teachers work out what they should use.

What should I read?

The best coverage I know of this material is Quinn (2005). Quinn also makes it clear that the question is far wider than I have made it appear here. She also discusses *whoever*, *whomever*, *whosever*, pronouns with relative clauses (*He who would valiant be*), the form in *We/us linguists need to understand this construction, This is a problem for we/us linguists*, and the use of *him* or *his* (etc.) in *Him/his giving us the news was thoughtful*. Unfortunately, its very thoroughness and authoritativeness means that it is not an easy read for the lay person. Another useful book, though one with a wider remit, is Wales (1996).

The question of whether English has case is overtly addressed by Hudson (1995).

Part of the question considered here is discussed in my earlier work, Bauer (1998). In a readable paper, Denison (1996) provides literary citations tracing the development of some of the changes that are discussed here.

References

Bauer, Laurie 1998. Myth 16: You shouldn't say 'It is me' because 'me' is accusative. In Laurie Bauer & Peter Trudgill (eds), *Language myths*, 132–138. Harmondsworth: Penguin.

Davies, Mark 2004. *British National Corpus* (from Oxford University Press). Available online at https://www.english-corpora.org/bnc/.

Denison, David 1996. The case of the unmarked pronoun. In Derek Britton (ed.), *English historical linguistics 1994: Papers from the 8th international conference on English historical linguistics*, 287–300. Amsterdam: Benjamins.

Hudson, Richard 1995. Does English really have case? *Journal of Linguistics* 31(2): 375–392.

Quinn, Heidi 2005. *The distribution of pronoun case forms in English.* Amsterdam: Benjamins.

Wales, Katie 1996. *Personal pronouns in present-day English.* Cambridge: Cambridge University Press.

17 *Is that your wife again?*

Possession

Andreea

Setting the scene

Lately, I have started to follow 'The Minimalist Life' on social media and as a result, my newsfeed is now filled with mindful advice such as *Your home should be the antidote of stress, not the cause of it* and *Minimalism is not about what you own, it's about why you own it*. While the world at large is only just beginning to take in our serious obsession with owning stuff, the world of linguistics has been preoccupied with this problem for well over a century.

Philologists and grammarians back in the 1930s (Stahl 1927, Thomas 1931, Timmer 1939, as cited in Rosenbach 2014) were already documenting how we talk about owning stuff, and exposing challenges in this area of language analysis. Researching possession (as it is known in linguistics) is big business! Over the course of its long history of study, the topic has been and remains a bustling place for ongoing exchange of ideas, with English being a key player on the scene. But the topic of debate is most likely not what you think, it is not to do with misplaced apostrophes, as captured by the well-shared internet meme *grammar is the difference between knowing your shit and knowing you're shit*. No, grammatical possession refers to a whole constellation of patterns used to point out who owns what, often by means of short words, like *of* or a single sound (*s*) whose alternation still keeps linguists on their toes.

How variation in the system has cluttered your grammatical space

In English, there are several options for expressing possession (some are given below), but probably not as many as there in other languages, as we will see later in this chapter. What the examples below have in common is that they all describe a relation of ownership between an owner (the *possessor*) and the object/person of ownership (the *possessum*):

(1) a. My home is an antidote to stress.
    b. The Minimalist person's home is an antidote to stress.
    c. The home of my best friend's sister is an antidote to stress.

DOI: 10.4324/9781003148999-17

d. My father bought an old book for children from the new bookshop.
e. A friend of Miriam's told me that her home was the antidote to stress.
f. The Minimalist person has an uncluttered home.
g. Few of my friends own homes of their own.

These sentences show that English grammar expresses possession either by using pronouns (*my* or *their own*), prepositions (*of* and *for*), the unusual-looking *'s* form (which we can view as a case marker), or certain verbs (*have* or *own*). Among the various options available, two major grammatical patterns immediately stand out as being dominant: the case marker *'s* and the preposition *of*. But it was not always so.

Back in simpler times, when (Old) English had overt case marking (see Chapter 16, on case), that is, bits of grammar whose function was to point out the role of various entities within a sentence, such as nominative case for 'doers' initiating the action (subjects), accusative case for those having something done to them (objects), dative case for receivers, and so on, there was also the genitive case – a historical relic we still keep today – one of whose jobs was to point out who owns what. Everything expressed as a possessive was [X's Y]: *John's mother, the politician's hair, the armchair's legs, the house's ceiling, the sugar bowl's sugar*.

Fast forward to the transition from Old English to Middle English, and case markings started to go out of fashion, with many being replaced by prepositions. As a result, the genitive *'s* was all but taken over by *of*. By the fourteenth century, *of* was beginning to enjoy the freedom and prestige of a new favourite grammatical form, according to calculations by Thomas (1931, cited in Rosenbach 2004, p. 216). This lavish existence is most likely due to influence from the usual suspect in English history: French (Allen 2003, p. 8). By now, possession was turning from [X's Y] to [the Y of X].

But, like many fads, the genitive was not altogether displaced by *of* and, eventually, the popularity of the preposition *of* declined. Come the twentieth century, we see a resurgence of the humble *'s*, with various studies reporting an increase of the genitive, a rise which continues today (Rosenbach 2014, p. 217). Some attribute the resurgence of the *'s* to pressures of economy in journalism and media: [X's Y] is shorter than [the Y of X] (Jankowski & Tagliamonte 2014). One can't help but wonder how desperate we are getting for character space if such a minimal saving makes a difference. Whatever the reason, we now find ourselves speaking an English variety with two competing strategies involved in a real tug of (possessive) war.

Space considerations aside, there is a key difference between the two versions of possessives, which has to do with what comes first. In genitive possessives (or Saxon genitives as they are also known; *'s*), the owner (the possessor) comes first:

(2) a. the Minimalist Life's newsfeed.
b. the company's director.
c. the book's many and diverse chapters.

In *of* possessives, the thing that is being owned (the possessum) comes first:

(3) a. the newsfeed of the Minimalist Life.
 b. the director of the company.
 c. the many and diverse chapters of the book.

The ordering of the parts matters because we tend to focus on that which comes first. The choice between possessive constructions (*'s* or *of*) can sometimes be made on the basis of what has already been mentioned or what is already established as a relevant topic at hand. Speakers are largely in control here because as far as possessive constructions go, English grammar helpfully allows the flexibility to put either possessor or possessum first (in either *'s* or *of* forms). While topical elements may indeed have a lot to answer for regarding the choice of possessive used, they certainly do not have the last word. The alternation between the two possessive forms turns out to be incredibly complex and the ordering of information is only one of the factors that influences it. But before we consider other factors, let's be clear that not every possessive construction is allowed to vary in the first place.

A troublesome alternation part I: that which varies and that which does not

While some possessive constructions allow a choice between genitive and *of* forms, others do not. During the Covid-19 pandemic, many New Zealand newspaper articles took to discussing *the lack of community transmission* (from *New Zealand Herald*, 2020), but nowhere was *the community transmission's lack* mentioned, nor was *the community's lack of transmission*. Idiomatic expressions like *the tricks of the trade* are seemingly structurally frozen, even though, if you look hard enough, it is possible to uncover the rare use of *the trade's tricks* (according to Rosenbach 2014, p. 224). The *school of life* is OK but not *life's school* (though we do have *life's lessons*). In these examples, the version with *of* works but the one with *'s* does not.

The converse constraint is also possible: the genitive construction may be acceptable where the *of* construction is not. We can talk about any generic book owned by or belonging to John using the phrase *John's book*, but the *Book of John* is a very specific part of the Bible. *John's car* is possible but *the car of John* is odd (*the car of John's* works however). The preference for the genitive is particularly prevalent with animate and human possessors, and indeed, when I was taught English, the rule of thumb I was given went something like this: if the possessor is animate, use the *'s*, otherwise use the *of* form. I come back to animate possessors shortly.

Sometimes, it may appear that an alternation is possible but the meaning of the two forms is not the same. So can we legitimately consider these to be alternative versions of the same underlying message? For example, *the love of my cousin* and *my cousin's love* can, but needn't, always refer to the same thing; the former expression is ambiguous between the person 'doing' the loving (*cousin* as subject) and the person being loved (*cousin* as object), the latter is not ambiguous (*cousin* can only be interpreted as subject). The ambiguity is not problematic for English speakers because it can be resolved by the surrounding context but it could be problematic for linguists or computers analysing large amounts of data automatically.

Cases in which only one form is available, either *'s* or *of*, are considered the knock-out context. Two questions arise at this point about the knock-out context. Why are some forms allowed to alternate and others not? And how do speakers know which alternations are possible and which are not? The first question has two main answers; the second is still awaiting one.

Knock-out contexts can arise from internal semantic or structural properties specific to the entities involved. For instance, in the earlier idiomatic expression *tricks of the trade*, it makes good sense that it should be 'frozen' in structure and therefore not allow alternation because that phrase has a very specific meaning (in some ways, it behaves a bit like a single word). Alternatively, knock-out contexts can arise from old (linguistic) habits, recurrent patterns leading to a fixation of sorts. One form becomes so common and dominant in certain possessor/possessum pairs that the alternative form, although possible in theory, never turns up in real interactions (see Chapter 2, on norm). For instance, we tend to say *his size* and keep *the size of him* only for contexts emphasizing surprise and exaggeration (e.g. *Look at the size of him!*).

The second question of how speakers 'know' which combinations are allowed is a linguistic black hole. Speakers rarely 'know' how they know anything related to their linguistic use, so asking them is not helpful. The matter is further complicated by the fact that there is disagreement between (native) speakers themselves about whether or not a given alternation is acceptable. So even if we could ask them, they would potentially give different answers.

A troublesome alternation part II: how do we *really* choose (and do we *actually* choose)?

Leaving aside the problematic knock-out possessives and turning to those cases which do allow alternations between *'s* and *of* forms, the next problem to sort out is how English speakers choose which construction to use.

As I hinted earlier in the chapter, the status of the possessor is an important and relevant influencing factor in the grammatical choice: *'s* goes with animate and especially, human possessors (*Jane's hair*, *the caretaker's son*, *Trump's presidency*), *of* is more common with inanimate possessors (*the parts of the chapter*, *the cogs of the machine*). This pattern goes hand-in-hand with what is topical.

Because we humans generally like to talk about (other) humans (e.g. animate beings), the human participant in any conversation, is often privileged and, thus, topical. So we tend to put this information first. In other words, it makes good linguistic sense to use the genitive structure [X's Y] when X is a human (or, at least, animate) possessor, because it allows us to put X first. This iconic arrangement is one of many wonderfully un-coincidental patterns observed in the fabric of language (Haiman 1983 illustrates a large array of these).

While the pattern seems reliable and explicable in cases where the possessor is animate and the possessee is inanimate, comparatively little is known about cases where both are inanimate; is *the cog of the machine* more common than *the machine's cog* or vice versa?

Of course, what is human and what is topical do not always coincide. We are happy enough discussing inanimate entities too. When the two factors of animacy and topicality come into conflict with each other, it becomes a numbers game, depending on what else is happening with the other relevant factors that come into play. In English, none of these factors are deterministic; they merely reflect tendencies. Thus, if required, we can have *of* possession with animate possessors: *the business of the mayor*, *the fault of the director*, and conversely, we can have inanimate possessors in genitive constructions: *the museum's shop, the desert's beauty, 2006's budget* (examples from Fiest 2012, p. 226). Studies of Canadian English, for instance, show a clear indication of a change in progress whereby collective nouns, such as *committee, team, school*, are beginning to take *'s* more frequently than *of* (Jankowski & Tagliamonte 2014).

Besides animacy and topicality, a third factor governing the choice of possessive construction is the length of expression identifying the possessor. Shorter possessors tend to occur with genitive forms and longer ones with prepositional forms: *branches of the big old tree* is more common than *the big old tree's branches* (see Ehret et al. 2014 and discussion in Rosenbach 2014, p. 227). Like animacy constraints, possessor length constraints also make good linguistic sense because it appears easier for our brains to handle long and complex chunks if they come later in the phrase.

Good texts start with short, familiar phrases and add the big, heavy ones at the end, by which point, the reader/hearer is (hopefully) ready for them. This way of presenting information is captured by what linguists call 'The End-Weight Principle', meaning 'do the heavy-(linguistic)-lifting at the end', a principle attributed to the work of Randolph Quirk and his colleagues at the *Survey of English Usage* project (Quirk et al. 1985).

And if you thought three factors is already a lot to take in when putting together a single noun phrase, wait: there's more. There are some factors relating to the familiarity of the possessor which amount to the fact that more familiar possessors tend to be coded by genitives: *the book's chapters* only makes sense if we know which book we are talking about, whereas *chapters of a book* is more natural if we are referring to any generic book.

Next, there are factors related to pronunciation. One specifies that in order to follow English intonation patterns of strong-weak syllable stress, a phrase like *the laws of God* is more likely to occur than *God's laws* (example from Rosenbach 2014, p. 232). There is also the business of sibilant sounds (Szmrecsanyi 2013), avoiding doubling up of /s/-like sounds in expressions like *the virus's spread* or *the virus's circulation* in favour of *the circulation/spread of the virus*.

And there is the peer pressure of priming (see Chapter 8, on comparison): if a genitive form occurs at some point in the conversation, we are suggestive beings, likely to be influenced in using a genitive too (as opposed to using *of*) or vice versa (*of* is likely to be followed by another *of*).

But last and most challenging of all is the semantic connection between possessor and possessum. What does it really mean to possess something?

But what is possession really, and does it even have to concern ownership?

It seems reasonable to assume that possessing something involves having control over it. And there is nothing we have more control over than that which is part of us to begin with. So the most obvious candidate for the relationship between a possessor and a possessum is a part-whole relationship, where the possessum cannot exist in isolation from the possessor. Examples include *Jim's arm, the book's introduction, the spoke of the wheel, the lid of the jar*, where the possessed entities are part of the possessor; the arm is (hopefully) attached to Jim, the introduction chapter cannot exist if there is no book to speak of, the wheel is integrally reliant on having spokes and a jar is arguably more useful and jar-like if it has a lid.

We can refine these possessive relationships into several types, such as kinship relations, *the man's mother, the boy's grandmother*, body parts, *Mary's finger, Lisa's broken heart* and *the man's leg*, and legal ownership, *my grandmother's house, the property of the school, Lawson's business*. Using European languages as a yardstick, Koptjevskaja-Tamm (2001) identified these three categories as being the most prototypical possessive relationships. Cognitive linguists are especially fond of prototypes (see also Chapter 3, on prepositions) because they capture adequately the variation observed in meanings of words, and allow the analyst to do away with strict boundaries, opting for fuzzy boundaries instead. Famous examples in (psycho)linguistic research involve furniture items: a *chair* is a good example of a furniture item, but a *telephone* is not (Rosch et al. 1976).

The three types of 'best examples' of possession listed above contrast with less prototypical examples, such as *Peter's usual bus, my most trusted mechanic* and *the president's auspicious speech*, in which the possessor is more loosely connected to the possessum. Peter does not own the bus, it's *his* by virtue of the fact that he regularly takes it; I certainly do not own my most trusted mechanic, I merely take my car to be serviced by him; and the president is not likely to have written the speech but is probably just delivering it.

'Looser' possession is also termed alienable possession, not because it comes from outer space, although it could in theory involve extraterritorial entities (*the orbit of the moon*), but because it reflects the fact that possessor and possessum are not intimately linked entities and can be disentangled from each other. I can potentially change my mechanic, and once I do so, he is no longer *my* mechanic. Alienable possession contrasts with inalienable possession, a category which includes the prototypical possessive types mentioned earlier, kinship relations and body parts, in which the possessum and possessor are harder to separate.

The alienable/inalienable distinction has some very real and noticeable implications for languages in which one grammatical form of possession may be used with alienable possessives and a completely different form is used with inalienable possessives. In many Oceanic languages, choosing which possessive construction to use is rigidly specified by the grammar and not a matter of speaker 'choice'. For instance in the language of Manam, spoken in the Solomon Islands, 'my father' is expressed by *tamá-gu*, where *gu* is roughly equivalent to English 'my', but 'my loincloth' is expressed by *ʔúsi né-gu*, where besides *gu*, the form *né* is also required to point out that the loincloth is more loosely connected to its possessor (Lichtenberk 1983, p. 278, 294). Going one step further, food items have their own specific possessive marker too: for example 'my taro' would be *baŋ ʔaná-gu*, where *ʔaná* accompanies the usual possessive *gu* (Lichtenberk 1983, p. 291). To English speakers, it may come as a surprise that any language should give such special treatment to (possessed) food items. Manam is not unusual in this respect. It is very much in line with other related Oceanic languages, including Kokota, Saliba, Kove, Lolovoli and various Fijian languages. It turns out that all across Oceania, there are markers used exclusively for expressing possessives involving foods. These markers can be traced back to the ancestral language which gave rise to the Oceanic languages we hear spoken today (Lichtenberk 2009). So really, to Manam speakers, it is English which is odd in ignorantly lumping what is a precious resource together with others of relatively less importance: *John's car, John's show, John's taro*. Did I mention that there are also special possessives for drinks (*my coffee* will involve a different *my* from that in *my taro*)?

In their work, Payne & Berlage (2014) identify no fewer than thirteen relationships of possession entering the (still somewhat constrained and specific) construction of [noun + *of mine*] in the British National Corpus (Davies 2004–). What these particular examples also show is that it is possible to have possession with both forms (*'s* and *of*), termed 'double genitives' (*mine* is a pronominal version of the *'s* form, equivalent in form to *a lover of Lucy's* or *a favourite of John's*).

(6) Semantic possessive relations (from Payne & Berlage, 2014, Table 1, p. 335)

interpersonal: *a lover of mine*	kinship: *a son of mine*
creator: *a short book of mine*	ownership: *an old T-shirt of mine*
human property: *any fault of mine*	evaluation: *a favourite of mine*
concern: *no business of mine*	performer: *another hobby of mine*
body part: *this wretched hair of mine*	place: *[a] local school of mine*
verbal noun: *no doing of mine*	membership: *this team of mine*
experience: *a recent experience of mine*	

In these examples, the possession relation is very loose or even metaphorical. But what about the example below? The kea bird is certainly not the scientist's kea in any way, why does possession come into it?

(7) I've got a kea [NZ native bird] just landed and I'm going to take off and see who that is. (Radio New Zealand trailer for a programme, 26 December 2019, noon, scientist speaking)

And then there are examples which make use of grammatical possessive marking patterns, but which do not seem to be clear instantiations of ownership, such as, *the university's prestige relies on its rankings* (does the university really own prestige?), *the day's sports line-up included rugby, netball and tennis* (does the day own the sports line-up?), or the Beatles' song *A hard day's night* (does the day own the night following it?).

Yet English grammar seems to require a possessive form despite the lack of possessive semantics: *university prestige* seems strained though borderline acceptable for some, *day sports line-up* is definitely odd but *daily sports line-up* works, while *a hard day night* is downright awkward. Of course, we can say that a university *has* prestige, a day *has* a sports line-up and a night following it, but having something is not always the same as possessing it (while this book may have eighteen chapters, no one would imagine the book owns them in any sense).

So possessive marking turns up in contexts we do may not expect it to, and the converse is also true. We sometimes reference what could be thought to be possessive meaning but we do not mark it explicitly: *the school hall, the road markings*.

Capturing the precise semantics of possessive constructions and the many different nuances that can be expressed by them remains an open problem in linguistics. Just where and how to draw objective boundaries between different types of relationships is tricky: are body part relations a sub-type of part-whole relations or a separate category of their own? Far from being just a theoretical quibble, these labels have implications for which possessive grammatical constructions are used to express them, so we want to be able to differentiate them. Even in English, where the distinction is not coded by the grammar in the same rigid way, we know that semantic relationship is one of the factors which enters into the possessive equation (deciding between the genitive *'s* and *of*). But it is even stronger than that. The semantics of the possession has implications for how we process it.

In a series of studies combining linguistics theory with experimental methods, Lichtenberk, Vaid & Chen (2011) and Vaid & Chen with Lichtenberk (2019) show that even when expressed by the same grammatical means, alienable and inalienable possession are in fact handled differently by English speakers. Inalienable possession is parsed much quicker – because *John's arm* is expected to be connected to John, my brain processes that association much faster than it would *John's book*, which I may be liable to borrow or steal at any time, thereby invalidating the possessive relationship. Furthermore, inalienable possessives have a much wider range of possible interpretations; *John's book* could be a book he owns, a book he has written, or a book he is currently holding for someone else, but *John's arm* is really (one hopes) only refers to the arm that is attached to his body; this being a good reason for the timing delays needed to decode *John's book* (compared to *John's arm*).

Wrapping up

Despite our struggles with the semantics of possessive relationships, we already know a lot about the factors which influence our choice of possessive form in English.

Still, one cannot help but wonder, do our brains really make sense of all these factors? Can my own brain realistically take in all this complexity and peruse such a wide array of possibilities (without consciously doing so!), while at the same time, being unable to complete a supermarket trip without a written-down grocery list (or maybe that explains precisely why I need the list)?

Having uncovered many of these factors, current research in English possession is now gearing up to assess what speakers actually do when conflicts occur between the various factor weightings. This is done by building complex statistical models from analysing large collections of real language data. It does appear that animacy of the possessor is indeed the most important factor which has the power to trump all others. This means that in learning English as a second language, the rule of thumb I was given all those years ago is still a good one to live by. Yet while animacy reigns supreme, the other factors can still bring about a change of grammatical choice if the context is right.

It may seem odd that such minute phonological and typographical units – the barely noticeable *'s* and *of* – have caused such a heavy workload for grammarians of English. Many speakers do not even register their existence. It just goes to show that some of the most challenging cases for language analysts can lurk in the tiniest of corners, but that does not diminish their importance!

Far beyond possession itself, this body of work also shows that, contrary to the perception that grammar is a fixed, independent and logical set of rules which can elegantly account for what we hear and say, the reality of grammar is that it is not just messy and grey but also inseparably tied to other parts of the language system. The grammar we use is influenced by the sounds of the words we choose, the relevance and importance of certain entities to the topic at hand, and what we (or others) have just said before us. The whole system is an interconnected web of linguistic possibilities, evolving in real time and jointly constructed by multiple speakers.

What should I read?

Rosenbach's (2014) review article is by far the best overview of the topic, but the terminology may prove difficult for non-specialists. For those who want to read more about the history of the genitive case marker in English, parts of Russell Thomas's (1931) dissertation may be satisfying, though not straightforward reading. Jankowski & Tagliamonte's (2014) article offers a look at how linguists gauge language change in progress. In general, the 2014 Special Issue of *English Language and Linguistics* on possession is a comprehensive, expert resource on the topic.

References

Allen, Cynthia 2003. Deflexion and the development of the genitive in English. *English Language and Linguistics* 7(1): 1–28. doi:10.1017/S1360674303211023

Davies, Mark 2004. *British National Corpus* (from Oxford University Press). Available online at https://www.english-corpora.org/bnc/.

Ehret, Katharina, Christoph Wolk & Benedikt Szmrecsanyi 2014. Quirky quadratures: On rhythm and weight as constraints on genitive variation in an unconventional data set. *English Language and Linguistics* 18(2): 262–303. doi:10.1017/S1360674314000033

Fiest, Jim 2012. What controls the 'genitive variation' in present-day English? *Studies in Language* 36(2): 261–299. doi:10.1075/sl.36.2.03fei

Haiman, John 1983. Iconic and economic motivation. *Language* 59: 781–819. doi:10.2307/413373

Jankowski, Bridget L. & Sali A. Tagliamonte 2014. On the genitive's trail: Data and method from a sociolinguistic perspective. *English Language and Linguistics* 18(2): 305–329. doi:10.1017/S1360674314000045

Koptjevskaja-Tamm, Maria 2001. Adnominal possession. In Martin Haspelmath, Ekkehard König, Wulf Oesterreicher & Wolfgang Raible (eds), *Language typology and language universals*, 960–970. Berlin: Mouton de Gruyter.

Lichtenberk, Frantisek 1983. *A grammar of Manam*. Honolulu: University of Hawai'i Press.

Lichtenberk, Frantisek 2009. Oceanic possessive classifiers. *Oceanic Linguistics* 48(2): 379–402. doi:10.1353/ol.0.0054

Lichtenberk, Frantisek, Jyotsna Vaid & Hsin-Chin Chen. 2011. On the interpretation of alienable vs. inalienable possession: A psycholinguistic investigation. *Cognitive Linguistics* 22(4): 659–689. doi:10.1515/cogl.2011.025

Payne, John & Eva Berlage 2014. Genitive variation: The niche role of the oblique genitive. *English Language and Linguistics* 18(2): 331–360. doi:10.1017/S1360674314000057

Quirk, Randolph, Sidney Greenbaum, Geoffrey Leech & Jan Svartvik 1985. *A comprehensive grammar of the English language*. London: Longman.

Rosch, Eleanor, Carolyn Mervis, Wayne Gray, David Johnson & Penny Boyes-Braem 1976. Basic objects in natural categories. *Cognitive Psychology* 8(3): 382–439. doi:10.1016/0010-0285(76)90013-X.

Rosenbach, Anette 2014. English genitive variation – the state of the art. *English Language and Linguistics* 18(2): 215–262. doi:10.1017/S1360674314000021

Stahl, Leon 1927. Der adnominale Genitiv und sein Ersatz im Mittelenglischen und Frühneuenglischen. *Giessener Beiträge* 3: 1–35.

Szmrecsanyi, Benedikt 2013. The great regression: Genitive variability in late Modern English. In Kersti Börjars, David Denison & Alan Scott (eds), *Morphosyntactic categories and the expression of possession*, 59–88. Amsterdam: Benjamins.

Thomas, Russell 1931. *Syntactical processes involved in the development of the adnominal periphrastic genitive in the English language*. Doctoral Dissertation, University of Michigan.

Timmer, Benno Johan 1939. The place of the attributive noun-genitive in Anglo-Saxon. *English Studies* 21: 49–72.

Vaid, Jyotsna, Hsin-Chin Chen & Franktisek Lichtenberk 2019. A Processing advantage for inalienable possession: Evidence from English phrase plausibility judgments. *Te Reo: Journal of the New Zealand Linguistic Society* 62(1): 155–173.

18 Conclusion

Andreea and Laurie

If we have left you with the impression that people know nothing about English grammar or that anything goes in English grammar, then we apologize: that was not our intention, and it is not true. We cannot even agree with science fiction writer Isaac Asimov (1980, p. 109), that 'English grammar is incredibly loose. It consists almost entirely of a collection of exceptions'. It is just that in this book we have focused on those parts of English grammar where, for one reason or another, the rules are in flux, and that means that we observe variation in the way that people use the rules. The reasons for such variation are relatively restricted, and not mutually exclusive. We have repeatedly come across some of them in this book. The most important of these factors are the following:

- The language is changing. Living languages change all the time – you cannot stop it – and it would be surprising if our language stayed the same. Sometimes, language changes quite quickly; other times it takes centuries for a change to be fully implemented. And even if a change becomes fully instated, some remnants may be left behind, for example, *How do you do*? and *by and large* do not make sense in terms of current grammar. While change is happening, people use, in effect, two grammars: the grammar of the old version and the grammar of the new version (which may not be fully understood yet). Because people hear the old alongside the new, they are easily confused about which to say. This factor has been relevant in our chapters on the definite article (Chapter 5), countability (Chapter 6), the present perfect (Chapter 7), the progressive (Chapter 9), gender (Chapter 12), case (Chapter 16) and possession (Chapter 17).
- Spoken language is not the same as written language. Spoken language comes first – both in the individual child and in the history of humans. Written language is derived from spoken language, is often more consistent, more explicit and more polished than spoken language. We cannot expect people to talk like books, though this is often what criticisms of spoken language boil down to. We often find constructions in spoken language which are absent from written language (and, indeed, vice versa), and this is normal. We have seen this factor being important in our chapters on comparison (Chapter 8), double *be* (Chapter 11), shadow pronouns (Chapter 13) and insubordination (Chapter 15).
- Language is not homogeneous. Automotive engineers know words and expressions that carpenters do not (and vice versa). Americans and Scots

DOI: 10.4324/9781003148999-18

speak different varieties of English. Men and women use slightly different types of English. When we hear speakers of other varieties on a regular basis, we may not realize that there are differences between the varieties, and use expressions or grammatical constructions that come from both. We have seen this factor at work in our chapters on double negatives (Chapter 4), the definite article (Chapter 5), countability (Chapter 6) and adjectives (Chapter 10).

- Some grammatical points are adopted as part of the standard language and others are not. The standard has an immense influence on literate speakers (who often meet it more in writing than in conversation). People who do not use the standard all the time may nevertheless adopt a standard form because of its prestige and influence. Sometimes it works the other way around, and a picturesque non-standard expression becomes part of the standard (the word *blackmail* comes from Scots, the phrase *have a butchers* comes from slang). We have seen this factor at work in our chapters on norm (Chapter 2), countability (Chapter 6), comparison (Chapter 8), adjectives (Chapter 10), double *be* (Chapter 11), shadow pronouns (Chapter 13), insubordination (Chapter 15) and case (Chapter 16).
- Sometimes, grammar reflects the meaning; sometimes it reflects the form in which the meaning is encoded. *A committee* is in form a singular unit, but in meaning it is made up of a lot of people. Where form and meaning contrast (as with *committee*), language users can follow the meaning or follow the form. This leads to divided usage. We have seen this factor in the chapters on comparison (Chapter 8), gender (Chapter 12) and number agreement (Chapter 14).
- Grammatical features can gain subtle new meanings, which may become more important or more frequent, with time. This factor was seen to apply in our chapters on prepositions (Chapter 3), the definite article (Chapter 5), present perfect (Chapter 7), the progressive (Chapter 9), insubordination (Chapter 15) and possession (Chapter 17).

On top of all this, we find cases where it seems that processing linguistic structures is so hard that the brain copes badly with them. Either we see speakers getting lost in the structures they create (as with cases of shadow pronouns, Chapter 13 and insubordination, Chapter 15), or the things that determine which grammatical form is used are so complex that we do not understand how speakers can resolve the issues involved (for example, in the case of comparative and superlative forms, Chapter 8 and possession, Chapter 17).

Finally, of course, we find that some of the things we say are determined not just by grammatical rules or constraints (although these certainly play their part), but by custom and usage (see Chapter 2, on norm).

What all this means is that although we know a lot about English grammar, so that we can often tell when people make genuine errors in what they say, there is still a lot we do not know, and there are areas where discoveries can still be made and new explanations provided.

Reference

Asimov, Isaac 1980. *Casebook of the black widowers*. London: Gollancz.

Glossary

Language for language

Andreea and Laurie

Here we provide a glossary of linguistic terms to help readers understand the jargon of grammar. Items in small capitals have their own entry in the glossary.

Accusative. See CASE.

Active. See VOICE.

Aspect. Relating to verbs, aspect provides information about a given event in relation to its duration across specific periods of time, whether it is an ongoing, stretched out event, a completed event or a general state. Aspect can be grammatically marked on verbs (grammatical aspect) or it can be built into their semantic content (lexical aspect or Aktionsart).

Progressive. The progressive (sometimes also called 'continuous') is a grammatical means for signaling that the action expressed by the verb is ongoing and stretched out. In English, the progressive aspect is marked by the AUXILIARY VERB *be* together with the *-ing* form of the verb, for example *He was walking*.

Perfect. The perfect denotes completed events. In English, these are formed by the AUXILIARY VERB *have* together with the past participle form of the verb, as in *Alicia has walked the Routeburn Track*.

Case. Case is grammatical marking on nouns and pronouns to show what role they play in a sentence (in modern English, case is mostly shown on pronouns). The individual classes, such as the nominative, are also called cases. Where cases are not shown grammatically, the names for the cases may still be used for the functions those cases usually perform. The precise cases may differ from language to language and from analysis to analysis. We mention just a few here.

Accusative. The accusative case shows the direct object (see ROLE). In *I accused him of stealing my whisky*, *him* is in the accusative case.

Dative. The dative is the name given to the case which shows the person to whom something is given, and similar things. In English, *I gave him a good talking to*, *him* can be said to be in the dative case. Since the accusative and the dative cases in English look the same, some people prefer to use the term 'oblique case' to cover both of them.

Genitive. Sometimes called the 'possessive', this case shows possession and related matters. In *Mary is John's grandmother*, *John's* is in the genitive case. In *a summer's day*, *summer's* is also in the genitive case, although summer does not possess the day.

Nominative. The nominative is the name of the case used for the subject of a clause (see ROLE). In *I think I saw a zebra*, both occurrences of the word *I* are in the nominative case, the first because it is the subject of the clause *I think* (*something*) and the second because it is the subject in the clause *I saw a zebra*. In some languages, the nominative is also used for the subject complement (see ROLE).

Oblique. When the nominative (which was once also called the 'upright case') is contrasted with all other cases, the others are called the oblique cases. In *I have him the packet*, *him* and *the packet* are in the oblique case.

Clause. Clauses are groups of words which function together as a SENTENCE or a part of a sentence. In English, they typically have a subject, a verb and any other elements accompanying the verb, such as objects (see ROLE). *I love clauses* is a clause, but the sentence *I do not know if this is a clause* has two clauses, one EMBEDDED in the other: *I don't know if this is a clause* and *if this is a clause*.

Main. Main clauses can stand on their own and form sentences by themselves. They do not depend structurally or semantically on other clauses, but they can subsume other clauses. In the earlier sentence *I do not know if this is a clause*, the main clause is *I don't know if this is a clause* (the entire sentence). In a sentence like *After he's been to the party, he will go home*, the main clause is *he will go home*.

Subordinate. Subordinate clauses contrast with main clauses in that they cannot form sentences by themselves (or so traditional grammatical theory goes) and they depend structurally and semantically on a main clause. In the previous examples under MAIN CLAUSE, *if this is a clause* and *after he's been to the party* are subordinate clauses.

Constituent (bracketing). See PHRASE.

Construction. Constructions are groupings of words which have a particular form and a particular function. For example, an imperative construction typically gives commands, caution or advice. Sometimes constructions have open slots: [*what with* X], where X is the reason for a particular event or decision (*What with John coming late all the time, I did not want to hang around anymore*; or *What with the weather being so unpredictable, Mary decided to take an umbrella just in case*) and sometimes they are completely fixed (*let the cat out of the bag* or *kicked the bucket*).

Copula. See VERB TYPE.

Dative. See CASE.

Declarative. See SENTENCE.

Ditransitive. See VERB TYPE.

Embedding. See PHRASE.

Form. See WORD.
Form class. See PARTS OF SPEECH.
Function. See ROLE.
Future. See TENSE.
Genitive. See CASE.
Grammar. *Grammar* has several related meanings. It can be a description of a (part of a) language; a book containing such a description; the mental ability to learn and use language appropriately; and finally, and most specifically, it can be a description of that part of a language that deals with the arrangement of meaningful elements, morphemes and words, into larger structures, namely words and sentences.
Imperative. See SENTENCE.
Interrogative. See SENTENCE.
Intransitive. See VERB TYPE.
Lexical class. See PARTS OF SPEECH.
Main clause. See CLAUSE.
Modification. See PHRASE.
Nominative. See CASE.
Object, direct and indirect and oblique. See ROLE.
Parts of speech. Parts of speech (also known as 'word classes', 'lexical classes' and 'form classes') provide a classification of words according to their grammatical usage. There is no fixed set of parts of speech, so only some of the common ones are given here. The same set of letters or sounds can belong to one part of speech in one sentence, and to another in a different sentence: for example, *cut* in *I cut my finger* is a verb, but in *I've got a bad cut on my finger*, *cut* is a noun. Words in the same part of speech can be substituted for each other, as in the sentences below.

Determiner	**Adjective**	**Noun**	**Verb**	**Adverb**
The	black	cat	mewed	loudly.
This	clumsy	boy	fell	regularly.
No	clever	child	failed	here.
My	yellow	vase	broke	yesterday.

Adjective. Adjectives provide more information about a noun or name, and typically appear immediately before a noun (in attributive position) as in *the black cat*, though they can also appear in predicative position following the noun (as in *The cat is black*). Many adjectives can have words like *very* and *rather* modifying them (as in *very silly*, *rather pretty*).

Adverb. Adverbs are often made from adjectives with an *-ly* suffix, but as can be seen above, other words can be adverbs, such as *here*, *now*, *not* and *yesterday*. Adverbs typically provide additional information about a verb or an adjective.

Conjunction. Conjunctions are of two types, coordinating and subordinating. Coordinating conjunctions join two or more words or phrases of the same type or sometimes which just play the same role. We can have *Bill and Susan*, but we cannot have *Bill and yellow*. The main coordinating conjunctions are *and*, *or* and *but*, and some add *for* 'because'. Subordinating conjunctions introduce a subordinate CLAUSE within a main clause. Examples are the *when* in *She came when I asked her*, the *that* in *I saw the man that stole my wallet*, and also in *We hope that you will accept*, and the *because* in *I fell over because I tripped.*

Demonstrative. Demonstratives point out entities in physical or discourse space. In English, there are singular demonstratives (*this, that*) and plural demonstratives (*these, those*) and they can locate things that are near the speaker (*this, these*) or further away from the speaker (*these, those*). Demonstratives can stand on their own (*This is a funny definition)* or accompany a noun (*This definition is funny*).

Determiner. A determiner is one of a set of types of words which can go before a noun. Articles (like *a* and *the*), possessive pronouns (like *my* and *their*) and demonstratives (like *this* and *those*) are all types of determiner.

Noun. A noun typically follows a determiner and can then be used as part of the subject of a sentence (see ROLE). *Lecturer* is a noun in *The lecturer was very clear*.

Preposition. A preposition is a word which typically goes in front of a noun phrase to show how that noun phrase relates to something else in the sentence. Prepositions typically show location (in space or time), movement or possession. Examples are the *of* in *I am proud of my children*, the *in* in *Susan is in the garden*, the *through* in *The men ran through the woods*, and the *since* in *I haven't seen her since her birthday*.

Pronoun. A pronoun is a grammatical word which makes up a complete noun phrase by itself. There are various types of pronoun, some of them illustrated by *I*, *me*, *mine*, *my*, *myself*, *who*, *whichever*.

Verb. A typical verb in English has a base form, which can be used, among other functions, to give an order (*Go!*), a form in -*s* which is used with *he/she/it* (or nouns which can be replaced by them) in the present tense (*It/The train comes every evening*), a form, often in -*ed*, which is used in the past tense (*She walked home last night*), another form, again, often in -*ed*, which is used to make the perfect (*It has developed smoothly*) and a form in -*ing*, used, among other things, to show the continuous (*He is smiling right now*). Irregular verbs deviate from this pattern in some forms. There are many distinct types of verbs, some of which are dealt with in the section on VERB TYPES.

Past. See TENSE.

Perfect. See ASPECT.

Phrase. A phrase is a grouping of words which is smaller than a SENTENCE and which hangs together as a coherent unit (for example, *a white mouse* is a phrase but **a white mouse of* is not a phrase). In a phrase, there is usually one word which carries the most important meaning in the unit, and which gives the phrase its name, for example, noun phrases have nouns as their most important word (*the white house*), adjective phrases have adjectives (*very white*), verb phrases have verbs (*going home at lunch*), adverb phrases have adverbs (*too quickly*) and prepositional phrases have prepositions (*on the table*).

Constituent (bracketing). Constituents are phrases or groups of phrases which form a coherent unit grammatically and semantically. For example, in the sentence *Susceptible people sneeze frequently*, *susceptible people* is a constituent, while *people sneeze* is not. Constituents are often conventionally marked with brackets in linguistics texts: [[[Susceptible] people][sneeze [frequently]]].

Embedding. Embedding (or 'nesting') is the process of including one phrase (or CLAUSE) inside another. For example, the clause *that I wore last night* is embedded inside the larger clause *Mum bought me the dress that I wore last night*.

Modification. The most important word in a phrase is said to be modified by other words which add further information about it; for instance, in a noun phrase like *little mice*, the ADJECTIVE *little* provides additional information about the NOUN *mouse* by means of modification.

Recursion. The repeated process of embedding phrases or clauses inside other phrases or clauses is called 'recursion'. The grammar of English allows to recursively embed, for instance, as many adjectives as we like inside a noun phrase (though in practice this is not recommended): [*the large, white, cute, furry, lovable cat*] or noun phrases inside nouns phrases: [*elephants* [*in reservations* [*in Africa*]]].

Present. See TENSE.

Progressive. See ASPECT.

Recursion. See PHRASE.

Role (function). The term 'role' is widely used to refer to the function a noun phrase or a prepositional phrase has in a clause.

Direct object. The direct object identifies the entity in a clause which is directly impacted by the action described. In the sentence, *Romeo sent a message to Juliet with one of his cousins, in Shakespeare's play*, the noun phrase *a message* is the direct object. Clauses can only have one direct object and if one such object is present, the verbs in question (and clauses) are termed 'TRANSITIVE'. If no direct object is present then the clause (and the verb in it) is classified as 'INTRANSITIVE'.

Indirect object. The indirect object provides information about participants understood to be recipients in a particular event. There are two versions of the following sentence:

(i) Romeo sent a message to Juliet.

(ii) Romeo sent Juliet a message.

Linguists disagree as to what is the indirect object. For some it is *to Juliet* in (i), for others it is *Juliet* in (ii), for yet others it is both. In this book we use 'indirect object' for *Juliet* in (ii).

Oblique object. Sometimes also called the object of a PREPOSITION, the oblique object is an object which occurs with a preposition. In the sentence, *Romeo sent a message to Juliet with one of his cousins, in*

Shakespeare's play, the prepositional phrases *with one of his cousins* and *in Shakespeare's play* are both oblique objects.

Subject. The grammatical subject provides information about the main participant or doer in a clause, and in English, it typically comes before the verb. In the sentence, *Romeo sent a message to Juliet with one of his cousins, in Shakespeare's play*, the noun phrase *Romeo* is the subject.

Subject complement. The subject complement is the ADJECTIVE phrase or NOUN phrase following the COPULA in clauses containing a copular verb. For example, *very happy* and *the main protagonist* are subject complements of the following sentences: *Juliet was very happy* and *Juliet was the main protagonist.*

Sentence. A sentence is thc largest unit in grammar, containing one or more CLAUSES. In written English, it is identified by a capital letter at the start and a full stop at the end. In conversation, it has recently been abandoned as a unit of analysis because it cannot be reliably identified.

Declarative. Declarative sentences are presented as factual statements, and receive a full stop in written English. Most sentences in this section are of this type.

Interrogative. Interrogatives are presented as questions though they may not always be used to seek information; sometimes they can be rhetorical (*Did you really think I'd never find out?*) or simply checking that the listener is still following the thread of the conversation (*So you turn right at the lights, yeah? And then...*). In written English, interrogatives end in a question mark. Interrogatives are formed in English by inverting the order of SUBJECT and VERB (*Have you seen him?*), or by inserting the AUXILIARY verb *do* (*Do you know the time?*), or with a *wh*-word at the beginning, as in *Who do you think you are?* and sometimes they have the same structure as a declarative but end in an interrogative tag (*It's finished, right/eh/yes?*).

Imperative. Imperatives are used to issue advice or commands and they can orthographically be marked by an exclamation mark (*Don't you dare talk to me like that!*). Their subjects are either the second person (*you*) but often, imperatives don't have explicit subjects at all (*Keep off the grass please!*).

Subject. See ROLE.

Subject complement. See ROLE.

Subordinate clause. See CLAUSE.

Tense. Tense is a grammatical category which is related to the general time at which an event named by the verb (see PART OF SPEECH) takes place. While many languages have highly developed tense systems, English has just two major grammatical tenses: past and present.

Future. Although many languages, such as French, have future tenses, and although English has ways of talking about the future, it is controversial to claim that English has a future tense, because the futurity in *He will be here in the morning* is carried by an extra verb, *will*, rather than by changing the form of the verb. Similarly, in *I am going to be sick!*, the futurity is shown by *going to*.

Past. The past tense is used to express events which have already happened. In *I saw a zebra*, the event of seeing a zebra took place at some time before now, and *saw* is in the past tense. The past tense is typically used for presenting a narrative in English.

Present. The present (sometimes called the 'non-past') is used to express general truths (which are true now and at all times) and events which are happening at the moment. In *Lions are animals* and *Smith passes the ball to Rogers, who scores*, the words *are*, *passes* and *scores* are all present tense verbs. The present tense in English can also be used to express future time, as in *Her plane arrives tomorrow at noon*, where *arrives* is in the present tense.

Present perfect. The present perfect is used to express various events, typically recently completed events (*He has just finished this book*), but also events which have started in the past but continue in the present (*They have been married for over 30 years*), experiential events (*I have never been to Ankara*) and events denoting results and consequences (*I can't go on holiday as I have spent all my money*). In English, the present perfect is formed by the present tense form of the AUXILIARY VERB 'have' and a main verb, as shown in the previous examples.

Transitive See VERB TYPE.

Verb type. Verbs come in many different flavours, and the different types are not always mutually exclusive. Several types are presented here, though the list is not exhaustive. For a definition of a VERB, see PARTS OF SPEECH.

Auxiliary verb. Auxiliary verbs support the lexical verb in producing complex verb groups. The verb *be* helps produce the progressive (continuous) forms (*She is leaving*) and the passive (*She was robbed by the bank*), the verb *have* helps produce the PERFECT (*He has gone to London*), the verb *do* carries the TENSE when it is separated from the lexical verb in INTERROGATIVES or negatives (*Does she still live here? She does not live here any more*). Modal verbs are also auxiliary verbs.

Copula (copular verb). A copula has a subject complement but no direct object (see ROLE). The verb *seem* in *She seems happy* is a copula, and the SUBJECT COMPLEMENT is *happy*. Unlike transitive verbs, copular verbs cannot be made passive: *Happy is seemed by her* is impossible.

Ditransitive. A ditransitive verb has two objects, a direct object and an indirect object. The verb *give* in *The child gave his mother a painting* is a ditransitive verb, the indirect object is *his mother* and the direct object is *a painting*.

Intransitive. An intransitive verb is a verb which has no direct object or subject complement (see ROLE). Intransitive verbs do have subjects. The verb *sneeze* in *The girl sneezed loudly* is an intransitive verb.

Lexical verb (main verb). The lexical verb gives the main content of the verb phrase. Words like *come, concatenate, cook, ensure, identify, specialize* are lexical verbs.

Modal verb. Modal verbs are auxiliary verbs always followed by a verb in the base form that have no *-s* form and no *-ing* form. Giving a list is not entirely straightforward. Many of the modals are usually presented in terms of their historical relationship as present and past TENSE, though in modern English, the forms are more regularly used in senses that are not directly related to tense.

The modal verbs

Present form	*Past form*	*Comments*
better		(for speakers who say *I better go now, bettern't I?*)
can	could	
dare		(for some speakers, used as a main verb; a modal in *The love that dare not speak its name*)
may	might	
must		
need		(for some speakers, used as a main verb; a modal in *He need not come if he doesn't want to*)
ought to		(the *to* makes this an unusual modal)
shall	should	(*shall* is not used in all varieties of English)
will	would	

Transitive. Transitive verbs have a direct object (see ROLE). The verb *hit* in the *The car hit the crash barrier* is a transitive verb, and its direct object is *the crash barrier*.

Note that individual forms may belong to contrasting categories in different sentences. *Is* is an auxiliary verb in *She is coming round the mountain*, but a lexical verb (and a copula) in *She is very intelligent*. *Has* is an auxiliary in *He has arrived*, but a lexical verb (and a transitive verb) in *He has no idea*. *Grow* is an intransitive verb in *Nothing grows in our garden*, a transitive verb in *We grow tomatoes* and a copula in *My eyelids grew heavy*.

Word. A word of English can be defined, for practical purposes, in terms of the spelling system of English. In our spelling system, a word is an element that occurs between two spaces on the page, or which occurs between a space and a punctuation mark. While this definition is useful, and identifies words most of the time, it is not the end of the matter, because there are some problems which it fails to take into account. With a few examples, such as *in so far as*, speakers are unsure how many words to write; if people write *rainforest*, does that mean that they have fewer words than people who write *rain forest* (both are sanctioned by dictionaries)? There are CONSTRUCTIONS such as *to get down to brass tacks* which behave like words in many ways, but which in spelling terms seem to be made up of several words – even though those words are no longer meaningful (there is no meaning of 'brass' in that expression).

Affix. An affix in English may be of one of two kinds: it can be a prefix, such as *re-* in *rephrase*, *in-* in *inlay* and *bi-* in *bicycle*, or it can be a suffix, such as *er* in killer, *-able* in *kissable*, and *-s* in *cats*.

Base. Affixes are attached to bases. *Phrase* is the base in *rephrase*, *cat* is the base in *cats*. In *discoverable*, *discover* is the base for the addition of *-able*.

Compound. A compound is a word whose constituent elements are themselves words. Examples of compounds are *armchair*, *sky-blue* and *sky-dive*. The spelling of compounds in English is not standardized, so that *rainforest*, *rain-forest* and *rain forest* are all attested for the same compound.

Morpheme. A morpheme is a meaningful unit that cannot be split into smaller meaningful units. Affixes and bases may be morphemes. The word *in-form-al-ity* is made up of four morphemes (separated by the hyphens), *elephant* contains a single morpheme (it is monomorphemic). Where words are made up of more than one morpheme, all the material in the word must be associated with one morpheme or another; there can be no left-overs. Note that morphemes are seen as meaningful elements within words. The analysis of a word like *feet* (in comparison with its singular *foot*) into morphemes is controversial, because, although it contains two bits of meaning, 'foot' and 'plural', both parts of the meaning seem to be associated with the entire form, *feet*.

Word class. See PARTS OF SPEECH.

Index

CPSIA information can be obtained
at www.ICGtesting.com
Printed in the USA
LVHW020403081221
705586LV00004B/138

9 780367 710279